Lying Down with the Lions

Ronald V. Dellums

Lying Down with the Lions

A Public Life
from the Streets of Oakland
to the Halls of Power

_____

and H. Lee Halterman

Beacon Press Boston

Beacon Press
25 Beacon Street
Boston, Massachusetts 02108–2892
www.beacon.org

Beacon Press books are published under the auspices of
the Unitarian Universalist Association of Congregations.

07 06 05 04 03 02 01 00   8 7 6 5 4 3 2

This book is printed on recycled acid-free paper that contains at least 20 percent postconsumer
waste and meets the uncoated paper ANSI/NISO specifications for permanence as revised in 1992.

All photographs, unless otherwise noted, are courtesy of the African-American Museum and
Library at Oakland.

Text design by Lucinda L. Hitchcock
Composition by Wilsted & Taylor Publishing Services

Library of Congress Cataloging-in-Publication Data
Dellums, Ronald V., 1935–
    Lying down with the lions : a public life from the streets of Oakland to the halls of power /
Ronald V. Dellums and H. Lee Halterman.
        p.   cm.
    Includes index.
    ISBN 0-8070-4318-4 (cl.)
        1. Dellums, Ronald V., 1935–   . 2. Legislators—United States Biography.   3. United
States. Congress. House Biography.   4. United States—Politics and government—1945–
1989.   5. United States—Politics and government—1989–   6. United States—Social
conditions—1980–   7. Civil rights movements—United States—History—20th century.
8. Berkeley (Calif.)—Politics and government.   I. Halterman, H. Lee.   II. Title.
E840.8.D45A3   2000
328.73′092—dc21
    [B]   99-32097

We dedicate this memoir
to those who have struggled throughout the modern era
to bring peace and justice to our nation and the world;
their anonymous efforts have made possible the victories for change
that characterized the 1960s

    and

we offer our gratitude
to those who were gentle warriors while serving on the staff
of Congressman Dellums but who have now departed this Earth:
*Dona Cutting, Carmen Flores, Richard H. "Max" Miller, Beverly Nickens,
Mary Thomas, and Joyce Williams*

    and

with love
to our children, *Pam, Brandy, Erik, Piper, Joshua, Alexander,* and *Kimiko*

Contents

Movements explain my public life. Without the progressive causes of the 1960s and 1970s to be accountable to, I never would have embarked upon the odyssey that became three decades of service in elective office. As a child, I had never sought leadership positions in school. As an adult, I had chosen a career path that satisfied my need to contribute to the betterment of community through social work and community organizing. Recruited to go to Brandeis University for a Ph.D., I was thrilled at the prospect of contributing my ideas and experiences to the mainstream of progressive thought and to the expanding tradition of African American intellectual expression.

At the end of the twentieth century, manifestly a period of individualism, it may seem odd to hear that somebody would drop his plans and change his life because the community called upon him for service. In 1967 it seemed the most logical thing in the world—irresistible, compelling, and urgent. Without a movement to make the demand, a political career would have been too personal a quest and one for which I felt neither destined nor prepared.

For me the decisive moment came during a period of extraordinarily intense political activism in American life. Society seemed mobilized on every important issue that confronts us. The activists and supporters of long-standing causes, such as the women's and civil rights movements, seemed to dig deeper for strength and determination. Confronted with the failure to achieve through established political and judicial channels the fundamental liberties and racial equality promised in the Constitution and the Bill of Rights, people were becoming angry, and often their rage boiled over into rebellion. The nightly news seemed to echo the Declaration of Independence's cataclysmic proclamation: "[W]henever any Form of Government becomes destructive of these ends"—of securing the "unalienable" rights and liberty of the people—"it is the Right of the People to alter or to abolish it."

But in addition to anger, there was hope. Certainly for many the late 1960s and early 1970s seemed like the dawn of a new era, one during which the wrongs of so many centuries could finally be righted. In that sense, the leaders of its movements saw themselves as the heirs to the revolutionaries who founded the nation, the abolitionists and suffragettes who fought to realize the promise of liberty for all citizens, and the labor leaders who fought for equity and dignity.

Despite our understanding of the long duration of these struggles, we wanted peace, and we wanted it now; we wanted freedom, and we wanted it now; we wanted justice, and we wanted it now. In short, we were a generation of people in a hurry, impatient with lingering oppression and with the political institutions that seemed unwilling to make the changes necessary to end that oppression. Hundreds of thousands of people would mobilize to fight injustice, to end wars, to promote equality, and to end poverty. It was hard to be a bystander, and, in the eyes of some, bystanders were agents against change—a "part of the problem." Like that of the Civil War a century earlier, this social schism would divide families as the fabric of our society began to unravel.

The political and social conflict that gripped the nation, indeed the world, reached a fever pitch in my community of Berkeley, California. Within the cauldron of the Bay Area, all of the movements for social progress had significant constituencies. Their militancy was palpable, and the demand to "be part of the solution" certainly forced one to defend any decision not to become involved. In 1967 I ran for a seat on the Berkeley City Council—and won. Once I was a public official, I felt it my duty to listen carefully to the protesters. I heard the legitimacy of many of their demands and worked to further these causes. I agreed to campaign to go to Washington as the U.S. congressional representative from my district only because I was willing to be a voice for these movements.

While many with whom I shared governance on the Berkeley City Council and then later in Congress would decry the protests, demonstrations, and other expressions of outrage as a discordant noise—incoherent and strident—I heard a chorus. I heard harmony in the claims for equality by African Americans, by Native Americans, the continent's indigenous peoples, and by Latinos and Asian Americans. I heard the counterpoint added by the assertions of women, lesbians and gay men, and the disabled, all of whom were being denied full participation in the economic, social, and political life of the community. I heard syncopation from the environmentalists and from peace movement activists, who were seeking to defend the life of the planet from ecocide and its people from self-destruction. I found inspiration in this music of protest and I believed that its powerful voices deserved representation in a body that all to often seemed to refuse to listen or to respond. In her essay "Where Is the Rage?" June Jordan, an African American and an extraordinary activist, poet, and professor, captures the legacy of that era: "unabashed moral certitude and the purity—the incredible outgoing energy—of righteous rage."

At the time, many felt that the ideas advanced by this loose coalition of social movements were not being vigorously articulated in the institutions of the body politic. By accepting the call to run for elective office, I entered a bond—a sacred contract if you will—with my community to represent the wisdom and the beauty of these ideas and ideals, and to articulate the "righteous rage" of those who had been the victims of injustice. My election—or the election of any single individual—could not be a substitute for community activism, but it could be a component of an overall strategy to achieve social change.

In the years to come, when harnessed to the political process, such powerful expressions from the community would change the world. But as an activist chosen to be an insider, I would often lament the failure of the community to mobilize in order to pressure the institutions of government, and the sometimes dispositive impact this would have upon efforts to stop a war, to redefine national priorities, or to achieve other significant objectives. I would wonder about the efficacy of continuing to serve in public office. During those times, only my faith in the ideals and the movements that had inspired me in the first place allowed me to carry out the duties of representation and governance.

Departing from public office after nearly thirty years provides both an opportunity and an obligation to share some insight on the public record. While in the beginning I sought to avoid the call to public office, I came to value such service as extraordinarily thrilling, challenging, and humbling. The jokes of late-night television hosts notwithstanding, I came to believe that elective public service is perhaps the highest honor that a community can bestow upon one of its own.

The experience of being an African American representing constituencies that were overwhelmingly white—first on the Berkeley City Council and then in the U.S. House—was complex and challenging. As a "left-wing radical" elected to a Democrat-controlled Congress—a Congress significantly influenced by its "Southern Barons" and one that shared power with Richard Nixon's White House—I found the challenge even more daunting.

The pressure from the White House came down on me early, even before my election to Congress. At a time when I had won only the Democratic nomination, the Nixon White House unleashed Vice President Spiro T. Agnew to attack me from across the nation. Speaking in Arkansas, Agnew challenged the right of the people who had chosen me as their candidate to have any voice in the Congress, by charging that I was "an out-and-out radical" who needed to be "purged from the body politic." This was not an idle threat, given that institutions such as the House Un-American Activities Committee (HUAC), established to enforce McCarthyism's efforts at rigid political conformity, still existed upon my arrival in Washington. Although the disclosure of the Nixon "enemies list"—and my prominent place on it—was yet to come, I found myself reviled by the White House and by many in the Congress because of my left-wing political views and those of the community I represented.

Much of what we accomplished during the first half of my tenure in the House occurred despite the pervasive influence of those who held that my values and positions were "outside the mainstream." Often those successes were achieved beyond the legislative chamber. When certain political leaders and much of the establishment press looked at me, they did not see Ron Dellums, a member of Congress the equal of all others under our system, where districts grant mandates to representatives through the ballot—they saw Ron Dellums, representative of that "commie-pinko left-wing community of 'Berzerkeley'" and a person whose ideas belonged outside the legislative chamber, if anywhere. By characterizing me as an extremist, and by efforts to marginalize the ideas I advocated, they sought to avoid the depth, integrity, and beauty of the political idealism that my constituents had sent me to Washington to represent. The attack was all too often personal in nature, focused on my credibility and authenticity as an American rather than as a challenge at the level of ideas. As it would for anybody in my situation, this caused me great personal pain and consternation over the years.

But the community kept returning me to Congress and kept insisting that I represent its urgent, progressive voice. Like the Southern Barons of an earlier era, I and other like-minded legislators became a group—in our case a group of urban progressives—who ultimately benefited from seniority, and whose ideas and ideals would begin to find their way more prominently into the debate and into the legislative product. By staying engaged, and by learning the legislative process and demanding that it accord our ideas the dignity granted to those of other coalitions, we began more and more to influence legislative outcomes. However, seniority alone does not account for our success. We depended very much on the presence of what the Reverend Jesse Jackson would later come to refer to as "street heat"—people mobilized to command the attention of the organs of power. Their activism always enhanced our ability to achieve success legislatively on behalf of their idealism and ideas.

Recently someone remarked to me casually that the mid- to late 1990s seemed to occasion the twenty-fifth anniversaries of many of the successes or manifestations of the progressive movement as a whole. Earth Day, the Stonewall demonstration in New York, the establishment of affirmative action programs and Third World Studies departments, the Supreme Court's decision in *Roe v. Wade*, the United States' withdrawal from Vietnam, the impeachment of Richard Nixon—these and many other events were the progeny of progressive campaigns that have changed the political, cultural, and social fabric of our nation. And yet recently the electoral ascendancy of the Far Right has threatened to reverse those gains, although it has also provoked a counterreaction to its overreaching efforts. Having lost sight of their earlier victories, many progressives now question their ability to bring about change or to resist right-wing reaction. A new cynicism arises, fueled in part by the press, which often fails to take a careful and comprehensive look at the conditions that continue to cause great pain in our society. Some who were past supporters of progressive movements now question even the necessity to vigilantly protect the achievements of the last three decades.

I remain committed to the belief that the view of justice articulated by the movements of the 1960s and 1970s remains the best and most noble course for our nation. It is imperative for a new generation of activists to take up the challenge and to build upon the victories of that era. I firmly believe that, in this respect, history *is* progressive. Although the forces of reaction will always resist change, the people will continue to move history forward toward equality and justice; they will refuse to be bound forever by tyranny and oppression. The question will always be, How will change be made—peacefully or not?

The events I have selected to discuss in this book are those that formed me before I entered public service and those that later contributed to my understanding of how to effect change through the use of government power. Our advocacy combined a knowledge of movements, the use of coalition, adherence to principle, and actions to create new awareness and new possibilities. It is my hope to do justice to the grand sweep of events that has done so much to change the world in my lifetime, and during my thirty-year political career. This is not an exhaustive history, but one that I hope will provide enough depth of analysis to be meaningful to the reader.

When I look at the world that confronts many young African Americans today, I see the despair and hopelessness that their situation evokes, and I remember my early life and how a similar despair gripped some during that era as well. I urgently want to instill in the current generation of youth the sense of power and righteousness that has animated centuries of struggle against racism and oppression, in this nation and throughout the world, and to provide some perspective on the victories that have been achieved. I hope that those aspiring to bring about positive changes in society will learn from my experience that entering public life can be both a principled and effective way to make a contribution.

The liberation of South Africa from the yoke of apartheid is one of the most important political and human rights events of my lifetime, and I consider having played some role in that process to be my greatest legislative and personal achievement. The history of that struggle—and of how the anti-apartheid movement in this and other countries contributed to the final outcome—should be studied in political science as a classic example for young people of how a community can manifest its demands and then organize to achieve success.

In 1973, the idea that a leftist and declared peace activist could someday chair the House Armed Services Committee was beyond imagination. When I did assume the chairmanship, twenty years later, during the transition period following the end of the Cold War, the new realities of international politics required me to be honest enough to challenge the continued value of my own Cold War–era paradigms. It was not enough to challenge the "hawks" to accommodate their thinking to the newly emerging circumstances; we had also to challenge the "doves."

Social progress occurs when the reach of justice, equality, and freedom are extended to all people and the economic foundation for healthy homes and communities is established. As an activist for justice, I agree with Dr. Martin Luther King, Jr., that a society cannot have justice without peace—or peace without justice. These are inseparably linked aspects of a community's condition; the absence of one is the absence of the other, and they can only be present at the same time. Hearing his articulation of this truth in Berkeley, California, would change the very basis of my political outlook and the nature of my commitment as a representative of the people.

Listening to Dr. King on the radio some time later, I heard him say that the most revolutionary act one could commit was to assert the full measure of one's citizenship. For thirty years of public service, I attempted to do whatever I could to help an entire constituency do just that. It seems to me that we must now revisit the foundations of our principles and understand the strategies that are necessary to achieve change in *these* times—and that an essential element of any such strategy must be to reassert our citizenship as vociferously as we did during the 1960s. As June Jordan wrote in her essay, "I do not believe that we can restore and expand the freedoms that our lives require unless and until we embrace the justice of our rage."

This rage must confront the continued misallocation of national resources, the erosion of our constitutional liberties, and the escalating threats against the achievement of constitutionally based equality. In the 1960s, Dr. King held a mirror up to the collective face of America and the view seen was so repugnant that the nation agreed it must affirmatively act to change the festering conditions of raw injustice that it saw. The prejudice and discrimination brought boldly into relief by the civil rights movement have yet to be fully eradicated, and the disingenuous claim that white workers and students are displaced from opportunities because of affirmative action misses the essential point. In an era of downsizing and the offshore migration of capital investment, opportunities must be expanded for all our citizens *while* the nation continues the necessary business of opening doors for those historically closed off from opportunity. Disturbingly, some who call themselves progressives question the need to deploy proven strategies to eliminate the lingering effects of racial inequal-

7

ity, in the name of a purely class-based politics. A truly progressive view should demand that we mobilize to address both issues—race and class—insisting on full employment and full education strategies while refusing to retreat from the principle that racism must end in our society and equality must become manifest. If we can mobilize in pursuit of such a high moral purpose, one that sets out to benefit all, we can again change the world.

Finally, I have been reminded throughout my professional and political career that working for progress in the real world demands that one learn how to escape the narrow confines of received assumptions and theories. This means constantly reassessing, moving forward, and refusing to be bound by old ways of thinking, while remaining true to core principles. Trained by a mentor social worker to understand this point early on, I came to comprehend that my public career did not allow for the luxury of ideological rigidity. Such rigidity constitutes a failure of intellectual rigor and is rooted in a misunderstanding of constantly changing material circumstances. This early mentoring, and the skills I learned at the university, would aid me throughout my career. For in one sense—whether as a caseworker, a group worker, a community organizer, or a national legislator—I would never stop being a social worker, no matter how far my calling stretched the boundaries of that profession.

chapter one

You Can Make It Out

When I was growing up in West Oakland, California, a constant part of our environment was the sound of the freight and passenger trains rolling along the nearby rail lines. The heavy rumble of the freights underpinned the industrial character of our neighborhood. The more elegantly pitched noise of the passenger trains promised that there existed a larger world beyond. The train whistles warned of danger, a reminder to watch your back.

In the years before and just after World War II, the railroad was the lifeline that bound black communities together across the nation. Still tied to their roots in the South, those African Americans who had headed west or north for jobs in the factories and shipyards would return to their people by train or send messages via travelers or the crews that plied the rails. The porters, stewards, and cooks who worked their trades in the Pullman cars provided important financial resources to their communities through their wages. For those unable to travel because they couldn't get time off from work or had limited financial resources, but who wished for their children to visit grandparents, the railroad workers would make certain that kids traveling alone would arrive safely at their destinations. Cosmopolitan and intellectually avid, the crewmembers also provided a transmission network for the discussion of social and political ideas, as well as matters of fashion and culture, linking Oakland with Harlem, Los Angeles, Atlanta, and countless other large and small communities around the country.

My dad, Verney, having followed his older brother, my uncle C. L. Dellums, to California from Texas, worked the railroad for a time—"runnin' on the road." C. L. and other community civil rights leaders later sought to integrate the waterfront, and my father was sent forward to break open the docks and work as a longshoreman. At first he got very little work on the waterfront; to make ends meet he managed the pool hall operated by the railroad union downstairs from its offices. This made it financially hard on my family, but in the long run my dad eventually succeeded, retiring after working as a longshoreman for more than twenty years.

As meaningful as the work was, my dad's career on the railroad and on the docks failed to deliver on the hope, nurtured by both him and my uncle, that leaving Texas would allow my dad to go to college. Both my father and C. L. had graduated from high school, and each of them pursued learning on their own throughout their lives. They were very dignified men, deeply interested in the social sciences, and they were masterful orators. Despite their lack of formal education, my dad and his brother were so learned, because of their voracious reading habits, that they seemed to be the intellectual equals of any college grad—in fact many believed that my uncle had received an Ivy League degree.

C. L. Dellums became a protégé of the legendary A. Philip Randolph, the labor organizer who had successfully led the strike that created the Brotherhood of Sleeping Car Porters, the first African American–led trade union in America. A spellbinding speaker whose stentorian voice could shake the rafters of a church or union hall, C. L. eventually took over the leadership of the union when Randolph retired. He loomed larger than life to me. He was a role model of success—well dressed always, he ran an office, had a staff, and was a leader in the community. In fact, C. L. was so well respected throughout his life that although Ronald Reagan, newly elected as governor of California in 1966, initially considered not reappointing him to the state's Fair Employment Commission, he yielded to the political reality that my uncle could not be denied his place on the commission. By then I was an adult, and it astonished me that somebody as conservative and strong-willed as Reagan would nonetheless feel obligated to seat my uncle—a staunch progressive of equal determination. Then again, as an adult or as a child, I never would have wanted to cross my uncle, and it ultimately made sense to me that neither would Governor Reagan. C. L.'s reappointment left me with the view that with enough political support one could press forward with progressive ideas even in the face of a seemingly implacable adversary.

Oakland in the 1940s was a city, but a small one compared to Los Angeles, Chicago, or Philadelphia. The West Oakland neighborhood where I lived was its own small town—racially mixed but unified by its working-class character. People tended to be employed, but whether Italian, Portuguese, Greek, Hispanic, or black, they were generally working-class folks. Hit hard by the Depression, many benefited from the jobs created during the military buildup of World War II—working at bases that would become a focal point of defense policy debate half a century later. These military bases and the shipyards of the Bay Area drew black people from throughout the nation to the West Coast, most of them coming from the South. West Oakland would be the "port of entry" for blacks in Northern California, just as San Jose was for immigrants from Mexico or San Francisco was for Asians. Most of the black migrants would disembark the train at Sixteenth and Wood Streets in West Oakland and settle within blocks of the industrial base that had lured them west in the first place.

Over the years of my childhood, West Oakland lost its integrated character—certainly its white majority—becoming more and more black, finally almost exclusively so. New black migrants filled the houses of the departing white ethnics, who were moving to neighborhoods in the northern and eastern parts of the city, or even out of Oakland altogether, presaging the "urban flight" that would begin in earnest in the 1950s. Although people working at the bases and shipyards earned good money, housing segregation kept black folks bottled up, primarily in West Oakland. Three and four families were often packed into what had been single-family dwellings; indeed, many garages in the community housed families despite the concrete floors and the dampness that often lingered in the infamously foggy air of the Bay Area. Some homeowners would rent rooms to individuals, whom we called "roomers." Throughout my youth I could hear the sounds of family life floating out of curtained garage windows and savor the scent of "down-home" cooking oozing through the cracks of garage doors. Our household, like so many others, contained three generations and multiple families.

Seventh Street was the heart of this vibrant community, lined with restaurants, hair salons, barber shops, nightclubs, cafes, and stores and other businesses bustling with activity. It provided the necessary commercial and social life for our neighborhood and the promenade to display Saturday-night or Sunday-morning finery.

My mom worked at the legendary Slim Jenkins's historic nightclub on "the Street," before trying her hand as a beautician in the neighborhood. In order to learn the skills required for her new endeavor, she enrolled in the only beauty school in the city. This offered her the opportunity to cut, style, and curl the hair of the school's patrons—but because of the segregated patterns of life in the city, these patrons were exclusively white. I can remember the smell of "frying hair" in our kitchen, as she hot-combed our neighbors' hair for practice, and the sound of curlers snapping as she perfected the skills that would be of use in *our* neighborhood. Not only was her personal training incomplete at the only beauty school in Oakland, that school was not preparing any of its students to serve the needs of an entire community. It was like so many other everyday realities in our lives.

Later my mother was the first black person to get a job at the downtown J. C. Penney store, and eventually she became a career clerk in the government offices that were located downtown as well. These new jobs put her in a world that did not yet fully accept the presence of a woman of her color, and she was fiercely proud of her achievement.

To go downtown was to leave the protection of the neighborhood, to become an outsider in your own city. Although the effect of the Jim Crow legacy was not so pronounced or unbridled as in the South, being black in the 1940s in Oakland meant watching your back. I remember many occasions on which police officers would harass black and Latino kids, or knock down and kick or beat up people of color. Although white kids were not immune from police harassment, the almost all-white force seemed to focus especially on people of color, particularly black folks. As West Oakland became less integrated, it increasingly took on the characteristics of a small Southern black community, with the white, urban police becoming more and more alienated from the people they were supposed to serve. This pattern of racial harassment and police alienation from the community would continue for decades, leading ultimately to the birth of the Black Panther Party in the 1960s.

Although it involved some financial sacrifice for a working-class family, my parents enrolled my sister and me in St. Patrick's, a Catholic school. Both of my parents had hoped to attend college. In fact, C. L. had sent for my father to move to California because they were going to secure Dad's enrollment in U. C. Berkeley's school of journalism, through which my dad could pursue his dream of becoming a sports journalist. But before he could enroll, he and my mother met and married. After marriage and children, they knew that some of their dreams would be fulfilled only through the lives of their children. Given their suspicions of the increasingly segregated schools in our neighborhood, they forked over scarce dollars for tuition to ensure that their children would be well grounded in the basics.

The nuns taught me well, and they were as concerned with the academic success of their black students as they were with that of any others. My report cards, while containing good grades, included comments from my teachers about how things came to me too easily, that I was smart and talented but that they encouraged me to work harder. I knew my parents wanted me to go to college, and at some level I saw myself going, although I had no concept of what this meant. My parents strove hard to impart to my sister and me their belief in the value of educational excellence and they pushed us to achieve, monitoring our work. As our neighborhood became increasingly "Southern," older folks—with their cultural roots in the experience of being black in the South—would say to us, "Go out and get you an education, because nobody can take that away from you."

These factors and the constant assurance by the nuns that I could make it to college would stick with me from my childhood Catholic school experience. The nuns always approached me as if I were intelligent, they never assumed that I was unable to learn something, and they always pressed me to work harder and to achieve to my highest ability.

The academic curriculum of school was augmented by the history I witnessed sitting in my uncle's office and by the discussions I had at home with my father and mother. My parents were very much concerned not only about my grades but about the content of my education. At dinner, my father would question me concerning what I had learned that day; he often corrected the historical record with the information he had acquired from his extensive readings. I learned from him to probe and question, never to accept without critique any assertions of fact or value.

My parents were especially proud of the accomplishments of African Americans, and they were deeply concerned with the problem of race in America. Forceful and persistent, arguing from data and fact, my father provided nuance and context to the lessons being handed down from the homogeneous view of history taught in school and the sometimes brutal reality of the streets. My mother, more philosophical and flexible by nature, asserted her pride and perspective in different and subtler ways. Their combined insight and enlightenment stood firm against the tidal wave of social pressures that threatened to drown the aspirations of ghetto kids. Having learned of and witnessed the great achievements of Africans and African Americans, they sought to instill in me a sense of boundless possibility. While my youthful visions of the future were of a life as a famous singer or baseball star, they honed my intellect and analytical skills, and pushed my language capabilities. As a result, many in my neighborhood would observe, "That boy sure can talk," or, "That boy is going to be a preacher or a lawyer."

People also began to talk about my "perceptiveness." I would comment about something I had heard, and the adults would say, "Now that boy understands what we are saying." Even if sometimes I really did not, this was a form of praise that I liked, and so I began to become more and more observant, taking the time to understand what people were saying rather than popping off verbally early in a conversation. This skill would be essential to me later, as a professional, as an organizer, and as a politician, and it never failed that I could more quickly achieve a desired outcome by understanding what it was that a client, an adversary, or a friend was saying.

Outside of the home, C. L.'s erudition and intellect left a powerful impression on me. Although he was handsome and charismatic, clearly it was his mastery of the language that led his union brothers to fall in under his lead; his mastery of strategy was what kept them loyal to his banner. The political heart of Seventh Street was my uncle's union office, and I loved to spend time there observing him in action. He touched everything that was happening politically, whether it was the NAACP, the Democratic Party, or the union. Although my family was generally well respected in the neighborhood, C. L. gave magic to the Dellums name throughout Oakland and beyond. It was obvious to me that he was "the man."

When I was twelve my mother and father separated. One consequence was that the tuition payments to Catholic school placed an even heavier burden on what was now a requirement to run two households. My sister and I begged and pleaded with my parents to allow us to join our peers from the neighborhood, who attended Prescott School, across the street. We could see them every day on the playground, and we desperately wanted out of St. Patrick's. My mom had rejected sending me to this neighborhood school because of her concern that there black youth were being tracked away from college prep programs and into the trades. We succeeded in getting out of St. Patrick's, but we were enrolled at Westlake Junior High School, a public school located outside West Oakland, in a neighborhood that was predominately white and middle-class. Using my uncle C. L.'s North Oakland residential address to secure admission, we soon found ourselves in an almost alien environment. It was a world completely different from either our own neighborhood, increasingly black, or St. Patrick's, naturally integrated by families from throughout the local parish.

Nothing in my childhood had prepared me to be a student at Westlake. In my first semester I was one of only fourteen black students and one of only two black males. The long commute from our community past Lake Merritt each day drove home the point that I was off my turf. In addition, most of the kids at school were well-off financially; the boys wore fancy shoes, Pendelton shirts, and cashmere sweaters. In Catholic school we had all worn uniforms, so economic class was not so obviously on display. Although my sister and I were always well dressed, our clothes would never match those worn by most Westlake students.

Although I had heard racial epithets hurled at blacks and Latinos in my life, they generally came from people outside of our neighborhood. Within the community, people—whether white or black—knew you by your name and were not socially awkward in the presence of racial difference. Westlake was not a situation of natural integration; the handful of blacks enrolled in the school were either outsiders like my sister and me or isolated neighborhood "block breakers," and the white kids of Westlake were not used to dealing with difference in a respectful manner. As a result, phrases like "the colored boy"—as in "let the colored boy play"—which would never have been heard in West Oakland, became a substitute for my name and always branded me as an outsider.

Although this degradation made me simmer emotionally, I worked hard to do well in school and succeeded in being accepted socially. Never a fighter by disposition, back in my own neighborhood I learned how to "play the dozens" by sneaking out of the house at night and listening to adults sitting on the corner, telling stories and verbally cutting each other. The rhyme and rhythm and style of the dozens, brought from the South, would stay with me. As I learned to best my adversaries verbally, cutting them down with words, some of the tougher guys in the neighborhood began to take up for me; they liked my verbal style. This worked for me because it meant that people in the community knew they couldn't mess with me physically or my "take-up buddies" would be around to settle the score. But my take-up buddies were not enrolled at Westlake.

One day during study hall when I was in the eighth grade, the teacher, also a counselor, went out of the classroom to work with a student. None of the rest of us—twenty or so students, of whom I was the only black person—felt like studying, and we got to goofing around. One boy was trying to cut me down verbally, but all my neighborhood practice was getting the best of him. With his wit failing him, and no doubt feeling humiliated, he suddenly leapt up and called me a "dirty black African." Rage exploded in me as I jumped to my feet and started punching and pounding him. I remember hitting him with more anger than I had ever hit anybody before. Then suddenly kids were shouting that the teacher was coming, and we all resumed our seats, heads buried in books. At that moment the bell rang, ending study hall, and we all quickly left.

Word about the fight spread fast, and soon I was a hero among the few black students at the school. Feeling pretty proud of myself for "defending the race," I wanted to rush home and tell my mother. I was sure that this proud black woman would be filled with joy over the victory I had won in behalf of our people.

When she got home from work, I told my mother how I had "whipped the boy" for calling me a dirty black African. She offered no congratulations and asked me to repeat why I had fought him. Then she sat me down.

"I work and you go to school every day," she said, "so I can't be there with you to help you decide to fight or not to fight. That's your decision. But since you brought it to me, I think you should have fought only because he called you dirty, if that made you angry enough. Not because he called you black, because you *are* a member of the black race. And not because he called you an African, because you *are* of African descent.

"Hundreds of adjectives could be used to describe Ronald Dellums, and two of them are that you are black and of African descent," she told me. "You are also many other things: a son, a brother, a friend, a baseball player, a student, and a newspaper boy. You're tall, you're intelligent, and so on. These are all adjectives of which you should be proud, including your race and your ancestry."

Then she said, "Although you might not understand it now, when you threw your fist into that boy's face, you were throwing a brick into a mirror—it was an act of self-hatred."

I was confused. Instead of bringing my mother joy, I had obviously caused her pain. I later walked by her bedroom and heard her crying tears of sadness.

Later still I asked my mother why she had been crying. She sat both my sister and me down and answered. "Maybe I've done something wrong . . . because I've brought both of you this far into the world and I haven't helped you to feel a sense of pride in your blackness and your African heritage. Maybe I haven't done enough to help both of you understand that being black and being African is nothing to fight against. . . . If somebody calls you black or African, you should smile and say, 'Yes I am, and I'm proud of it.' It was my responsibility to help you gain that pride and I haven't done it, and I feel badly about it. I believe I have failed you both."

She began to bring home books and magazines from the library and to teach us more about the history of black people in America and about our African heritage. Although I was only thirteen, she worked to instill in me a confidence about my rightful place in society and a recognition of the fact that other people's lack of insight was not demeaning to me. Her efforts forced me to confront the reality that you have to start by dealing with people as they are and seek to change their views from where they start, not from where you want them to be. It was a lesson that would be invaluable in both my professional and political careers, for at that point my mother chose not to reinforce my anger. Instead she sought to reinforce my humanity, my sense of pride in who and what I was.

When I graduated from Westlake, my assigned school was West Oakland's McClymonds High School, an athletic powerhouse and overwhelmingly black. McClymonds counselors decided that I was really not college material. They based their view solely on my declining junior high grades, the consequence of young love and the distractions that adolescence brought, and despite all the protestations of my parents, the counselors would not relent; they were used to channeling black students into the trades and they could see no other future for me.

Once again resorting to the artifice of my uncle's North Oakland address, my mother secured my enrollment at Oakland Technical High School—"Tech"—her alma mater and a school that offered solid college preparatory courses. Based on my academic success at Catholic school and my earlier junior high grades, Tech's counselors were persuaded to place me into the more rigorous college prep classes.

I succeeded at first. At the end of my first year, my grades were so strong that my biology teacher went to the administration to see whether or not an academic scholarship might exist to which I could aspire, and discovered that there was a scholarship to the prestigious University of California for an academically qualified black male student from Tech. Although the high school was 30 to 40 percent black by enrollment, I was one of only two black male students in college prep, and the other—Pervis Atkins—was surely going to get a football scholarship. The scholarship to U. C. was mine if I could maintain my grades. My parents were thrilled. As with the nuns before, many of my teachers were strongly supportive. They often wrote encouraging notes on my report cards and would call my parents to urge them to push me to pursue my education beyond high school. (Time and again, I would remember their confidence in my abilities, which would help me to believe in the possibility of success despite many failures.)

The scholarship was not to be mine. I was preoccupied with becoming a big man on campus and getting along with the fellas, and my interest in girls and "running the streets" would once again derail me from my academic pursuits. I talked on the phone instead of studying. I did not want to be the "sundown Ronnie" of my younger days, always having to be home by evening to do my homework. I wanted to fit in with the crowd, and most of them were not enrolled in college prep.

In addition, I was crushed emotionally when I did not make the baseball squad, something I wanted more than anything else. I was actually a pretty good pitcher at the time, playing with guys like Frank Robinson—*the* Frank Robinson who would become a star with the Baltimore Orioles. My dad would spend his few extra dollars to buy me special equipment, and my grandmother—Gram—would massage my arm to keep it limber. I was certainly good enough for the team in the tenth grade, at least junior varsity. When I was turned down by the varsity team for the second time, in my junior year, my father's inclination was to sue the school district, with the help of the NAACP, on the grounds that few black guys who tried out made the team, even those who were pretty good ballplayers. I did not want to do that, thinking that it would detract from my personal accomplishments if it were said that "Dellums got on the team through a lawsuit, not because of his arm." Perhaps my father was right; perhaps by failing to assert my rights at the time I was allowing myself to become less than a full citizen. Perhaps, like many of those who argue today that they have achieved everything on their own, I failed then to recognize that sometimes it takes collective action to obtain the enforcement of our rights, which in turn allows each individual to achieve to their best ability.

In any event, my rejection by the baseball team took my spirit away and contributed to my loss of interest in high school. In combination with all the other temptations and distractions, this caused my grades to drop. Through artifice—and with the help of girlfriends in the school office—I figured out how to avoid having my parents know the real state of my academic situation. As a result, I went to my graduation night not knowing if I would even receive a diploma. Meanwhile, my mom and dad went telling their friends that my scholarship to U. C. would be announced from the stage. When that did not occur, it was crushing to my parents, who had worked and sacrificed to make college achievable for me. I felt I had failed them and promised that I would make good on their dream.

That fall I enrolled at San Francisco City College, in engineering—a profession I was so disinterested in that I dropped out of the program before the end of the first semester. My mother bemoaned this action; she felt that by leaving school I was forswearing ever acquiring a college education. Having promised my parents that I would go to college, I felt terribly guilty, but I just couldn't continue in school. Worse than my sense of guilt was the feeling that my life was in complete disarray.

In January 1954, less than a year out of high school, I was adrift—unemployed and seemingly unemployable because I was too young or too untrained, or maybe because I was just plain black.

A few friends from the neighborhood had decided to go into the military. Military service was not anything I had ever actively contemplated—and the Korean War was underway—but more and more the idea grew on me. I could get out of town, see part of the world, earn some money (which I was dramatically failing at by staying in Oakland), and I could use the GI Bill to go to college if I wanted to do so later. But I did not want to go into the service without a buddy.

I talked with my dad about it, and he suggested I should go into the Coast Guard. "You don't have to end up in some backwoods fort; the Coast Guard is located in lots of large metropolitan centers," he argued. So I talked with my buddy Rudy Harrison and spent a week convincing him that we should try for the Coast Guard, although he seemed set on the Air Force. We went over to San Francisco to the Coast Guard recruiter, who told us in a split second that they were not enlisting at the time; they had just had a round and wouldn't be recruiting again for another six months. His active disinterest in talking with us any further was obvious: we were being told to take ourselves to some other place.

By then I was pretty excited about serving on a ship and traveling around to see the world. Rudy persisted in his interest in the Air Force, but after several days I wore him down and we headed to the Navy recruiter in the Oakland Civic Center/Post Office building downtown (the very building that would later house my congressional district office). There the recruiter told us that we could go into the service with stewardship ratings: in other words, we could cook or wait tables. I didn't have a problem with people who cooked or waited tables—hell, the Brotherhood of Sleeping Car Porters had made a profession out of such service, and I knew lots of such people and respected them for what they did—we had come here, though, to enlist as seamen, and I found the recruiter's attitude to be racist. He wasn't asking us if we wanted to be stewards or cooks, he was telling us that this was the field to which blacks were limited.

After a few words were exchanged on this point, he relented and allowed us to take the seaman's test. I passed with higher marks than Rudy, with the practical result that I could go in now but he would have to go in later. We went back and forth with the recruiter, arguing that he could get us both in at the same time, and all during this time the Marine Corps recruiter kept trying to get us to consider his branch of the armed services. The Marines, their recruiter said, could take us both right now, and we would serve with an Alameda County platoon.

Rudy still wanted to try for the Air Force. Since he had gone along with me to the Coast Guard and the Navy, it was only right that I pursue his interest now. So we walked across downtown Oakland to the Air Force recruiter and took the enlistment test for the Air Force. We both passed, but because I had gotten very high marks, the Air Force was willing to enlist me right away, with Rudy having to wait for a later opportunity. It was the same story. We wanted to go in together, so we left the building and started walking, talking about our future, our dreams, and what we should do. We found ourselves back at the Civic Center building and sat down on the steps.

Rudy was much more practical and realistic than I was at the time. He also understood that despite our friendship our paths were differently marked. He said that he really thought he wanted to make a career of military service, but could not see himself in the Marine Corps for the long haul. On the other hand, the Air Force really interested him. He told me what I already knew.

"You're not interested in a military career; you want to get a job. You want to get out of town. You want to earn the GI Bill and go to college, man. As your friend, I think you should take the two-year Marine Corps deal. You can do *anything* for two years. In two years you can come back and go to school. Me, I've got nothing else to do and a military career sounds good to me. That's what I want to do, make a career in the Air Force."

"Besides," he said, "if you don't get out of town and just keep hanging around, you're going to get in trouble with the police and maybe even end up in jail—you never know." That was happening to a lot of fellows in the community, what with the police always seeming to home in on black guys for things for which people of other races seemed not to be bothered. "You're the only one—maybe you and Theus—who can make it out and get into school. You've got to do it."

So Rudy and I cried a little, we hugged and we shook hands—and though we promised to stay in touch with each other we both knew at that moment that our lives had changed forever. Things would never be the same between us. (Rudy did go into the Air Force, and while home on leave he died, in a tragic accident, on the Fourth of July. Because he was known as a gifted athlete and a strong swimmer, nobody really believed he could get into trouble in the water, and he drowned as hundreds ignored his cries for help.)

We ran back up the stairs to the recruiter's office. I guess he had seen us sitting on the steps, because he had stayed at the station after closing hours. While Rudy ran down to the nearby courthouse to get a copy of my birth certificate, I took and passed the entrance test. I signed the papers right then, and when my mom got home from work that Monday night I was to shock her yet again: her son was leaving two days later to become a marine, and everybody was predicting that fighting would soon break out again in Korea. I tried to assuage her fears and told her I was doing it so I could secure the GI Bill funding that would allow me to go to college—and make up for the lost scholarship to U. C. I also explained to her that I needed to get away from home and get my head together, grow up a little bit and take some of the pressure off of her. (That's precisely what would happen, although not without risks.) Mom was not persuaded. She thought this was the worst decision I had ever made and that nothing good could come from it.

Within forty-eight hours I was in boot camp at the Marine Corps Recruit Depot, in San Diego, California. Basic training was shockingly strenuous and sometimes brutal. I thought it was the most horrible thing I had ever gotten into. People were screaming and cursing at us and pushing people beyond the limits of their physical endurance. Drill instructors would march their platoons into each other just to provoke fights. If your family sent you candy, they would force you to eat all the candy at once, or they'd make you smoke a whole pack of cigarettes at once if that was the gift you got in the mail. Although my senior drill instructor, Staff Sergeant Allen, a black man, was decent and professional and obviously cared about all of his marines—especially the few blacks under his leadership—I encountered a lot of Southern, unsophisticated, and blatantly racist junior drill instructors. Between the sadism, general harassment and intimidation, and the racist barrage, I gave thought to running away and quitting. But it became a fleeting thought when I remembered Rudy's admonition that one could do anything for two years. I decided I needed to finish what I had started. I decided to just live it out, to survive, to endure.

One day Staff Sergeant Allen called me into his office. He told me that I had gotten the highest score in my training battalion on the battery of tests administered when we first arrived in boot camp. He said that there were representatives from Officer Candidate School (OCS) in a Quonset hut down the road. They had come to interview me for possible selection for officer training. The sergeant told me to report to the hut, but on my way out the door I saw an odd look on his face, one that I would not understand until after the interview.

By this time, I was actually doing well in the Corps, and I thought with pride that OCS might be a way to get ahead in my career and to get into college. All sorts of ambitions began to fill my head as I double-timed it across to the hut. I entered the small building and snapped to attention in front of the two officers sitting behind a small table. "Sir. Private Dellums reporting as ordered, sir."

The two officers looked at me, looked at each other, and looked back to me again. One of them asked, "What race are you, Private?"

"Sir. I am a Negro, sir." I replied, with all the pride my mom had helped me to acquire.

The same officer said, "That's what I thought. Get on back to your outfit, son."

With a broken heart and shattered dreams, I did an about-face and left the building. It was all too obvious that I had been rejected for OCS on the basis of my race, but I could not understand why I had been ordered to report in person if they would not take blacks into the officer corps. Clearly these officers had been surprised by my appearance.

It turned out that when my paperwork was processed at boot camp—after my hair had been cut and I was moving quickly through lines along with scores of other recruits—an admitting clerk had glanced up and entered "Caucasian" on my forms. The OCS officers had come to interview a white lad with a college prep back ground, some college, and the number-one score in the training battalion—a prime candidate for OCS as long as all of it was true. They hadn't asked me any other questions, or undertaken to learn anything else about me. When they saw I was black the interview ended.

From that day forward, I counted down every day and hour until my discharge. I found the discipline of the Corps challenging, and it helped me to mature, but I could never forget that early incident and saw that the Corps was not where my opportunities would lie. In the meantime, I began to feel in charge of my environment and understood the values and principles that the Corps sought to inculcate within us—on its better days. I was in great shape. I gained a sense of independence, of competence, of being on my own. I gained a tremendous amount of confidence in myself. My father, upon seeing me return home for the first time, cried and hugged me, declaring, "My son went away a boy and came back a man." Despite my mother's dire concern, joining the Marines would not be the worst decision I would make. It brought me a discipline that would serve me well for the rest of my life.

When I thought people were being treated unjustly in the Corps, I brought it to the attention of my fellow marines. Sometimes the only way we could handle this was to do a little brawling, but other times I was able to mobilize a group of people in order to change the circumstances. One night I saw a young black marine being arrested by a squad of military police, and that he was being badly hurt in the process by an all-white crew; it was completely unjust as I viewed it. So I rounded up scores of marines to protest what was going on. First I went to the black and Latino marines: they would immediately grasp the injustice. Then we went to the Caucasian marines and told them what was up. There was too much brotherhood at stake for the white guys not to join us in the protest—at the end of the day you have to know that the guys you will be with in the field will defend you with their lives.

I brought these hundreds of marines right up the parade field to the MP company and went in to demand that they release the man they had unfairly arrested. They refused, so I went to the officer of the day. Seeing that a riot was almost at hand, they let the guy go. Without having thought about the possibility that mutiny charges could have been brought against me (the authorities apparently did think about it for a while), I was determined to oppose such blatant racist behavior and brutality—and I felt that the Corps should have known it was not well served by such conduct. (I was lucky. Events a decade earlier at Port Chicago, near Oakland, had demonstrated how merciless the military could be with protesters within their own ranks—taking to court martial scores of black sailors who had refused to load weapons ships under dangerous conditions. Events decades later aboard ships in the Navy, events that I would investigate from my seat on the House Armed Services Committee, showed how slowly progress would be made within the military to end the comprehensive effects of racial discrimination.)

Balancing high performance with a refusal to yield to the injustices I witnessed or experienced, I managed to make it through my two years in the military without any serious disciplinary problems. I never was sent to serve outside of California, despite repeated efforts on my part. I was often assigned to work in positions above my rank, and was sometimes placed in the awkward position of supervising marines who outranked me. This was partly because the Corps never gave me the rank I deserved while serving, although they promised it to me if I would reenlist. By this time, however, I had decided that I wanted to go back to school, and I was tired of the capricious nature of life in a supposedly ordered universe. With newfound maturity, discipline, and a sense of purpose, I was ready now for college and had become ambitious about enrolling.

During my time in the service I had met and befriended a really great guy, Vernon Fulcher, who had come to the Marines from Kansas. About the same age, he and I had both started community college and dropped out. Fulcher was an avid reader and got me into the habit of reading—mostly novels but also a lot of books about race and the problems of race in America. Reading had provoked me to stand up for brothers in the Marines whom I thought were being treated unfairly; it also generated within me a new excitement about learning. Like my father and uncle before me, I had discovered that other worlds existed beyond the horizons of my personal experiences—and that the experiences of others could inform my judgments about the events of my own life.

After the service our intellectual paths would continue in parallel. Fulcher took an associate of arts degree from Los Angeles Community College; I took one from Oakland City College. He went to Los Angeles State; I went to San Francisco State. He went to UCLA for graduate training in psychology; I went to U. C. Berkeley for graduate training in social work, with an emphasis in psychiatry.

Getting through school took its toll. Although I was strongly motivated, I remembered my earlier college experience and did not want to overcommit myself. Because I took only a two-thirds load in my first semester, I qualified for only $120 a month in GI Bill financial support. I had gotten married, to my first wife, Arthurine, and had a child, my daughter Pam, while in the service, so that was not going to cut it financially. With the help of veterans preference, I got a job working on an early IBM computer system at the Naval Supply Center—one of those bases that had drawn an earlier generation of black folks to the West Oakland community. With the couple of hundred dollars a month from my work added to the GI Bill money, we could make ends meet.

I worked the swing shift as a tabulating machine operator—GS-2—from 4:00 P.M. to midnight and attended school from 8:00 A.M. to 2:30 P.M. Basically, I went straight from school to work and from work to home, at which time I had to study. It was an incessant wheel, turning over and over every day—working to provide for my family, studying to provide for my future. By January our relationship was a shambles, and my young wife and I separated and eventually divorced after less than two years of marriage.

I went to my dad and explained my situation. I needed help and he responded by welcoming me to move in with him, even though he had only a tiny, one-bedroom apartment. I would spend the next five and a half years sharing my father's space. It was an extraordinary opportunity to get to know him beyond his role as my father. We became fast friends. He became my confidant, my buddy, and my roommate. I lived with him until I remarried, in January of 1962.

A few months after my separation, and well into my second semester of school, the base acquired a larger and more sophisticated computer system. It was going to reduce the workload. Told by my supervisor that I would have to work days, but a day job was mine if I wanted it, I knew that I couldn't take the job and also stay in school. I explained my situation and asked to be kept on the swing shift, but my request was denied. I went all the way up through the system to the base commander, finally appealing to him as a fellow service member. He would not relent. "Report to work at 0800 Monday morning or be fired," he said. Our meeting was over.

The walk from his office to my work station was one of the longest I had ever taken—even though I'd marched far longer distances in the Marines. I knew as I thought about my situation that I had reached another cross-roads moment in my life. When I got back, my shift supervisor asked what was the outcome of the meeting with the commander. I told her exactly what he had said.

"So what are you going to do?" she asked.

I answered, "I've been thinking about that. If I quit school and stay here and work the job, I might become a GS-4 or a GS-5 in a few years' time. Or maybe someday—with luck—I might become a shift supervisor like you. But if I quit the job and stay in school, my opportunities are unlimited. I respectfully tender my resignation."

It was like leaping off a cliff, having faith only that something would break the fall and save me from another disaster, another disappointment.

Within a few weeks I had secured a job as an after-school recreation director at Lafayette Elementary School in West Oakland. I would continue to work in Oakland Recreation Department programs through my first year of graduate school. The opportunity to work with youth provided me the insight of the constantly changing and honest perceptions that kids bring to community affairs, culture, and political life. Despite the fact that school and work were both substantial commitments, I availed myself of every training seminar that the staff were offered to improve their work skills. I took art workshops, drama workshops, and even obtained a certificate to teach crew, so I could take kids from West Oakland to Lake Merritt, in the center of the city. I marveled at their joy in learning to work as a team, employing their collective strength with precision. I was learning again how to listen, and how to be educative, skills I would use for the rest of my life.

| *chapter two* |

Sit Down, Man—We're Going to Win This

As soon as I received my master's degree in social work from U. C. Berkeley, I took the State of California's civil service examination for social workers. I was tremendously enthusiastic about what I had learned in school and had a great desire to do well in the field. I aspired to develop new treatment modalities and to contribute to a new and better understanding of how to help individuals manage their complex lives and cope with the various pressures that impinge upon the human condition. Having passed first among all who took the exam at that sitting, I had many job opportunities, at sites throughout the state. I chose to work in Oakland, with clients from the type of neighborhoods throughout the city with which I was so familiar.

As a black man, I understood fully that many of the obstacles that individuals face during their lives are social and structural—some especially arduous, such as racism—rather than personal. On the other hand, I knew from my own life that personal issues and struggles had at times derailed me from the path of success that my parents had tried to keep me on. With my education and training providing a professional overlay to my childhood and adult experiences, I had come to believe that by listening, paying attention, and appropriate intervention I could help people to better cope with the various factors that affected their lives.

I believed that social work could make a difference in people's lives— that a well-trained professional could help them to gain control of their environment and succeed in society. I chose a specialization in psychiatric social work because at the time it would place me on the cutting edge in the field. I wanted the intellectual challenge, and I wanted to give myself the best shot at securing a good job.

Like most of my colleagues, I had a large caseload of psychiatric after-care patients, "on leave" from state mental institutions, into and out of which many of them rotated regularly as their conditions degraded or improved. In most cases—unless the individual was a danger to himself or herself, or to others—I worked hard to prevent people from being routinely returned to institutional settings. For at the end of the day, I observed, an individual's problems were in the home, family, neighborhood, and community, and eventually my clients would have to return to those environments. Thus, I concluded, treatment was best undertaken in the community and at home whenever possible.

I worked with many challenging and memorable clients, and one in particular changed my life by altering my view about how to use my newfound skills. Making me adopt a more explicitly economic and political view, he caused me to rethink my whole career.

This particular client was a black man diagnosed as a very aggressive, hostile, and paranoid person. He was in his mid- to late forties and had fallen through the cracks economically. My supervisors had assigned me the case, I think, because they believed he could better relate to me, a young black man, than to a white caseworker, that I might have greater success with him than had previously been achieved. It was very tough going. In the beginning I made very little apparent progress with him. His anger, hostility, and violence always simmered just below the surface of our interactions, making communication difficult. But, as Gram would often say to me, "Nothing beats a failure but a try." I continued to try.

One day during an appointment in my office he interrupted me. "I don't need all this 'psych' bullshit," he said. "I don't need to feel good; I need a goddamn job." I knew from his file that that at one point in his life he had been successfully employed and apparently very productive at work. Then, for reasons I now no longer remember, he had lost his job. Probably he was laid off; I do not think he was terminated for cause. After that, he had never been able to get back to square one economically. As a black man only marginally trained and skilled, he was not prepared for many of the jobs available, and those he obtained were short-term. As a man in his forties, he was rapidly approaching unemployability. He was the type of person society throws away; but of course human throwaways do not disappear, they linger on the margins of our society and intrude upon the system as they seek to reassert their humanity.

Gainfully employed, he had been able to cope. When he lost his job and his economic stability, he also lost his sense of himself. As the bottom started to fall out and his life began a downward spiral from which there seemed to be no escape, he fell apart emotionally and psychologically. It was not that psychiatric issues were not present for him when he had been employed, or that he could not have benefited from treatment then. They had and he could have. But the reality was also that he had once been able to cope with his problems and maintain his social and economic balance; without economic hope, his coping abilities cascaded away and he became increasingly antisocial. This, of course, complicated his already difficult search for new employment.

That day he leaned in closer and said, "I appreciate coming here to meet with you. You're a black man and I'm a black man; you and I understand what it means to be black. I feel that as a black man you really care about me; I think that as a social worker you really want to help. But all of that won't help me. I don't need to talk about my feelings. What I really need is a job. Nobody has tried to help me and the world is stacked against me."

The elemental validity of his assessment of his situation was very powerful. Right after the interview I discussed the case with my supervisor and other colleagues. There was truth in this man's sense that things were stacked against him. Although there were existing treatment modalities and referrals to help someone in his situation, I began to feel that I wanted to challenge the factors that were destabilizing people like this client throughout the community rather than continue just to work with individuals one at a time. I began to feel the need to move on and become more directly involved in an effort to end the economic conditions that created such pain and disruption in people's lives. I felt a need to get at the causes, rather than the symptoms, of individual dysfunction. Creating employment, providing training and education, and eradicating the structural barriers to employment seemed the necessary things to do—a quest that would occupy me for the rest of my life. In that one moment, in that particular exchange with that particular person, I awakened from my dream of becoming the black Sigmund Freud.

A short time later, I left my job as a caseworker to become the program director of the Bayview Community Center, one of several agencies participating in the newly established and experimental Youth Opportunity Center (YOC) in San Francisco's Hunter's Point neighborhood. Envisioned as a supermarket of job placement, training, and other services for sixteen- to twenty-year-olds in this predominantly black neighborhood, it was on the cutting edge. I had always been somebody who wanted to master a set of skills before embarking on a project; taking this job was a total breach of form for me. Everything I would learn about job training and development would be "OJT"—on-the-job training.

But I found out quickly that the principles of social work that I had learned in the university and through my internships would serve me well in working my way to increasing competence in this new career. My professional training reinforced the lesson my mother had taught me: that one had to start working with people where they were, not where you wanted them to be. As I became engaged in broader activities, keeping this principle in front of me at all times was helpful, although it required patience and a great deal of hard work. Another professional tenet I'd learned forbade either condemning or condoning behavior: by forbidding passing judgment on a person, this principle allows the social worker to focus on understanding behavior and its roots, and better understanding enhances the prospect of problem solving.

Like my earlier decision to quit work to stay in school, this career change required a leap of faith that an exciting but unknown world would be professionally and personally satisfying. I eventually became associate director of the agency, having been promoted by its director, Herman Gallegos, a Latino labor organizer who told me, "Look, if us minorities don't give each other opportunities, who will?" When he departed, I became director, closing out the program when its funding ended. I then moved on to a variety of other positions with other community programs and agencies.

My first job with the Hunter's Point–Bayview Community Center, as program director, constituted my reinitiation into "the 'hood." No longer secure and comfortable in a downtown office, I was back on the street working with "at-risk kids"—many of whom were only several years younger than I was. I could feel all of their energy and chemistry, and I could see in their eyes a combination of cynicism about the program's real commitment to them and a simultaneous hope that their cynicism was wrong.

The Ford Foundation and the federal government had funded a number of experimental programs around the country, collectively known as the Great Cities Program. The project was designed to test and develop initiatives that would address the problems of poverty and discrimination, especially in urban areas. The Youth Opportunity Center in Bayview/Hunter's Point was one such program, the goal of which was to equip low-income youth for successful and complete integration into the economy and the polity. This was a tough assignment in 1964, for this generation had seen a president shot down and the police turn dogs and fire hoses on those who were trying to secure their constitutional rights. Many young people were beginning to believe that violence might be the only solution to the problems of racism and economic oppression. Communities were exploding across the nation.

In response to this growing unrest, and borrowing from the experiences of projects like the YOC, a variety of comprehensive programs were legislated and funded. Within short order, President Johnson's War on Poverty was in full swing.

The Reverend Martin Luther King, Jr.'s observation that the most revolutionary thing one can do is to assert the full measure of one's citizenship is a powerful idea: it means demanding access to power and equality of treatment, and requires the discharge of one's duties. It does not promise outcomes, only impact, and embraces the notion that self-determination requires the ability to speak and to be heard politically. It respects the dignity of the democratic process.

One of the most radical things to emerge from the War on Poverty was the mandate embedded in the Economic Opportunity Act of 1964, which required the program to be operated with the "maximum feasible participation of the poor"—what the community would call "max feas." This provided the legislative imprimatur for a King-like vision of fully engaged citizens, empowering previously disempowered communities to assert their voices in the distribution of program resources and in the planning of program requirements. Life in the "poverty business" would never be the same.

Very quickly, "the poor" realized that "maximum feasible participation" meant that they should control—not just influence—the distribution of millions of dollars to improve conditions in their communities. Excitement and hope rose among those who saw the potential of this mandate.

In equally short order, community leaders came to realize that they did not have to confine themselves to acting within the limitations of the various federal antipoverty programs but could also challenge existing institutions—governors, legislatures, mayors, school boards, city councils, and boards of supervisors—that had been remote from them and unresponsive to their needs. They could demand that these institutions step in to meet legal requirements when the federal programs came up short on funding. They could demand more and better services for their neighborhoods. They could demand more equitable distribution of local and state resources. They could demand an end to police harassment and more attention to the problems of their communities.

People's involvement in governance through the new antipoverty programs gave them an opportunity to gain a better sense of the factors that inhibited, harmed, or affected their lives on a daily basis. From this, they could better determine where to put pressure and what levers to pull. Growing from these experiences, they rapidly saw that the ultimate act of controlling their lives would be to engage in the political process—fulfilling in practice Dr. King's injunction. "Max feas" imbued the community with the hope that comes when the possibility exists to control the dynamics of one's own life. A new political force was born.

By going to work at the Youth Opportunity Center, I had put myself in the midst of a number of young activists trained across a number of academic disciplines who were attempting to figure out how to grab this new opportunity for community action and self-determination. Like me, they had grown up as kids in the 'hood and had been encouraged by older folks in the community to "get some learnin'," to "go to school and make something of yourself." They had done so, and had become architects, lawyers, and planners—as well as leaders of the Congress on Racial Equality (CORE), the NAACP, the Urban League, and other groups. They committed themselves to working within the low-income community at the grassroots level, using their skills to move the community's agenda forward.

My engagement in this process led to a total immersion in community politics at a very intense time in our history. Beyond the nine-to-five demands of running our own programs, we were always attending community meetings. A coalition of groups met every Sunday, and Will Ussery of CORE held regular "grits and gripes" sessions, using the lure of breakfast to bring out more people from the community, thereby expanding participation. Everyone involved felt a new sense of engagement and partnership. Not only was the community learning how to utilize power and set its own agenda, we were learning how to assess its needs. Like a psychiatric social worker trying to understand the forces at work in a client, we had to understand the forces at work in the community. Otherwise our collective effort—the analogue of treatment for an individual—would be off target and would fail to achieve its objectives.

All of this allowed me to understand and deeply appreciate the power of political activism and community organization, of deliberate and purposeful planning, and of strategy. I learned the strength and power of bonding with people in the community, of bringing people with you rather than pushing them, of building bridges, alliances, and coalitions on the basis of mutual self-interest. In short, I got an education in the fundamentals of community organizing, grassroots participation, and militant activism. It was an exciting and challenging time.

The key to success was the willingness of these young leaders to come together and identify common interests among the different groups within the community. As their sophistication grew, this same tactic of coalition building was used to organize across community lines—and across racial and ethnic lines. Once we were ready, we were "kicking down the doors of City Hall" to demand of San Francisco mayor Jack Shelley the full promise of "max feas."

A group of us had secured a meeting with Mayor Shelley, and we all had different roles to play, some louder and angrier than others. Mine was summation—to lay out our demand for the power to control our own destiny as a community. Shelley agreed to a community-wide meeting to discuss the issue of governance with respect to a wide range of programs and issues, and pledged to abide by the outcome.

By the time of the meeting, the outcome was a foreordained conclusion. Forty-nine community groups were completely mobilized to demand community control. One spoke against. In this effort, I learned close-up how the political establishment could be made to respond to a well-organized political effort on behalf of supposedly powerless people. You could bring the system to you; you could make things happen. Community organization had prevented the traditional "divide and conquer" tactics from succeeding. The politicians could no longer ignore the demands of the city's low-income residents that they receive the full range of services enjoyed by more prosperous neighborhoods, because the previously divided communities—people of all colors—had stood united.

While we were pressing the political system to secure the power of "max feas," newly established federally funded legal service offices began to undertake a series of class action lawsuits on behalf of the community. In expanding their efforts beyond providing services in individual cases involving (for instance) divorce, eviction, or credit problems, they too were responding to boards controlled by the poor, who demanded help with larger issues of social justice as well. Recognizing that the legal service resources available to low-income citizens would go a lot further if class action litigation secured broadly applicable rights, they undertook a strategic plan to use the courts to break the economic and political system open. (The counterreaction this would provoke continues to this day, with the Legal Services Corporation constantly under attack and its survival still in jeopardy.)

As powerful governmental and business interests clamored for relief from the increasingly effective onslaught of community activism, the principle of "maximum feasible participation" also provoked a counterreaction in the form of efforts to eliminate the transfer of real power to the previously powerless by eviscerating the programs which fell under its mandate.

While it existed, however, the "max feas" provision allowed for both the implementation of power and the training needed to continue the struggle once the federal support and sanction for these programs was withdrawn. Those of us working in San Francisco saw both the potential created by the provision and the certainty that it would be snatched away once reactionary forces had a chance to secure legislative change. That moment eventually came in 1967, when U.S. Representative Edith Green of Oregon successfully offered an amendment to limit participation of the poor to one-third of the membership of a given antipoverty program's governing board. This action would cause great harm to communities and to the ability of these programs to deliver on their original promise.

During the interim, though, we mobilized to move our agenda forward as far as we could. The militancy that had been causing rebellion in the community in reaction to the oppression under which people were living was now being turned toward making a revolution within the political system. For however long the programs existed, we vowed, we would use them to advance the ends that the community was organizing to achieve. We were also preparing for the day when federal financial support would end but people would still confront problems within their communities—and still need to organize to solve them.

The War on Poverty was actually a magnificent idea and its components embodied the appropriate conceptual response to the requirements of the time. It provided the substantive answers to the follow-on questions raised by the civil rights movement. The right to sit at a lunch counter or to buy goods and services in a store wasn't real without money; the Equal Opportunity Act represented the needed economic response. The right to buy or to rent a home in any community, established by successful legal desegregation efforts, was meaningless without the economic wherewithal to do so; jobs and economic development programs made real the promise of home ownership. An integrated workforce was not open for people lacking training; job training, job creation, and economic development programs set out to solve that problem. Winning the right to attend colleges previously off limits because of racial segregation could mean little to those not properly educated in high school; new education programs were established for students of every age and grade level.

And so it was with regard to health care, child care, Head Start, and numerous other programs designed to create the conditions that would vindicate the dreams of the civil rights movement. The War on Poverty sought to identify and address the full range of problems that needed to be solved to bring about the integration of all our people into the social, political, economic, and cultural life of the nation. The problem was not in its promise but in the execution.

It angers me now that for twenty years or so the dominant political view has cavalierly assumed that these programs were failures—the implication being that they represented the wrong strategy. The reality is that these programs were never adequately funded, and political compromise often meant that scarce resources were diverted into less needy communities. It goes without saying that some programs were ineptly administered, but that was most often because of overbureaucratization within institutional power structures rather than because members of the community were allowed real control. And, finally, the guts of the original mandate—the "maximum feasible participation of the poor"—was constantly being undercut and was ultimately denied. I believe firmly that the achievable promise of these programs was short-changed both literally and figuratively.

Like Dr. King and many others, I began in the mid-1960s to challenge a distant war in Asia that was robbing the American taxpayers of the resources to fund the critical effort to achieve social and economic justice at home. The under-financing of antipoverty programs and the abandonment of the principle of "max feas" helped feed the cycle of despair and cynicism that would create so much social dysfunction in the 1980s and 1990s. Hope began to fade again, and social and economic programs became less effective at a time when their very rationale was coming under attack. Youth became convinced they had no future or opportunity, and when people feel hopeless they become nihilistic.

While still at the Hunter's Point–Bayview Community Center, I met the first black man whom I knew to have a Ph.D., Dr. Louis Watts, educated at Brandeis University. Brought in from Brandeis as director of the Youth Opportunity Center, Watts assumed enormous stature within the larger organization. The pride I felt, and the esteem in which I held this man, are beyond my words. One day, word was sent to the community center where I worked that he wanted to see me at the headquarters office. Still at the point of gaining confidence, I was nervous over what I might have done to merit his attention. With trepidation I went to his office. When I got there he asked me to sit down and we chatted briefly. He handed me a book, *The Shoes of the Fisherman*, and asked that I read it and return to see him when I had done so.

When I returned sometime later, he asked, "Why do you think I asked you to read the book?" Seeing the perplexed look on my face, he responded to his own question. "Because it's about the loneliness of leadership." Then he said that he had watched me carefully and thought of me as a potential leader. "You need to prepare yourself for the isolation that leadership demands," he continued, "and learn how to avoid the loneliness that leadership often imposes. What you are doing here is pioneering work. We are breaking new ground."

I was floored. Although teachers and some of my "take-up buddies" had said similar things, I had never really internalized a notion that people would look to me for leadership. Maybe I had a good rap and could think through a problem, but leadership was different and something I had never really sought. Being a leader would mean that people would rely upon my thoughts, my vision, and my judgment—and that was a significant responsibility. It also meant that people could turn on me and reject me—very publicly. During our meeting, Dr. Watts asked me to read another book, a political and philosophical tract on the value of being open to change, growth, and new ideas.

Young people, of course, think they know everything. I was not much of an exception—especially now that I saw myself as older and mature, well-trained and battle-hardened. It was a personal challenge to read this book and to understand that embracing its message would mean that I would constantly have to challenge my own thoughts and conclusions. Like my mother, father, and grandmother, who fought to educate me beyond the teachings of my schools, Dr. Watts was trying to give me the tools to question, critique, and search. This book would provide the seeds for my view that truly progressive political values could never be stagnant or unyielding—that they could never become dogma. The very idea of "progressivism" was rooted in the concept of progress, and would always connote movement and dynamism. Watts wanted me to see that the responsibility of leadership would be to press forward at the political edge to promote progress as rapidly as was achievable. He knew that this would lead to loneliness and isolation, and he wanted to steel me for this possibility.

Shortly thereafter, Dr. Watts suggested that I pursue a Ph.D. of my own. He knew that I had already completed my M. S. W. at U. C. Berkeley, but he felt that I needed the "union card" of a doctorate if I was to succeed in gaining acceptance for my emerging social and political analysis. "It's not so much that you need to go to school to learn, because I think they will learn more from you that you will from them. You are the one working on the cutting edge," he said. For me, the idea of pursuing a doctorate was as remote as thinking about traveling to Mars. I had been remarried while in graduate school, to Roscoe Higgs. I had a new family, children, and no financial resources that would allow me to leave work in order to spend years in an academic program. But Dr. Watts persisted, and intervened with the dean of Brandeis's Florence Heller School for Advanced Social Policy. The upshot was that I was accepted at the school for the fall semester of 1967, with assurances of substantial financial aid secured with the help of Dr. Watts and professors I had studied with while at U. C. Berkeley's School of Social Welfare. My wife and I discussed this carefully. We both had been raised in the East Bay and were not at all confident that we would like life on the East Coast. Grandparents would be unavailable to our children; they would lose contact with their friends and we with ours. It seemed like an overwhelming idea.

Kermit Scott, one of the "Young Turks" who had taken me under his wing as a protégé, and others questioned my decision to leave our work in the community. I told him that my education was just a two- or three-year detour and that I would return to the movement when I was finished. I told him that I wanted to acquire the tools that would allow us to have specific, well-reasoned answers when somebody said, "I hear you rapping—but what's the program? Just *how* do you plan to solve the problems of poverty, hunger, poor housing, inadequate education, and unemployment?" I wanted to be the man with the plan.

In the end, my wife and I decided to risk it, to give up the comfortable familiarity of home and strike out on this new adventure. For me, it seemed like a chance to find out how to make a contribution to the intellectual life of the nation in the tradition of our great black thinkers and commentators on the social condition, a contribution that would have widespread and long-lasting value for all, but especially for the black community. We began to make plans to move east in the fall of 1967.

Then, on a cold, winter night in January, with the sun having set early and the damp air shrouding our little apartment on Wheeler Street in Berkeley with mist and fog, I got a call from my friends Don Hopkins, Ernie Howard, and Otho Green. They wanted me to attend a "black unity" meeting at Wilmont Sweeny's home, a meeting that had been called to pick a candidate for the Berkeley City Council. They also informed me that my name was among those on the list for consideration. I told them I really wasn't interested, what with planning to leave town and all. They insisted, though. "Put your coat on, man. We'll be by in twenty minutes." I was glad to be home and wanted to settle in for the night, but I couldn't turn down my buddies. Waiting for the doorbell to ring, I explained to my wife what was up, and that I'd be back by nine-thirty or ten.

I had gotten involved in East Bay politics during the run-up to the previous year's election, to replace California State Assemblyman William Byron Rumford, who had retired. Rumford, the author of California's controversial Fair Housing Act, was a legendary civil rights leader, only the second black person elected to the state legislature. Two young "brothers" had vied for the seat: the victor, a young attorney named John Miller; and the candidate I'd supported, the same Otho Green who was dragging me to this meeting. I had done some political speaking on Green's behalf and had even become his number-one surrogate. Whenever somebody was needed to represent Green before a group of welfare rights activists, black militants, the peace movement, or some other left-wing or militant faction, I'd been tapped. I hadn't always known what Green's position might be on an issue, so sometimes I'd just articulated my own thoughts. As a result, I had quickly developed a reputation as someone with a strong progressive vision. John Miller and Otho Green had both enjoyed substantial support among mainstream Democrats in both the black and the white communities, and it had been a tight election all the way to the end.

By speaking around town so much, I had gotten to know Bob Scheer, later to become a nationally prominent reporter for the *Los Angeles Times*. In 1966, he was challenging Jeffrey Cohelan for Cohelan's seat in Congress. Cohelan, a former union official and liberal Democrat, supported President Johnson's Vietnam policy; Scheer represented the burgeoning antiwar and "New Left" movements in his effort to unseat the Democratic incumbent. Not only was Scheer a great analyst and a powerful speaker, he had hundreds of campaign volunteers in his organization. At the time, I tried to convince Green that he should come out in opposition to the war. Not only would this instantly link us with Scheer's strong campaign, I argued, it was the right thing to do: all our experiences in the antipoverty effort had persuaded me that our community was being shattered because our nation's resources were being drained into the killing fields of Vietnam.

During the campaign, Green never came out against the war, but in the end, John Miller offered some modest criticism of war in general, and that was enough. On election morning, thousands of "Scheer-Miller" doorhangers blossomed throughout the community, placed by the legions of antiwar activists drawn to Scheer's campaign. It was not enough to elect Scheer to Congress, but Miller prevailed in the narrow race for the Assembly.

I was disappointed and saddened that neither Scheer's nor Green's campaign had succeeded, especially in light of the fact that they had never hooked up. But getting to know Scheer had led me to further contacts with individuals who would subsequently form part of a multiracial coalition that would dominate East Bay politics for more than two decades. (At one point on the campaign trail, he had even turned to me and quietly asked, "Why aren't *you* a candidate?")

For me, these previous efforts in East Bay politics were in the past, and on the night of the unity meeting, I had no interest in staying out late to discuss issues or debate ideology, strategy, and tactics, much less become a candidate.

Wilmont Sweeny, a moderate and the first black person elected to the Berkeley City Council, led the meeting, which was also attended by Maudelle Shirek, one of the community elders, who had cut her teeth on the radical politics of the 1930s. The room was packed with members of Berkeley's black intelligentsia, people of all political stripes. At stake was unity in support of a black candidate who could secure election to the Berkeley City Council—a neat trick for the ideologically torn gathering.

Four seats were at issue, two held by Republicans and two by Democrats. Of the Democrats, Bernice May was running for reelection, but Art Harris, a local icon, had determined not to run. He had announced that he would be honored if the Democrats would endorse a black candidate to join Sweeny on the council; he felt that having only one black person on the council was tantamount to tokenism. In response, the Berkeley Democratic Club (BDC) had come to black community leaders and promised that they would abide by the choice that emerged from the black community. An alliance between the Democratic Club and the black community would give such a candidacy a very strong base—and, of course, it would aid the candidacy of Bernice May as well.

That night we all took part in discussing what the issues in the election ought to be. I argued that even national issues like the impact of the Vietnam War should be raised, and that certainly the issue of racial injustice deserved major attention. I also asserted my disinterest in being thought of as a candidate.

A number of individuals were actively seeking the nomination. Sometime after 2 A.M., a blackboard with seven names on it was placed in front of the room. Somebody said, "Take Ron Dellums off the list. He's not interested." But before my name could be erased, Maudelle Shirek, who had been pretty quiet throughout the meeting, spoke up. "Wait, I want to ask the young man a question."

'Yes, ma'am," I responded. I stood and turned in her direction. Given her political history and her age (beautifully declared by her dignified white-haired Afro), I wanted to give her the respect of my individual attention.

"I like what you had to say," she said. Then she asked, "Why would you refuse to run if people in the community think you can do the job?" I answered that I wasn't interested in a political career. (At the time, I didn't think it was relevant to raise my personal plans in a public meeting, and this instinctive view that my private life was not the public's business would stick with me throughout my thirty years in public service.)

I couldn't cater my views and actions to the beliefs of others, I told her. "I don't have a conservative speech or a liberal speech. I have my own viewpoint. I'm not really ready for politics, and politics isn't ready for me," I said with a smile.

She was undeterred. "If you could run on your own terms, would you do it?" I realized that she was challenging my integrity and questioning my sincerity; she was asking me whether I was for real or just another young cynic blowing hot air. She was coming straight at me.

I hesitated for a moment, thinking, then answered with a response I would revisit later at moments of despair and when disappointment in the political process gripped me: "That's the only way I could do it—on my own terms, stating what I honestly believe. I'd listen and try to understand what people had to say, but then I'd act on my beliefs. That's the only way anyone should run for office."

Shirek turned to the front of the room and said, "Leave his name on the list because he's going to get at least one vote."

I thought, "Please, lady, don't do me any favors." My friend Don Hopkins gave my jacket a yank, pulling me down into my chair. "Sit down, man—we're going to win this thing." And we did, although it did not feel to me like my victory. As a psychiatric social worker would say, maybe I was ambivalent.

By two-thirty in the morning I was the candidate. People began signing pledge cards and pressing donations into my hand. I was confronted with the painful choice of frustrating either the community leadership's expectation that I would run for office on their behalf or my family's expectations about our planned move. I felt confused, beleaguered, and adrift. It was like I had been run over by a freight train, but I had never heard the warning whistle. To have been called to public service by the community was a request that I could not turn down lightly. If the community was of the belief that my candidacy and the potential of my service on the council could better the lot of the "brothers and sisters" suffering daily, I had better have a damned good reason for declining. Yet this was going to turn upside down all the plans we had made as a family.

For a week I was the black unity candidate, but I couldn't sleep at all, and I was paralyzed by the fact that I had been thrust onto the stage in a role I had not sought. Five days later I got up and went to Otho Green's house and told him, "I can't do it. You've got to get me out of this." With tears streaming down my face, I said, "You guys are my friends and I love you. But this is what *you* want for me, not what I want for me. I want my life back, I want to go to school."

Green looked at me with a pained expression. "It's too late, man," he said. The Berkeley Democratic Club had agreed to endorse the candidate that had emerged from the unity meeting, and there was no time to re-convene—and no obvious candidate to select—before their meeting the next morning. He agonized with me and told me he never would have pushed so hard if he'd realized how traumatic it would be for me; now, though, he said, I would just have to press on.

At that point I knew I had to suck it up and just do my best. After another night of reflection I was prepared—had my game face on and was ready to give it my all. Throughout the election the nagging thought remained that maybe I would not win and could escape this new fate, but my pride did not allow me to do anything less than everything I could to win the seat.

The liberal/moderate Berkeley Democratic Club endorsement was mine because of the deal struck with the black community leaders at the behest of Art Harris. Its ratification at their endorsement meeting went smoothly. I was now one-half of the Democratic tandem. A large billboard in the center of town read, "Elect Bernice May and Ron Dellums to the Berkeley City Council."

With my candidacy a reality, the left-wing forces that had pressed so hard to elect Bob Scheer to Congress—now organized into the Community for New Politics (CNP)—had to deal with me. Scheer called to invite me to their endorsement meeting. I respected his political analysis and oratorical skills and told him I would be there.

For me, securing the endorsement of the Left was important because it was where I stood politically. But upon hearing of my intention to speak before the CNP convention, some in the more centrist Democratic Club expressed their consternation. In response, I said, "I've been invited to speak before their convention. I should be willing to go anywhere and everywhere I've been invited. If I let you start telling me where I can and can't go, then next you'll be deciding what I should say. I refuse to have anybody tell me where to go or what to say." As I had said to Maudelle Shirek on that fateful night such a short time earlier, I had to do this my way. People could support me for their own reasons, but I was going to act on the basis of my beliefs.

When I arrived at the CNP meeting some folks protested the consideration of my endorsement on the grounds that I was the Berkeley Democratic Club candidate. The schism between the BDC and a succession of left-wing organizations would constitute the primary battleground in Berkeley politics to the end of the century. But the attitude expressed at the CNP meeting angered me, just as the earlier confrontation with some BDC members had done.

When the time came for me to speak, I said to the huge gathering, "I haven't come here to tap-dance or foot-shuffle with my hat in hand, begging for your endorsement. You invited me. You can hear out my politics and make your own judgment. You can choose however you want. That's your right. But don't judge me before you know who I am and what I stand for." They quieted. I spoke. They asked questions and I answered their questions. With that process over, I proceeded to leave the podium.

Before I could get out the door, a voice erupted from the floor of the convention hall: "We can't afford to ignore the fact that Dellums has been selected by the black community as its candidate. If we're ever going to build bridges to that community, we need to respect its choices."

Two things struck me at once: that this person understood the importance of coalition building, and that, given my politics, I could be that bridge.

My nagging wish for a different kind of life went unfulfilled: I was elected to the Berkeley City Council in April and seated in May. On top of my full-time job, suddenly zoning questions, finances, community planning agendas, and all the issues arising in the city government were mine to master—and all without staff. In addition, I was determined to be the kind of council member who was plugged into the community. My antipoverty program experience had led me to understand the need to ensure that people had access to their government, as well as the value to government of input from the community. The promise of my campaign had been that I would be open and accessible. I set out to apply the principle of "max feas" to myself. To begin with, I regularly sat down with the community in meetings at the South and West Berkeley community centers. The result was long hours and constant exhaustion.

In addition to representing the interests of the black unity coalition in alliance with the liberal/moderate BDC, I soon became the only council member to whom the Left would have access for its political agenda.

Shortly after my election, a group of people opposed to capital punishment visited me and asked me to introduce a resolution before the city council that would condemn the death penalty and urge the California state legislature to end this barbarous practice in California. Their cause was made urgent by the impending execution of Caryl Chessman in California's gas chamber—an inhumane device that painfully sucks the life from its victims.

Not only did I support them on the substance of the issue, I believed that my responsibility as an elected official was to provide a channel for the voices of a community crying to be heard. As an organizer, I understood the value that would flow to their effort if a municipal government put its imprimatur on the anti–death penalty cause, even if the authority to institute or abolish capital punishment lay with the state government. As with the divestiture movement a decade or so later, which would contribute so significantly to the dismantling of apartheid in South Africa, I believed that "local" efforts could have far-reaching effects.

Another issue that I was asked to bring before the council was a resolution condemning the arrest and indictment of Huey P. Newton, the Minister of Defense of the Black Panther Party. Newton had been arrested as the result of a police shoot-out in which he was injured and a police officer was killed. I agreed with others that an unrepresentative grand jury—one that did not reflect the entire community—could not hand down a constitutionally valid indictment. For this reason, and because of my conviction that First Amendment rights to redress grievances legitimated bringing such issues before the council, I introduced the resolution.

Because of the actions I took on these and other issues, I became the elected official to whom the feminists, black liberationists, peace activists, and members of other movements would turn in their efforts to secure government action on behalf of their views. Once a community activist/organizer, I was now a politician who had to employ all the skills at my command to build legislative majorities on the nine-member council. And as my relationships with all of these movements grew, I came to rely upon them as they had come to rely upon me.

Political events in the 1960s often threatened to spin out of control and into violence. As unrest threatened to engulf the city, the conflict between police and the community grew and grew. On one such night, the small Berkeley City Council chamber was packed with people protesting the university's acquisition by eminent domain of a parcel of land in the south campus area. During the meeting I slipped into the offices behind the council chamber. Looking out the window, I saw hundreds of police in riot gear assembling below. It was clear that if the crowd did not disperse and tensions continued to rise, people were going to get hurt.

I went outside and asked a young Panther brother to go find Bobby Seale. When Seale arrived, I took him back to the window and showed him the amassed police force, and I told him that it was his responsibility to get everyone out of the council chamber and home safely. "Bobby," I said, "be a leader and lead."

I then pressed the mayor to allow Seale to speak to the city council. Seale rose to the occasion. "I don't hate you," he said. "I hate what you are doing to my people. We came to protest in peace and we have. Now we will leave in peace." The disorderly crowd hesitated to follow him for a moment, but he sternly announced, "I said we will leave in peace, *now!*"

With that, the crowd settled down and marched out of the chamber in an orderly fashion. The situation was defused, and although even greater confrontations would occur in the days to come, I have never forgotten the powerful leadership Seale demonstrated that night, avoiding senseless bloodshed while making the point that people have the right to protest government actions directly *to* the representatives of government.

Ultimately, Governor Ronald Reagan placed Berkeley under martial law in response to community efforts to resist "imperial" actions by the university to expand into the residential community of the south campus area. This escalation of the crisis began with a dawn invasion of the city by legions of police and county sheriff's officers, called upon to defend those whom the university had hired to put up a fence around—and thereby deny community access to—the blossoming park just off Telegraph Avenue. Responding to this, students and community activists marched to the park, and a confrontation ensued. When Reagan called in the National

Guard, the entire community mobilized against the governor, the military occupation, and the university's arrogance. People were beaten, tear-gassed, and shot—one was killed—over this patch of earth that would come to be called People's Park.

I joined with the community in the protest, walking with the marchers and demonstrators. I requested the opportunity to speak about the occupation of Berkeley on KPFA, the Pacifica Foundation radio station and voice of the Left in Berkeley. I convinced Warren Widener, a young black man who had been elected to the Berkeley City Council in 1969, to join me. As a result of that talk, my actions before the council, and my marching with people on the street, I became in the eyes of some the titular leader of the Left in Berkeley.

Another result of my accessibility was that community leaders requested that I sue the Bay Area Rapid Transit District (BART)—the commuter rail service then under construction—to keep its promise to put its train tracks in Berkeley underground. With my attorney, Matt Weinberg, going single-handedly against one of the largest law firms in the Bay Area, we succeeded. My first foray into the legal system would give me the confidence to bring a variety of lawsuits to court to protect the Constitution and the rule of law in the future, but the victory had other consequences in the present.

The chairman of the board of directors of the San Francisco Economic Opportunity Council, where I had become the director of the Concentrated Employment Program, made it clear to me that he disapproved of my litigation against BART. I shared my concern about the situation with Ernie Howard, another "Young Turk" in the San Francisco War on Poverty days and my associate director as we closed down the Youth Opportunity Center. He agreed with my stand, and felt that I should not be looking over my shoulder, worrying about the personal cost in terms of job security, whenever the community sought my help to "do the right thing." Howard had started a consulting firm, Social Dynamics, Inc., and he invited me to work with him. I accepted. In 1968, we were audacious enough to believe we could change the world, and Howard wanted to make sure that I had the personal resources to continue to make my contribution to the struggle through public service.

The coalition had been forged—white, black, Latino, Asian American, and Native American, young and old, female and male, gay and straight—

and it would move forward to capture further political offices based upon its strength, forever changing the nature of Berkeley (which in 1969 still had a Republican mayor!). The events surrounding the People's Park crisis and the military occupation of the city had transformed my relationship with the East Bay's predominantly white students and leftists. Years later, after my initial run for Congress, my friend and colleague Roz Kane offered her opinion that this set of events, probably more than any other, brought together the final pieces of the alliance that ensured the success of that campaign.

Meanwhile, in response to my actions and my outspoken positions on the council, the press began to characterize me as a "dangerous leftist," a "Panther sympathizer," and so on, even trumpeting its disapproval with headlines like "Dellums Shares Stage with Known Communist: Betina Aptheker." This characterizing of me as an extremist rather than confronting the validity and substance of the ideas I was espousing gave me a prominence beyond Berkeley and would prove dangerous to me and to my family.

Threatening phone calls became a constant, to the point where friends from the community, and the Panthers as an organization, mobilized to escort my children to school, my wife to work, and me to my council duties. People with a knowledge of cars volunteered to check out ours to make sure they were safe to start. During one period of particularly persistent threats, friends camped out with us for two weeks, staying in the front and back yards as well as in the house.

On one night, this insanity nearly led to catastrophe. Michael Jones, already at my house and armed with a shotgun, drew on my friend Joel Dorham, who was himself armed with a pistol, when Joel entered through the back door without announcing himself. (The terrible irony was that Joel—who might have lost his life at the hands of Michael—had already most likely saved mine years earlier. He had driven up on a situation in which my friend Harold Theus and I were in a fight against six other guys, who were armed with tire irons and other weapons. Joel had leapt out of his car, and because he was known to these other fellows he was able to call off the fight. He protected us from a beating so severe that Harold and I might not have survived.)

The danger to me, my family, and my friends left me bitter at a press that could be so consistently shallow and cavalier in its treatment of me, without regard to my safety or the substance of my politics.

47

Despite the stress my family and I endured, my time as a city council member in Berkeley honed my political skills and helped me to broaden my vision.

In 1967, Dr. Martin Luther King, Jr., came to Berkeley to give a speech to defend his decision, announced at the Riverside Church in New York, to oppose the Vietnam War. Dr. King had been attacked by many in the civil rights community for diluting the priority of the civil rights struggle and for taking a position that seemed "anti-American" in its condemnation of an aspect of U.S. foreign policy. In my view, his antiwar stance needed no defense, but he was traveling across the country to explain it, and to use his moral authority to move the civil rights movement to a higher level of moral engagement. In the speech he gave at Berkeley, he laid out five points that changed forever my thinking about my responsibilities and the focus of my activism as a public official.

First, King noted that there were two kinds of leadership. "One," he said, "waits until a consensus forms and then runs swiftly to the front of the pack to lead, but only after the process of consensus formation has been completed. The second form dares to go forward to mold the consensus, to challenge the regular order of things . . . I am of the latter; it is important to go forward." From my training and perspective as a social worker, I knew this meant that he believed he had to be part of the educative process.

Second, he said, "I cannot segregate my moral concerns." He could not compartmentalize his outrage. In taking a moral stance, he argued, one had to challenge immorality in all the forms in which it is visited upon people. For him, this meant that he not only had to press for the realization of civil rights for all people and work to overcome the pain of bigotry and hatred, he also had to oppose the war in Vietnam as immoral. He had to speak to peace.

Third, he argued that nonviolence was not simply a tactic or a strategy for change, but an alternative way to live. For him, to speak out against war and violence was fundamental and not simply a tactical maneuver. He argued for the need to seek an alternative way for people to function with each other, for resolving grievances between people or between nation states.

Fourth, and most significantly from a policy perspective, he argued that "peace is more than merely the absence of war, it is the presence of justice." When I heard these words, it immediately made sense to me that the ultimate movement is the movement for peace, for without justice there is no peace. Therefore, to pursue peace it is necessary to challenge all forms of injustice. By working for peace you must work for justice; by working for justice you work to bring about peace. They are inextricably linked. Dr. King had started as a civil rights leader, but now he was a leader in the peace movement, challenging racial, social, economic, and environmental injustice as part of his effort.

Finally, Dr. King spoke to the issue of national priorities in eloquent terms: "We are dropping bombs that are exploding in the ghettos and barrios of America." In this breathtakingly simple phrase he accomplished three things simultaneously: he challenged the mentality of war and condemned the development of armaments to destroy human life; he challenged the nation's priorities and their adverse impact upon the poor, the disadvantaged, and the needy; and he made vivid and immediate the connection between the two.

His exhortation to all to translate the "jangling discourse of stridency and discontent," to deliver the message in terms that did not disturb the ear and therefore could be heard, related to my experiences in the antipoverty campaign and on the city council. I was beginning to learn that if you proffer the message and people are turned off by how you say it, then you are talking to yourself. You need to conceptualize and articulate issues in terms that allow you to be heard, terms that invite people to come to your side. That was King's strategy—take the stridency of the antiwar movement and replace it with the tones of the civil rights movement so that people of all political persuasions could hear the beauty and truth of the argument.

Bobbie Avakian, then a young Berkeley militant, had urged me to make the war a major part of my campaign for city council. Dr. King's words forced me to reflect on issues of violence and nonviolence—on the pathways to change—and to choose the better path. He made me a warrior for peace and his influence led me to adopt a more comprehensive view of all the issues that came before or touched upon the city council's activities.

chapter three

Revolution Inside the System

At the end of the 1960s, the whole Bay Area, especially the East Bay, was in constant ferment. At U.C. Berkeley, Third World students demanded ethnic study programs that could offset the perceived Eurocentric bias of the academic canon and provide for a more complete and accurate academic program. Women, on and off campus, pressed for an end to gender discrimination and stereotyping, reinvigorating the feminist movement. The very epicenter of the disability rights movement was located at the university, spawning leaders such as Ed Roberts, Hale Zukas, and Judi Heumann, who were committed to literally breaking down the barriers to their full participation in society.

Trade unionists closed down the campus on behalf of nonacademic employees; antiwar demonstrators raised the volume and frequency of protest. The Oakland Police Department was in more or less open warfare with the Black Panther Party. And the People's Park struggle, which had led to martial law and the occupation of Berkeley by the National Guard, had placed that city even more firmly in the national consciousness as the seat of "revolution" in the United States.

As a member of the Berkeley City Council, I was constantly called upon to represent the voice of protest within officialdom. Even the Third World Liberation Front approached me, to support their strike across the Bay at my alma mater, San Francisco State University. This confrontation found me, along with other community leaders, challenging S. I. Hayakawa's unwillingness to yield to student demands. (Then the president of the university, Hayakawa would soon be elected to the U.S. Senate, largely on the strength of his Reagan-like determination to resist the so-called radical protesters.)

Fleeting doubts within the Left that may have existed because I was a registered Democrat, had run in an alliance with an openly Democratic candidate (although the election was nonpartisan), and had been endorsed for city council by the Berkeley Democratic Club had long since faded away. During my nearly three years on the council, I had gone from being the soft-spoken social worker to being the person with an open door to the Left, to militants, and to community activists. As a result of my belief in the validity of the analyses to which I was exposed in countless conversations and meetings, I had become an increasingly vocal and public advocate for all of these "outsiders." Our relationships grew constantly stronger as I increasingly displayed my convictions about the integrity of the ideals advanced by the people on the streets: equality, peace, justice, and environmental preservation.

At times during this period I seriously questioned once again whether public service was the most effective way for me to contribute to the advancement of these noble ideals. But whenever I voiced my doubts, people in the community always strengthened my resolve by telling me that I had to stay. Access to official power was important to the advocates for change; my seat gave them a voice within "the system"—and in a democracy or a republic such representation is critical.

In 1969 they offered me a new challenge.

Jeffrey Cohelan (the man Bob Scheer ran against in 1966) had first been elected to Congress in 1958. A solid Democrat and a former leader of the milk drivers' union, he had served ably as a liberal member of the Berkeley City Council before his election as the district's representative in the House. The Americans for Democratic Action (ADA) authenticated his liberal standing, consistently rating him in the high-ninetieth percentiles on their "issue scorecard." Despite two Democratic primary challenges based on his continued support of President Johnson's war policies in Southeast Asia, he had chosen not to break publicly with the administration. Although Cohelan was now, in late 1969, beginning to change his tune on the war, many felt it was too little, too late.

John George, the second of those who had tried to unseat Cohelan, came to meet with me alone one day. "I ran for this seat the last time," he said, "but I want you to know that I don't have squatter's rights on it." Elaborating on his thoughts, he went on. "I believe that you can win this, and I want you to run. I want you to think about it."

I liked and respected George, so I told him I would think about it, but immediately after he left I regretted having said so. The end of my four-year term on the city council was in sight, and, as with my service in the Marine Corps, I was counting down the days to my discharge. I wanted to recapture my life. Though it was not as vivid as it had been three years ago, I still held the dream of going to Brandeis to secure my doctorate.

Perhaps detecting my disinterest, and being persistent by nature, George asked for another meeting. This time he brought a group of young black, white, and Latino activists. He wanted me to understand that the views he had expressed earlier weren't his alone. He also was trying to assure me that if they could persuade me to run, they would "have my back." It was a moving meeting. I was looking into the youthful faces of a multiracial coalition—people who had come to ask me to represent their common interest in the ideals I shared.

I told them, "Give me one or two weeks to think about this and I'll make a definitive decision." Once again I was torn between alternative visions of the future for me—and for my family.

Two weeks later, George called. I asked him to reassemble the group. I went to that meeting feeling (once again) ambivalent but hopeful that some way, somehow, I would yet get out of this. It would be the community that would take me off the hook; I wouldn't have to be the one to say no.

I began to lay out my conditions. "If I run, I have to run on my own terms." Obviously they wanted to know what those terms would be.

"First, I have to have the freedom to stand on my own ground. I will listen to what people have to say, but I'll take the stands I feel are best. I refuse to be coerced." They said that would not be a problem; they respected my judgment.

"Second, I won't take any funny money; the campaign will have to raise all its financial support from the people." They didn't blink; of course a campaign could be mounted from the grass roots.

"Third, the campaign must be run as a coalition, because I believe coalition politics are sophisticated and difficult but exciting—and it's the only way to win. You have to agree to work to bring all kinds of people together." I knew that, after all, I was meeting with the seeds of such a coalition and should not have been surprised at their enthusiastic agreement on this point.

"Fourth, I want to carefully document and study the campaign. If we lose, other people will need to analyze our effort and understand where we made mistakes so they can avoid them in the future."

They agreed: "Okay—deal!"

In hindsight I realized that once the question of my candidacy had been put to me, my fate was sealed. There was no way, at that moment in our history and with so much on the line, I could have refused.

John George pledged to serve as election committee cochair. Kermit Scott, ever the master strategist during our War on Poverty work in San Francisco, came aboard as campaign manager. John McElheney, a stalwart Berkeley Democratic Club member, enlisted as campaign treasurer. And Roz Kane, a colleague at Social Dynamics and one of the most brilliant political analysts I have ever met, "worked the numbers."

Numerous other individuals offered their support and energy—including a nineteen-year-old leftist and conscientious objector who walked in to stuff envelopes and ended up working with me for twenty-eight years, and who would eventually serve as policy director for the House Armed Services Committee for a time. Our collaboration continues through the writing of this book.

We opened campaign offices in the heart of the barrio and in the low-income neighborhoods of South Berkeley and North and West Oakland, as well as in the heart of the south campus student community. Left-wing activists provided an office in central Berkeley. Our campaign to change national priorities and end the pain in our communities—to stop repression, end racism, and bring home the troops—was on its way.

The strategic question was, How could a left-wing black candidate secure a majority of voters against a liberal incumbent in a congressional district that was 72 percent white and only 17 percent black—a district in which left-leaning Berkeley constituted only a quarter of the voters? As I had told John George and his group, the answer was coalition politics, a theme and strategy that Jesse Jackson would popularize in his national campaigns for the presidency a decade and a half later.

I went to house meetings and block parties all around the district, constantly inveighing against a system that routinely excluded so many of its citizens, urging that we "bring down the walls." Against the backdrop of the 1960s, some would interpret this as a call to violence, but I was not looking to promote violence; I was calling for a revolutionary and radical restructuring of society along egalitarian lines. And, in the context of political organizing, I was appealing to people across the divides of race, class, gender, sexual orientation, and disability status to identify the common interests that could unite my community in pursuit of Dr. King's goals of justice and peace.

My work with Ernie Howard and Roz Kane at Social Dynamics had placed me in a position to travel around the nation consulting with communities on how to employ the tools that had been made available by the federal programs that constituted the War on Poverty. As a consequence, I had come to understand at first hand the significant commonality of social conditions and the need to speak to people on the basis of their own mutual self-interest.

Everybody needs work and financial security or support. Nobody should be discriminated against or shut out of the economic and political process. Clean air and water, and an absence of toxins in the environment, are universal requirements for a high quality of life, or even for survival itself. Health care is essential to all. Human dignity and due process of law are necessary to peace in the community.

These were unifying themes to me, and in my campaign for Congress I appealed to the community to rally together and join in pursuit of these common interests.

Logistically, we received a significant push when President Nixon ordered U.S. military forces to invade Cambodia in April of 1970, in an incredible strategic miscalculation which would ultimately propel Cambodia into the xenophobic abyss of the Pol Pot regime. Nixon's order galvanized the East Bay's peace movement, providing an army of precinct workers for my campaign. Literally thousands of angry and energized peace activists tried to fit themselves into my too-small campaign headquarters, awaiting their assignments. In some of our key precincts we had an unheard-of eight or ten get-out-the-vote workers working to secure the largest possible turnout.

During the campaign, some would challenge what they saw as my preoccupation with the war, in the same way many had challenged Dr. King's determination, so strongly articulated in the year before he died, to extend his moral vision beyond the issue of civil rights. Informed by King's vision, my answer to my critics was, "Our people have over the years carried the burden of racial, social, and economic oppression. They should not have to carry the burden of ignorance as well." I felt obliged to carry on King's effort to educate the community about its stake in ending the Vietnam War—and in ending war and militarism in general. As I saw it, my responsibility as a candidate for Congress was to be educative and to pass on to the community my understanding of King's brilliant and provocative ideas about peace, equality, and justice.

I moved among the various different constituencies within my district, attempting to mobilize a majority on the basis of commonality—including their interest in peace. Equality and justice were themes of relevance to women, to trade unionists, to those with disabilities, and to seniors, just as they were to blacks, Latinos, Asian Americans, and Native Americans. I sought to hear the voice of each of the many smaller communities within the larger whole, which entailed listening to the various strains of the chorus of protest that had found expression in the East Bay.

It was as important to this campaign that Cesar Chavez walked the streets of the Fruitvale with me as it was that volunteers from Women for Peace addressed envelopes and made phone calls. It was critical that young white students and Berkeley leftists were animated to become involved—not just because of my opposition to the war, but also because they recalled my efforts to end the state of siege that had brought martial law to Berkeley over the People's Park issue. Students mobilized from the community colleges as well. Sandré R. Swanson, then president of the Laney College student body, delivered scores of students to the effort. He later joined my congressional staff and rose to the position of district director, in which capacity he would perform outstandingly on the issue of the conversion of local military bases to civilian use.

My first congressional campaign was also fueled—in terms of significant fund-raising and other volunteer efforts—by the charismatic involvement of Edith Austin and other Dames for Dellums, members of a group that would reconstitute itself after the campaign as the very successful Black Women Organized for Political Action. Kermit Scott had previously learned the same organizing tactic, and daily sought out ways to build links with Catholic social justice activists, Jewish community leaders, and leaders of church-based medical and food clinic services.

This coalition of movements and grassroots efforts would not be denied. At the end of the night on June 2, 1970, they had secured for me the Democratic nomination for California's Seventh District seat in the U.S. House of Representatives. Considering the district's overwhelmingly Democratic affiliation, the nomination was practically tantamount to election in November. Unless something dramatic happened, Washington, D.C., was about to get a dose of straight-ahead movement politics.

Those at the tiller of the ship of state desired to forestall such an event, and they reached across the country in an effort to derail the movement juggernaut before the question could be put to the people. During the quiet days of summer, when campaigns tend to fall into a lull until Labor Day ends summer and kicks off the fall election season, Vice President Spiro Agnew attacked my campaign—and me—during a speech he gave in Arkansas. In the overblown alliterative style for which he was famous, he condemned the campaign of a dangerous extremist running for Congress from Berkeley, California, declaring that I needed to be "purged from the body politic." In post-McCarthy America there was still no room, in the view of the Nixon White House, for serious and substantial dissent.

The confrontation between the counterculture, centered on the "Left Coast," and the Nixon White House was a political and cultural conflict that would transcend these players and endure through to the end of the century. It would find expression in the implacable hostility directed against President Bill Clinton by congressional Republicans and pundits a quarter of a century later. But in 1970 it catapulted me suddenly into national prominence even before my arrival in D.C.—helping to create a caricature of me that would linger for decades.

On the night of Agnew's speech, the phone rang late in the evening. Kermit Scott was on the line, saying, "Ron, you won't believe this. You've been attacked by Vice President Agnew." Exhausted from the pace of the campaign, I'd already gone to bed, and the phone call had awakened me from a sound sleep. I was in no mood for a joke like this—and my staff *had* joked around about how great it would be if Agnew would bring some attention to our campaign during his nationwide campaign against the "rad-lib" senators who were opposing the administration's war policy.

"Don't joke around with me," I said. "I'm bone-tired. This is the first night I've had a chance to get a decent night's sleep in quite a while."

Scott protested. "No, no. It's true. He called you a radical extremist at some big fund-raiser in the South."

Now fully awake with nervous energy, I was stunned. "Really?" I paused to think for a moment. "Call a press conference for ten o'clock tomorrow morning and I'll be there." I hung up the phone. My heart was pounding. Despite my exhaustion it took me hours to get back to sleep.

The next morning I was nervous as I dressed and then drove across Berkeley and into North Oakland to attend the press conference. After parking and before I could cross the street to our campaign headquarters, I looked over my shoulder and saw an elderly white woman walking toward me very slowly with the aid of a cane. She looked in my direction and asked, "Are you Ron Dellums?"

I said, "Yes, ma'am. I am."

"That's good," she said. "I've just walked ten blocks from my apartment to give you this check." She reached into her pocket and pulled out a check for five dollars. "It's not much, but it's what I have, and I walked all the way here to give it to you. Anyone that Agnew attacks has to be a good person, somebody I want to support." Her face was so warm and her expression so sincere that it brought tears to my eyes. I suddenly found myself embracing her. Then I stepped back and thanked her as I accepted the check. She turned to walk the ten long blocks back to her apartment.

I wiped my cheek and crossed the street and entered our campaign headquarters. It was jammed with local, national, and international press. In terms of media, this was the biggest thing that had happened in the campaign—even bigger than our decisive victory over Jeffrey Cohelan in the congressional primary.

Kermit Scott met me at the door. As my campaign manager, he had a great interest in trying to manage the conference for maximum advantage. He handed me a press statement that he had worked up with Mal Warwick and other campaign staff. "I don't want to read a statement," I told him. "I have nothing to be defensive about. I don't need to hide behind a statement."

My response troubled Scott; he was sure that improvising was not the right way to approach a situation involving this much press scrutiny. In his mind, this was an event a candidate dreams about: the press would provide millions of dollars' worth of free publicity—or notoriety. He wanted me to take my time and speak carefully.

"At least read through these, so you'll know what he said," Scott urged. He handed me a stack of a couple of dozen press clippings.

As I took them, I realized that my hand was trembling and that I was literally too nervous to focus on and read what was in front of me. Even had I wanted to, I probably could not have spoken from a prepared text. But with the eyes of scores of reporters from throughout the world glued on my every move, in order to mask the trembling and nervousness I acted as if I was speed-reading the clippings. The truth of the matter is that I never saw a word. When I had finished flipping through to the last page, I looked up at Scott and said, "Time to go." I had no idea *where* things were going to go; I had no idea what I was going to say. I had decided to just make myself available and see what would happen.

I sat down at the press table as Scott announced that the press conference would begin. The camera lights went on. "I have no opening statement," I said. "I am prepared to answer your questions."

After a moment of stunned silence, one member of the press took the initiative: "Vice President Agnew charges that you are a radical extremist who should be purged from politics. How do you respond to that charge?"

Leaning into the glare of the lights, toward the mass of microphones nearly dripping off of the table, I answered, "If it's radical to oppose the insanity and the cruelty of the Vietnam War, if it's radical to oppose racism and sexism and all other forms of oppression, if it's radical to want to alleviate poverty, hunger, disease, homelessness, and other forms of human misery, then I'm proud to be called a radical."

Another hesitation, and then the second and what would be the final question: "Vice President Agnew charges that you advocate bringing the walls down. How do your respond to that charge?"

"If Vice President Agnew had been diligent in carrying out his duties, he would have determined that my statement was made in the following context: We have built walls very high and very thick in this country dividing the races, the classes, the sexes, the generations, and even the religions. I believe that if we bring down those walls that divide us, what we will find are millions of people of all sizes, all shapes, and all colors leading desperate and miserable lives. Once we understand that fact, we can then bring all of those people together into a coalition to improve the quality of their lives.

"So, yes," I said, "I do advocate bringing down the walls—the walls of racism, sexism, and all the other 'isms' that represent the way we victimize and oppress people. Next question, please."

There were no other questions. Reflecting now on that moment, as I have done many times since then, I recall that it was very clear to me at the time that most members of the press didn't care *who* Ron Dellums was—they came to see a caricature engage in a defensive dance in an effort to deflect the "charges" put on the table by another politician. But what they found was the same person who had stood up in Wilmont Sweeny's living room and refused to run for public office on anybody's terms but his own.

In those few moments when one finds oneself at the center of controversy and in the white-hot light of public scrutiny, an opportunity exists to be educative. Rather than get trapped in personality or defensiveness, I have always sought a way to communicate the larger message. If the administration felt threatened by our politics and our movement, I was going to seize this opportunity to tell millions of people, most who might never have heard of me, what it was we were really up to in Berkeley. I was searching for the phrases and the tone that could communicate our message on the broad winds of the media's frenzy to other potential members of the coalition that was emerging from the East Bay.

I was also angry that the press had been willing to be so easily used by the administration in its reaction against the movements I represented. Why else would the media merely reiterate Agnew's "charge" instead of asking what political differences existed between Agnew and me that would have sparked his diatribe? It disappointed me that the press did not seem to see the manner in which it was being used to advance the White House's interest in its fight with the movement. In addition, the press's lack of interest in the ideas at issue was disheartening.

The question, Was I a radical? had made me realize that I could not allow the media or Agnew to define my politics, or me. I had to define both, and with my response I believe I not only took away the "legitimacy" of the attack, but also advanced my own vision of the process and substance of necessary political change in the country. The second reporter's question provided an extraordinary opportunity to define and underscore the whole notion of coalition politics and the potential that existed in people coming together on the basis of their mutual self-interest.

Nearly twenty years later, all of my instincts and experience screamed for Governor Michael Dukakis to understand the need to answer boldly and to shift the paradigm in a similar fashion when he was asked to respond to the Bush campaign's charge that he was a "liberal" and a "card-carrying member of the ACLU." Regrettably, his defensive answer not only betrayed his lifelong political record, but it allowed Vice President Bush— again with a complicit media doing his service—to inappropriately define his opponent throughout the balance of the election. I believe that had Dukakis defined the substance of his beliefs and declared the label "liberal" either applicable or irrelevant as one wished, he would have moved his political agenda forward and avoided loosing control of his own campaign.

In the wake of Agnew's cross-country attack against my candidacy and all that it represented, I was deeply honored when Coretta Scott King offered to come to the district to speak on my behalf. I will never forget the elegance and grace that she brought to our headquarters. Sitting at the same table where I had recently confronted the press, she invoked the memory of her husband and leant the legitimacy of her husband's quest to our campaign. The generosity of her act and the significance of her statement fill me with pride and thanks to this day.

It never ceases to amaze me that the press—despite the public's growing distaste for negative campaigning—continues to take the political characterizations that candidates make against each other at face value and turn them into "news." Certainly it is the extremely rare candidate who runs against somebody by saying their opponent is a great person, but to dignify unfair charges, name-calling, and mudslinging degrades the political process and ill serves constituencies who need information on a candidate's program—not slurs by his or her opponents—in order to discharge the most solemn obligation of citizenship.

Years later I would upbraid my own campaign's decision to characterize an opponent as a "Reagan Republican" and would publicly condemn the scare tactics used by candidates whom I had endorsed for municipal election. "It is not for us to characterize our opponent," I told my staff. "Just tell people what we believe and stand for, and then let them make up their own minds about how to cast their votes."

In the end, I came to believe that the vice president's behavior constituted an extraordinary example of the paranoia and hostility aroused in some circles by the movement for justice, equality, and peace. It struck me that winning this election might be more meaningful than I had earlier imagined; that it was crucial to prevent the administration from delegitimating a point of view shared by millions of Americans; that serving in public office might after all be the best way for me to contribute to the advancement of a noble set of ideas. In my heart I knew that eventually the nation would have to acknowledge the value of our analysis if we were all to avoid the social trauma and dysfunction that arise when the needs of the people are constantly ignored.

Although I tried to depersonalize the continuing attacks on me and to understand that they were part of a larger assault on the politics of the movement, the psychic wounds that had resulted from the earlier spate of death threats and the seemingly implacable hostility of the press were still very raw when I arrived in Washington, D.C., in January of 1971, as the duly elected congressional representative of my district.

As I walked onto the House floor for the first time, to attend a meeting of the Democratic Caucus to select our leadership, I heard one member of a small group clustered near me say to his colleagues, "Where is that radical son of a bitch?" I could see that one of the others then noticed me and quietly tried to point me out. I pretended not to have heard the comment, but if this was how some of my Democratic colleagues viewed me, I shuddered to think what Nixon's Republicans imagined.

What I was getting ready to do in the Democratic Caucus would further alienate me from colleagues such as those in this small group—and potentially from the Democratic leadership—by confirming the worst suspicions of some that I had come to Washington to challenge everything, including even my own party. To the extent that I would have to fight them to achieve my goals, they were right. I represented an impatient movement. But I had made my decision to fight for our goals from the left wing of the Democratic Party, rather than from outside the party altogether.

I strode past the whisperers and pointers to the well. I had to set aside their comments, for in the meantime I had to nominate Michigan Representative John Conyers to be Speaker of the House of Representatives.

I understood that this would be perceived as a direct challenge to the proposed leadership of Carl Albert, whom I later came to know as a very able leader and a nice man, who was running to succeed the retiring Speaker, John McCormack of Massachusetts. Such a challenge would perhaps do little to help me in my quest to secure the Education and Labor

Committee assignment I wanted, but I kept in mind the words that I had spoken to Maudelle Shirek when I vowed (it seemed like a lifetime ago) that I would only run for office on my own terms. Now I made a quiet promise to myself that I would only *serve* on my own terms. Balance would be the key, for I had not come to the nation's capital to needlessly alienate the people whose votes I would need for my legislative efforts to help change our national priorities.

All of these thoughts had crowded in on me the night before—my first night in Washington since my election in November. My family and I had checked into the Congressional Hotel and were excitedly awaiting the swearing-in ceremony and the start of the congressional session. Conyers had called in the late evening, and after a few pleasantries, he had requested that I place his name in nomination for Speaker at the next day's Democratic Caucus meeting. "Why me?" I asked him. "I'm just a freshman member." He said that my successful candidacy, like those of other newly elected members, represented a new political day. He wanted his candidacy for Speaker to be based in the future, and to challenge the old, established ways of doing business.

I knew there was no way for me to say no. I represented perhaps the most progressive district in the nation, a community that had produced leaders like Mario Savio, as well as fostering the free speech, antiwar, ecology, and feminist movements, and many others. By asking the question, Conyers had established the answer. I told him, "I would be honored."

As I took the lectern in front of the majestic Speaker's desk that faces the assembled members of the House, I knew that I had to both establish my *bona fides* as a representative and satisfy myself politically. The House floor was packed; many members told me later that they had come at that moment specifically to see just what "a Ron Dellums" was.

I had only a few minutes to make my speech, so I had to get to the point quickly and make it effectively. I explained that I had taken the floor to nominate Conyers because I wanted to "advance the candidacy of a person for whom I have respect and whose vision is a vision that I share. I do not take the well of the House in opposition to any other candidate, but in support of this candidate. . . . I do not know all the candidates, so it would be arrogant for me to oppose anybody. But based upon my sense of John Conyers and what I know he stands for, I nominate him for Speaker of the House of Representatives for the Ninety-second Congress." I was trying to communicate to all who were present that I took my politics seriously and would always align myself with like-minded persons, *and* that I tried to make my decisions based on information and not ignorance or prejudice.

I finished my brief nomination speech, and, to my surprise, applause arose from throughout the chamber. I could tell as I walked up the aisle to take my seat that I had accomplished what I had set out to achieve. I was able to nominate Conyers with the level of seriousness and respect that his candidacy deserved, while at the same being able to maintain my own dignity and the option for relationships as yet unformed.

My nomination of John Conyers constituted the beginning of a wonderful legislative partnership that would last until my departure from the Congress. This partnership quickly expanded to include Parren Mitchell from Baltimore, Walter Fauntroy from Washington, D.C., and Charlie Rangel from New York. Both within the Congressional Black Caucus (CBC) and beyond it—working with Bella Abzug, Henry Gonzalez, and other progressives—we would press hard to secure legislative victories on behalf of our communities.

For me, the starting point of the effort had to be to end the war in Indochina, because that cause spoke to both the moral character of the nation and our ability to reorder national priorities. But we had our debates. One ongoing dialogue proved to be prophetic. Rangel and I would argue about whether the war or drug abuse was the most significant issue to address. I remain convinced that had the resources squandered in Vietnam and on the Cold War been available for economic development, recreation, health care, and drug abuse prevention programs, the drug scourge that decimated the African American community over the next decades might have been avoided. Instead, the rage and hopelessness created within a cast-off generation has exploded into self-destruction, leading to violence and mayhem reminiscent of the mob wars of the Prohibition era.

In addition to nominating Conyers for Speaker, I joined with my CBC colleagues in another challenge to the Democratic Party's old-guard leadership. We sought to unseat the chairs of the committees on Rules, Agriculture, and the District of Columbia, on the grounds that they had been elected by a segregationist Democratic Party in Mississippi whose delegation had been unseated at the 1968 Democratic National Convention in favor of that of the Mississippi Freedom Democratic Party, led by Aaron Henry, Charles Evers, and Hodding Carter III. At the start of the Ninety-second Congress, we argued that these chairmen did not belong to the real

Democratic Party and were therefore members of an independent party. It flowed logically that they should lose their Democratic seniority, and with it their chairs. We lost the fight, but it was one more reminder to the Democratic establishment that I and others were willing to work to bring down the cozy order of the House of Representatives that was, in our minds, contributing to the devastation of our nation.

Once the organizational and procedural disputes were settled, and my staff and I had moved into our cramped offices, progressives from around the county sought our engagement with their causes. Among the first that we would take up was the effort to expose the true character of the war being fought in Vietnam.

Convinced that U.S. citizens needed to be told about the profoundly immoral acts being committed in Vietnam in the name of U.S. national security, we began to work with Tom Hayden, Jane Fonda, and the Citizens Committee of Inquiry on U.S. War Crimes in Vietnam. I introduced House Joint Resolution 296, calling for a full-scale inquiry into U.S. war crimes, and allowed the foyer of my office to be used to display a photo exhibit documenting such crimes. When it became apparent that no official congressional inquiry would be forthcoming, I agreed to organize and chair a set of ad hoc hearings on war crimes in order to create a forum for such an investigation.

Under the rules of the House, I had to ask the Speaker for permission to use a hearing room within its part of the Capitol complex. Many colleagues expressed a willingness to sit with me to receive testimony from former U.S. military personnel about the events that they had observed. I asked for the Cannon Caucus Room. Use of this particular room was intended to communicate to the press and the world that serious business was at hand. I was not required to indicate the subject matter we would be pursuing, and I had not done so.

In short order, Carl Albert, now the Speaker of the House, summoned me to his office because of the controversial nature of the hearing topic. Meeting with me personally, he advised me that many colleagues, as well as other forces off the Hill, were angrily besieging him because he had granted use of a House hearing room for our inquiry into alleged U.S. war crimes. "I gave you the Caucus room, why didn't you tell me why?" The implication was that I should have anticipated the trouble I had caused for him. "I was told that all I had to do was ask for the room," I said. It was clear to me that Albert's integrity would not allow him to withdraw the decision; and it was also clear that he hoped I would withdraw the request.

Recognizing that, I said to him, "Mr. Speaker, I'm terribly sorry about the pain and the stress, but I have been granted the room and planning has gone forward. There is no way to stop the hearing." I told him I felt strongly about it and had made a commitment myself.

"Well, I have to think about this," he responded. A short time later, he advised me that he would not withdraw his approval but would stipulate ground rules: no press—print or electronic—would be allowed in the room, and no press conferences were to be held in the building. With his grudging approval and now constrained by these rules, we marched forward to educate the American people about the illegality and horror being committed in their name.

As we knew it would be, the testimony offered by numerous soldiers, sailors, marines, and airmen, some of the "cream of the crop" of U.S. military officers, was damning and horrifying. Twenty years later, one of those officers, Ron Bartek, a distinguished West Point graduate, would work for me as a professional staff member on the House Armed Services Committee during my chairmanship. His testimony, and that of his fellow officers and the enlisted personnel who came forward, was heart-wrenching.

What the public had been led to believe was one isolated instance of inhumane brutality at My Lai was revealed instead to be part of a much more persistent pattern of behavior. Equally troubling was that the culture that allowed for individual atrocities to occur appeared to be rooted in the policies and methods by which the military was conducting the war. Fighting in Vietnam was as much based on "free fire" zones and "search and destroy" missions indiscriminately employed against the populace in hopes of damaging a ubiquitous enemy as it was on the planning and execution of "force on force" conflict. Both policies failed to account sufficiently for the need to discriminate between civilians and combatants in a war zone.

Helicopter gunships had strafed the jungle, fields, and villages on the assumption that everybody in a given zone was the enemy. Napalm had defoliated forests and fields alike, burning to death anybody in its path. The effects of the use of dioxin as a defoliant later forced the services and the Veterans Administration to confront the issue of the ecology of war as it affected our own troops—but there were no follow-up examinations for the Vietnamese men and women, children and grandparents residing downwind. With policies such as these, and with success measured by body counts, it was no wonder that transgressions against the fragile conventions of war and the rule of law would follow.

It was some of the most emotionally traumatizing testimony I had ever heard. Those who opposed the hearing did not, I supposed, want this information validated by the gravity of a House setting. Speaker Albert's compromise partly achieved that goal, from one point of view, but it did not prevent us from publishing the hearing transcript for public distribution.

I believe that in providing a platform for the antiwar movement within the halls of Congress, we did our part to end U.S. military involvement in Vietnam. Furthermore, we were beginning to figure out how to use the tools of governance to achieve our ends; we were learning how to bring "the revolution" inside the system. Our engagement in issues was like a system fueling itself; our involvement was attracting attention and more people were coming to us for assistance and alliance. We became engaged and involved with all aspects of what we called "the struggle." Like Dr. King, we saw an unbreakable link between local, national, and international issues.

One of my first trips away from Washington was to Bangor, Maine, at the behest of Ron Willis, a young Baptist minister trained in theology at Berkeley. Willis was organizing welfare recipients and was providing a ministry to the homeless. He asked me to come to a march and rally being held to dramatize the plight of the poor in this Northeast town.

As had happened at meetings I had attended during my War on Poverty and Berkeley City Council days, I found myself sitting in a room full of angry people—only this group was overwhelmingly white and primarily female. I was deeply moved as I heard of the heart-wrenching tribulations forced upon these people by extreme poverty, and again when I heard similar stories at a meeting with Native Americans from the same area. I had stepped outside the inner city, but here too found pain and poverty.

I was reminded that there were millions of people outside the economic and political mainstream, placed there regardless of race, and of the potential power of a multiracial coalition that could address the issue of economic oppression.

It was an extraordinary experience to be a black member of Congress from California leading a nearly all-white march in Bangor, Maine. The addition of a small number of Native Americans to the march drove home the point that economic pain refuses to acknowledge the color of one's skin. Mayor William S. Cohen, a Republican, joined the marchers, as he had joined us in the previous evening's meeting. Cohen, a thoughtful man, went on to win a seat in the Senate and later served as Secretary of Defense; this early meeting provided the basis for a working relationship that spanned two and a half decades and ultimately allowed us to work together across ideological and political differences.

Reflecting on the late 1960s and early 1970s from a vantage point at the end of the century, I am left to wonder what might have happened within our nation if Dr. King had lived to continue to lead and inspire us and to carry forth his "poor people's campaign." In organizing nationwide across racial lines, he had understood that if communities could step beyond the confines of their own pain and see how painful circumstances manifested themselves in other communities, larger political forces could have been awakened. He understood that a leader must assume responsibility for the knowledge that he or she possesses, and for passing it on beyond the boundaries of color or race.

Within a year of taking office, I was asked to meet with a group of workers from the Polaroid company's New England plant. They were concerned about how their photographic products and technology were being used for repressive purposes in the implementation of South Africa's notorious pass system. I was alerted and inspired by their concern, and within months I introduced legislation to end U.S. support for the apartheid regime in South Africa.

My office also worked with prisoner rights and anti–death penalty groups to extend basic civil rights protections to the incarcerated and the condemned. John Conyers's position on the Judiciary Committee was critical to our efforts to highlight the civil rights issues confronting prisoners; he and fellow Judiciary Committee member Don Edwards, a California colleague, would be the mainstays of efforts to defend and expand U.S. civil rights and liberties.

These efforts eventually took me into the bowels of San Quentin prison, to investigate the circumstances surrounding the death of the black revolutionary George Jackson and the subsequent disappearance of Jackson's young lawyer, Stephen Bingham (whose uncle was a colleague). Once inside the gates, it became necessary to insist upon a respect for the dignity of my office and my person, and I refused to be searched by the California Department of Corrections guards. "I am a responsible community leader," I told them. "Why would you possibly think I would come here armed or with contraband?" This resulted in a standoff. I left the prison and was outside explaining to the press my refusal to be searched when word was sent from the warden, Raymond Procunier, that I should be granted entrance without being searched. Despite being extended this courtesy, seeing the guards on the towers and knowing that anything could happen in a prison once you went beyond the view of the press and the public reminded me how difficult it must be to be an inmate, never mind how hard it is for anyone to ferret out what has happened behind those imposing walls.

Our work on behalf of political prisoners in particular would continue throughout my congressional career. And in one case our efforts contributed to the stunning victory of the release of Elmer "Geronimo" Pratt, a Black Panther Party member and an apparent victim of the FBI's "COINTELPRO," whose murder conviction was set aside in the mid-1990s, after which the Los Angeles County district attorney declined to retry him.

Early on in my congressional career, I made connection with a group of progressive doctors, nurses, and health workers who called themselves the Medical Committee for Human Rights. I had read an article by the group which had discussed the principles upon which they believed a national health care system should be based. Their article advocated that in order to provide for the most effective delivery of health care, such a system would have to be comprehensive, universal, community controlled, and not-for-profit, and that the emphasis would need to be on maintaining wellness—on preventing disease rather than waiting to intervene once there was an onset of illness. They argued for more resources to be directed at education and prevention, and noted that diet, prenatal care, community health, mental health, and other issues needed serious attention. As a social worker, I was intrigued by these values. As a policymaker, I was most interested in the assessment that such a comprehensive system—focused appropriately—was not only affordable but might achieve overall resource savings for society as a whole.

I told my staff to read the article and to contact the organization to advise them that I would be interested in hearing more, and in working with them to develop their ideas, perhaps even to introduce legislation based upon their principles. Roberta Brooks and Marilyn Elrod of my staff worked closely with the group, beginning the several-year process of drafting what became the National Health Service Act (NHSA). This landmark legislation provided a blueprint for implementing the principles laid out in that earlier article—what some would criticize as "socialized medicine," relying on a pejorative buzzword to truncate the debate, and appealing to people's fear of something "foreign" rather than engaging in a debate on the substance, merit, and scope of this program and the public policy alternatives.

Most of the media and its pundits consistently portrayed the NHSA approach as beyond the mainstream. This was remarkable, considering that our approach enjoyed the support of several major labor unions, the Gray Panthers, progressive organizations of medical professionals, and, if the polls were to be believed, approximately a third of all Americans. Even our efforts to ensure that news stories discussing the raging health care debate included a mention of the NHSA, at the very least, seemed to be met with what we could only conclude was cynical rejection.

With regard to the press, this provided the one last piece of weight on the scale that tipped the balance: one could only conclude that the media had formed too cozy a relationship with those in power, that they were helping to limit the policy debate rather than reporting fairly on it. Whether such coziness is purposeful, thoughtful, or inadvertent, it subverts the fundamental principle that democracy only works when there is an enlightened and informed electorate. Such a state is achieved only when people have a shared basis of reliable information, one in which all points of view and approaches and options find expression and are fairly reported.

Despite our conviction that the NHSA was by far the best approach to providing affordable health care to all the country's people, we nonetheless determined that universal access to health care was by itself an important issue—one that was within reach. At the height of the health care debate of the late 1970s, around 70 percent of Americans supported either our NHSA approach or the insurance approach being advocated by Senator Edward Kennedy of Massachusetts. From my vantage point, I realized that if we could guarantee health care access we would have reached an important goal. Once that was secured, we could go on to fight for the remaining principles embodied in our proposal. I decided to make common cause with Kennedy. This helped to accelerate consideration of his legislation, and serious discussions ensued between Jimmy Carter's White House staff and the senator's office. Sadly, at the moment that we seemed on the verge of achieving this initial goal, a potential agreement between President Carter and Senator Kennedy was abandoned at the eleventh hour. It is tragic to note that as of this writing more than forty million people still have not gained effective access to the medical delivery system.

Aside from our support for the NHSA approach, our involvement in this major issue demonstrates my view that it is essential for a progressive to advocate from the left and to offer a principled alternative for debate and vote, and to work to shift the center of that debate. By being true to that advocacy, a progressive would, ipso facto, redefine the issue. Without our presence in the debate, the so-called liberal position becomes the left position, and the center of the debate slides to the right. With a progressive alternative on the table, some will be compelled to consider the new ideas and approaches it represents, others will be provided "cover"—they will be able to point to their rejection of the most "radical" position in defending their support of a position that their constituents might otherwise have considered too far to the left.

In 1977, the time was right for such a strategy on health care; by introducing our health care bill we made everything else immediately more reasonable. As would happen so frequently on other issues, one could hear the refrain: if you don't like this health bill, then wait until you read the one Dellums is offering.

Sadly, over time a regrettable pattern emerged: the Left itself would often cut its deals too early and support an "attainable" liberal outcome, without understanding the essential requirement to keep the pressure on the system by validating popular support for the most progressive legislative alternative. No matter what the issue, any time that elements of the left wing abandoned the progressive alternative in favor of an achievable liberal outcome, the day would be lost. First, the political legitimacy of our view would be undermined with other members of Congress—they would justifiably confront us with the reality that the progressive community was with them, not with us. Second, the battle would be pitched several degrees to the right, making the inevitable compromise come out farther away from the desired outcome than was necessary. Obviously, compromise is almost always inevitable in the legislative process, but I took the position that it would always be important that progressives refrain from yielding to the temptation to strike these deals prematurely.

Environmentalists, Native Americans, people from the women's movement, and countless others streamed through the office, pressing demands and asking us to add their cause to our agenda. Our activism across the spectrum made it seem as if we were everywhere at once. From my assigned seat on the House District of Columbia Committee, I advocated enfranchising one of the last colonies in America—the District of Columbia. In a similar spirit, I testified before the United Nations in favor of ending the colonial status of Puerto Rico. I will always remember the teaming crowd that arrived at the UN offices to hear an elected official of the United States proclaim solidarity with their liberation struggle— although federal law constrained me to testify as a private individual. Within two years I became chairman of the D.C. Committee's education subcommittee, providing an official forum for exploring potential paradigms for the improvement of education in the nation's urban centers.

Toward the end of my public career, a constituent met me in an elevator, and after introducing himself to me, he said, "I really am glad to meet you and find out that you're only one person. For a while there you seemed to be everyplace, and I just thought there was no way you could be just one guy."

To which I replied, "But I *am* more than one person. There is a corporate Ron Dellums made up of members of my staff, and backed by other groups and individuals who share the same vision. I could never do what I do without the help and support of all of them."

Looming over our activity across a wide range of issues, there was always the war, still raging throughout Southeast Asia. I continued to feel the urgent requirement to do whatever I could to help end the killing.

Within months of my taking office, the antiwar protest came to the steps of the Capitol. Thousands descended on Washington and mounted Capitol Hill to "petition their government for a redress of grievances." Their objective was simple—to get the Congress to end the war. I joined several congressional colleagues in agreeing to receive this "petition" and to speak to the group about our shared commitment to their goal. Before we could finish, the Capitol police ordered the crowd to disperse and arrested those who refused, detaining them for hours at the Robert F. Kennedy football stadium. Although I was not arrested, I believed at the time that my rights as a member of Congress had been violated as surely as the rights of the petitioners had been.

Shortly after the arrests, I was approached by the American Civil Liberties Union to become the named plaintiff in litigation to vindicate the rights of the people who had been arrested and those who had been denied their rights to speech, petition, and association under the First Amendment to the Constitution. I agreed without hesitation.

My experience with the lawsuit against BART in Berkeley—along with my knowledge of the victories won by Legal Aid lawyers and Thurgood Marshall's NAACP Legal Defense Fund—had imbued me with a belief that such cases could be won in the courts. Rights could be vindicated by legal action—and a failure to assert them could result in large and small injustices (I remembered even my father's desire to sue the Oakland School District for discrimination and wondered whether he had perhaps been right).

We won the case and prevailed on appeal, and *Dellums v. Powell* took its place in the body of precedent establishing that citizens cannot be denied their right to petition and speak and that officials may engage them at the seat of government to understand their concerns. For the first time, the court also determined that money damages could be awarded to those whose rights under the Constitution had been violated. Although many inside the halls of Congress were seeking to delegitimate or marginalize our ideas and our position on the war as "un-American," the courts ultimately concluded that the Constitution of the United States guaranteed our right to freely express them. All ideas belong in the public debate, and ensuring the health of that debate demands that the people be able to carry it on at the door to the chambers of the seat of government.

Speaking on the floor, in other venues in Washington, D.C., and in my district had become routine, but soon engagements also took me to many other parts of the United States, and my new status as a federal official took me abroad to meetings sponsored by groups such as the World Peace Council and the Socialist International (SI). In 1970, at the height of the Cold War and before substantial rapprochement with either Russia or China, such affiliations were "politically dangerous," and when added to whatever issues had brought me to the attention of the Nixon White House during my campaign, they contributed to my earning a spot among the Top Ten on the infamous Nixon enemies list. The administration's paranoia was breathtaking, for it seems that they believed that I, along with my colleague Bella Abzug of New York, was on a par with Russia or China as posing a danger to the United States!

In the mid-1970s, I became a vice president of the SI's United States affiliate, the Democratic Socialists Organizing Committee (DSOC), later renamed the Democratic Socialists of America (DSA). I shared an affinity with DSOC's view that the government had a moral obligation to engage itself in confronting economic inequality and to stand as a bulwark against the ravages of unfettered capitalism. In other words, providing for the common good will sometimes require economic management by the government. In addition, though, my reasons for joining had much to do with my observations about what happens to public officials who serve for extended periods of time.

I was becoming aware that after several terms, elected officials, including myself, have learned how to fight off the predictable challenges to their reelection and figured out where they fit in the machinery of government. Along with the advantages gained by seniority, including the ability to steer useful patronage to one's district, this provides for the kind of political comfort that quickly breeds complacency. I had decided that I wanted to push myself back toward the political edge. By joining the DSOC, I was declaring to my colleagues and my constituency that I was taking my own maxim about progressivism seriously: one must constantly evolve, keeping open to new ideas and always attempting to move forward.

On those days when I questioned our reach and my ability to speak to the many different constituencies I represented, I recalled Dr. King's moral commitment to oppose injustice in all its manifestations. Like him, I could not compartmentalize my moral outrage. If I and my allies and supporters wanted peace, justice, and equality, we had to be everywhere all the time.

To be the legislator in Congress representing and articulating such a broad and radical vision made me the Washington-based embodiment of the cultural and political "sedition" that provoked programs like the Nixon-era COINTELPRO, designed and established to spy upon American citizens. My staff reported strange occurrences on the telephone. Many GIs, marines, Air Force personnel, and sailors called our office for assistance of one kind or another; some of them were AWOL. If they gave their location over the phone (something my staff always discouraged as we sought to arrange their return to military authority), they would as often as not be quickly picked up by the military police. The only explanation for their prompt apprehension, after sometimes lengthy periods of unauthorized absence, seemed to involve the telephone call itself.

Our suspicions were confirmed by information we received from a member of the Communication Workers of America, advising us that a monitoring program against our office was in place. At one point, a University of Maryland professor volunteered to use electronic "bug-detection" equipment to determine whether or not our phones were tapped and our office bugged; the phone lines were, and he signed an affidavit to that effect. It seemed that my presence on the Nixon enemies list had led to surveillance of my offices—a disgusting intrusion into the legitimate activities of a representative of the people.

As the months and years went by, I saw evidence that the system was corrupt in other, subtler ways; that some government officials, including members of Congress, were incapable of escaping the clutches of special interests; and that the scales were tipped permanently in favor of the powerful. My frustration mounted and I sometimes became discouraged.

Every two years, as I thought about whether to stand for reelection, I sought a solitary moment of reflection on the House floor in order to ask myself the same questions: "Do I need this? Should I give this up and do something else with my life?" As much as I felt honored by the opportunity to serve, I never wanted to become dependent on the privileges of office. I never wanted to need the status conferred by my office so much that it would cause me to retreat from principle or abandon a struggle. I thought I was all right as long as I could answer, "No, I don't need this. But I can accomplish something here." Then I felt comfortable going home to campaign, to be refortified by the community I represented.

At times I wanted to scream at my colleagues to open their eyes and understand the pain and misery their actions and inattention were causing—to force them to see the bombs of war exploding in the jungles of Vietnam *and* in the ghettos of America. I desperately wanted people to understand that our political viewpoint could provide programmatic solutions to problems at home and abroad.

During a speech I gave in Milwaukee, Wisconsin, in the summer of 1971, my frustration boiled over. I castigated many of my colleagues as "mediocre prima donnas," caught up in an inflated sense of self-worth and self-importance, with no real understanding of the pain and human misery being visited upon our people. Little did I realize at the time that in coining this particular phrase and giving vent to my feelings I had sown the seeds of a confrontation that would ultimately transform my approach to legislative service.

Shortly after giving this speech, I was speaking on the floor of the House in support of an amendment I had offered to restrict trade with Brazil due to reports of torture and other human rights abuses committed by that country's armed forces. During the debate on my amendment, Representative Wayne Hayes, a senior Democrat from Ohio and chairman of the House Administration Committee, rose to ask, "Will the gentleman yield?" I answered, "Certainly, I will yield to the distinguished chairman."

Referring to a newspaper clipping that he held in his hand, he addressed the presiding officer. "Mr. Chairman, I have something here that I think every member of the House would be concerned with and I hope I can have your attention. I especially want to ask the gentleman from California a question. I have a quote here . . . from the press in Milwaukee." Hayes proceeded to read the quote to all assembled, then turned to me. "Did the gentleman make that statement?"

"Yes, do you want me to explain it?" I asked.

"No, I do not need you to explain it. I just wonder if you then want a bunch of mediocre prima donnas to pay more serious attention to your amendment?"

The situation escalated from there, and after a heated exchange I found myself confronting him face to face; colleagues intervened to cool things down between us, but blows had figuratively been struck.

Later, back in my office, I reflected on the incident, and all the principles of my upbringing and social work training flooded back to me. By confronting me with my own words, Hayes forced me to take inventory of those principles and my utilization of them—or failure to do so—in pursuit of my goals.

I reminded myself that a social worker does not condemn or approve of individuals, but accepts them as they are. A social worker's job is to understand the sources of behavior and to work responsively from the point of view of the individual, group, or community in question. A social worker must understand motivation, beginning with the other person's frame of reference and point of view. In order to make progress it is critical to start from where people are at present, and not from where you think they ought to be. A social worker must be an educator, must help people to see and accept their interest in choosing a different course of conduct. I realized that these personal and professional principles were equally applicable, and significant, to my role as national legislator.

In having agreed to carry the burden and the responsibility for advocating for people who felt they had no voice, I had also internalized all of their anger and frustration. To a certain extent I had pledged to bring all of that rage inside the system, because I had made a commitment to speak out faithfully, to challenge and to advocate. But handling all of the stress of what that commitment really entailed, trying to develop my role as I went along, was proving to be a very large burden. In the wake of my confrontation with Hayes, I realized I could not afford to let myself become cynical—which was the implication of my statement in Milwaukee.

I had not come to Congress to attack and alienate my colleagues; I had come to challenge their ideas. I needed to step back from the personal. I needed to stop challenging the legitimacy of my adversaries and focus instead on challenging their ideas. I had to return to the educative role that Dr. King had laid out in his challenge to leadership. I needed to become better informed, to understand my opponents and be able to best them in open debate. I had to bring them along with me, not demand that they reject themselves. I was reminded that we need to express anger and frustration, but in ways that allow us to harness it and use it constructively.

I had to decide, once and for all, whether I was going to be a rhetorical activist who happened to hold a seat in the Congress, or an effective legislator committed to securing social change through the process of governance. By challenging me on the floor with what was, in essence, a cheap shot, Hayes had unintentionally served a higher purpose. He had forced me to look in the mirror. If I wanted my political opponents to take me seriously, to accept my political legitimacy and listen to what I had to say on behalf of my constituency, then I had to concede that every one of my colleagues had also been elected to serve and that I had an obligation to respect their legitimacy and the legitimacy of their constituents as well. If we want respect we must be respectful of others.

I had become a controversial person, which was not why I had made the journey to Washington. I could not be content with a role as the radical outsider if I wanted people to pay heed to our radical ideas. I needed to develop arguments that my fellow legislators could take home to *their* constituents and imagine articulating at *their* constituents' day meetings.

It would take time, much more time. As I stated from the well of the House Chamber on more than one occasion, "You helped me learn two of the most difficult lessons of life. They are the lessons of patience and humility."

And in later years I would often, in speeches to professional social workers' associations, jokingly ask and answer: "What do we call a social worker working one-on-one? We call that person a caseworker. What do we call a social worker working with a group? We call that person a group worker. What do we call a social worker working within a community? We call that person a community organizer. What should we call a social worker who addresses the problems of a whole nation? That person is a politician."

In October of 1973, Egyptian tanks rolled crossed the Suez Canal and attacked Israeli forces stationed in the Sinai Peninsula. Simultaneously, Syrian tanks pressed an attack against Israeli forces in the Israeli-occupied Golan Heights. The attack occurred on Yom Kippur, the holiest day of Judaism. It seemed as if the Syrian and Egyptian blitzkrieg might prove fatal to the young nation of Israel.

Within hours, President Nixon took action to provide material support to Israel, under a standing authorization provided by Congress. Once mobilized, and with American support arriving in the region by airlift—and because of a pause by the Egyptian forces in the Sinai to consolidate their beachhead—the Israeli military was able to reverse the onslaught, first in the north and then in the Sinai.

By December of that year, legislation had moved to the House to provide Israel with two-plus billion dollars' worth of military equipment, which included the approximately one and a half billion dollars' worth of support that had already arrived in Israel. But between October and December, the military situation had already stabilized, and, in fact, the qualitative military edge that Israel had enjoyed before the war had been reestablished, largely due to the initial influx of U.S. aid. I was being pressed to vote for this extended military assistance package, something that I did not believe would be in the long-term interests of Israel or of the establishment of peace in the region—and it was peace in the region that I believed was Israel's best guarantee for survival.

Knowing that this was a powerful and significant issue, I did everything within my ability to become fully informed about the nuances of the diplomacy, politics, strategic balance, and other factors associated with the proposal to send more aid to Israel. I listened to advocates from all sides and received briefings from U.S. intelligence sources and Israeli officials. I met with lobbying organizations and I discussed the situation with my colleagues and with experts on the region. By December 11, the time had come for me to vote, to make public my decision.

Everybody I talked with knew of my reluctance to send more arms into the region—it was already a powder keg, and I had decided to oppose the request for further military aid. The night before the vote, I talked to my family about what would occur the next day. I explained to my kids that I was going to cast a vote that would probably mean that we would be leaving Washington, D.C., to go back home to Berkeley, that voting against the arms aid bill would probably cause enough people to vote against my re-election that I would lose.

"It's not that they dislike your dad, it's that they disagree with my position," I told them. "I don't want you to worry, because that's all right. I'm telling you this because there are times when you have to do the right thing and be willing to live with the consequences of your decision—and that's okay." I asked them if they remembered my talks about peace and flashed them the peace sign. Their eyes lit up and they made the peace sign back. Then we hustled them off to bed.

The next day, during the debate, I took the floor to explain my position. "Mr. Speaker, a vote can be a cruel thing. You can't vote 'yes, but' or 'no, however.' . . . I came to Congress committed to peace, and if I'm not doing that, I shouldn't be here. As an American and a human being, I want this country to stand for the possibilities of life and freedom, not power and death. I also want Israel to survive, to flourish, and to live in security and peace with its neighbors. This isn't in contradiction to the first principle; it is a consequence of it. Israel's only future lies in peace."

I explained that I felt that if the United States poured more money into the arms race in the Middle East, the weapons then available to Israel's adversaries—which Israel could counter effectively with its defense forces—would inevitably give way to more sophisticated and longer-range weapons that would make a military defense more difficult, more costly, and maybe even impossible. If Israel's defense became more difficult and strategic warning more elusive, then greater instability would develop. Looking at the recent war, I could only imagine how impossible things might be if Israel had had only minutes rather than days to mobilize. Unless peace could be established, I argued, Israel's security would always be hostage.

I hoped to convince my colleagues to help "break the cycle," to move discussion toward a creative strategy that would help all parties in the Middle East not just to a higher level of "armed instability" but to *real* security and stability through peace. Unfortunately, the cycle of violence and reaction continues to play itself out even through to the time of this writing, the Camp David Agreement and the Oslo Peace Accords notwithstanding. Despite the bravery associated with these brilliant gambles for peace— fatal in the mid 1970s for Egyptian President Anwar Sadat and in the early 1990s for Israeli Prime Minister Yitzhak Rabin—peace has remained stalled by the absence of justice. King's prophetic words loom over the process: without peace there can be no justice; without justice there can be no peace.

In 1973, many members of Congress were stunned by my speech and by my vote; they had believed I would yield in the end to practicality. The prospect of the passage of the bill by an overwhelming vote should have, in their judgment, provided cover for me to vote to support the military aid package—and there was no way my vote could affect the outcome negatively. They knew this was a "hard" vote, one that would alienate a large portion of my constituency. One senior Democratic congressman from the South came up to me on the floor and said, "I just found out that you have a majority white district and one of the largest Jewish constituencies west of the Mississippi. Is that right?"

I said, "Yes sir."

"Well, I just want to tell you I admire your courage. And I have even more respect for you now than before because I realize you truly are a man of peace. I was over with a bunch of my guys, and I said, 'Son of gun, this guy's for real.' "

He told me that he and bunch of other conservative Democrats who saw themselves as "hawks" had been standing in the back of the chamber watching how the "doves" would vote on what the "hawks" saw as an issue of war and peace.

He took the time to tell me, "Many of your colleagues who advocated peace in Vietnam are not advocating peace in the Middle East. I have respect for your courage, but I'm saddened by your vote if it means you may not come back here. Because even though you and I don't agree on many things, I've come to realize that you need to be here and you have a right to be here."

I looked at him and he looked at me, and we shook hands—a white "good ole boy" from the South and a young black man from Oakland-Berkeley. I realized then that my decision to focus on being educative, respecting my colleagues, and, most importantly, staying focused on the issues was going to work. It might be one member at a time, and it would certainly be years before the personal attacks against me would end, but I was on the right track.

Despite substantial rumblings in my district and opposition in the Democratic primary, I was reelected in 1974.

Nonetheless, profound suspicions lingered among a large number of Jewish constituents about my vote that December, and some people expressed disbelief in my protestations that I was committed to the survival of Israel as a nation. Their doubts were aggravated by my view, also expressed in 1973, that Israel should negotiate with the Palestinian Liberation Organization (PLO)—or whatever other chosen representative of the Palestinian people might emerge—if it wanted to secure a real peace in the region. As Prime Minister Rabin would say twenty years later, "You do not have to make peace with your friends. The pursuit of peace is hard." But in 1973 my position provoked great anxiety and my vote against further military aid for Israel was viewed as anti-Israel rather than as a vote for peace and therefore for that nation's survival.

Twenty years later, I stood in the Rose Garden at the White House—as chairman of the House Armed Services Committee—and witnessed Prime Minister Rabin and Palestinian Liberation Organization Chairman Yasir Arafat shake hands and consummate a peace agreement. I prayed silently for those who had lost their lives to all the strife and violence in the intervening period.

In the wake of my 1973 vote, I took care to remain in regular communication with Jewish community leaders. This effort served me well, providing me with an opportunity to seek information and input from a concerned and informed constituency, on the one hand, and ensuring that I would be able to share and articulate my views—unfiltered by the media—on the other. Over a long history of mutual communication we would, on occasion, have to agree to disagree. But I would be educated by their observations of the state of affairs in the Middle East, and they by mine. I had taken a stand based on strongly held and well-informed views, rooted in principle. I was willing to take the consequences of doing what I believed was right.

The pathway to a Middle East peace was complex, and devising a solution that met the aspirations of all parties would be difficult. But I remained convinced that adherence to the pursuit of peace over war, and the development of mutual respect rather than toleration of the festering hatreds that plagued the region was the key to long-term peace there.

By mid-decade, the United States had withdrawn from direct participation and financial involvement in the wars of Southeast Asia. Having first tragically intervened on behalf of the colonial French to preserve their empire, we had laid waste to a nation that never deserved to be our enemy. Along the way, our nation had seen its economy dramatically disrupted, confidence in its government and leaders significantly eroded, and a president forced to resign from office following revelations about his abuses of power directed against those who dared challenge his war plan.

I saw a new opportunity for the progressive movement as a whole to complete the unfinished business of our time. Having secured an end to the fighting in Southeast Asia, we needed to change the way America engaged with the world and with the millions of its own citizens whose lives were being destroyed by the continued unwillingness of the nation to deal with the problems confronting our communities. To achieve social justice would require a reordering of national priorities, including profound changes in the way the United States approached its foreign and military policies. In my view, it was not enough for a few legislators and Washington-based lobbyists to argue that we should "beat our swords into plowshares"; the antiwar movement needed to become a peace movement in the terms of reference laid down by Dr. King.

We needed to compel the United States to base its foreign policy upon the principles of respect for national sovereignty, and upon the promotion of democracy, individual human rights, and sustainable economic development. We needed to build upon the successes of the treaty on the nonproliferation of nuclear weapons (NPT), the atmospheric test ban treaty, and other agreements designed to slow down and then to reverse the nuclear arms race. Our failures on both counts led to massive intervention in the affairs of the nations of Central America and to a continuing escalation of the nuclear arms race that would literally threaten world survival.

The huge "Watergate class" of freshman Democrats was poised and itching for a fight. Reform was in the air. The committee barons were being brought to account to the Democratic Caucus for actions inconsistent with party policy. It was our moment: we could return the nation to the course upon which it had embarked before the war and the machinations of the Nixon administration had derailed the Great Society effort.

I looked around expectantly, but the movement we had ridden to victory in forcing a political end to the war had gone home to celebrate its success.

Unfortunately, for many, what I had seen as a progressive movement on many fronts had been simply an anti–Vietnam War movement. What I thought of as "the movement" relaxed its pressure on the government, leaving behind a faithful few lobbyists and organizations. Despite the continuing efforts of these Washington-based groups, without the active, vocal support of millions of Americans they would be unable to compel politicians to pay attention to their demands for social change. My entreaties to my colleagues to cut the military budget and begin to reinvest resources in our cities was met with dismissal: "Ron, we're still in a mortal struggle with the Soviet Union; we cannot abandon our military investments, especially now that Saigon has fallen."

Before, my colleagues had acknowledged that I articulated the views of millions of people—some of whom were their constituents. Now they looked over my shoulder and saw that these millions had gone home. The progressive movement had made opposition to the war mainstream; without that unifying issue, our ideas about how to reorder national priorities were once again outside the mainstream. Ron Dellums was no longer speaking on behalf of a mass movement; now a progressive like me was simply Representative Dellums from California in the eyes of my colleagues.

Without the "street heat" generated by public opinion against the war, the burden of argument, education, and information about other issues fell more heavily upon our shoulders. It became even more imperative to learn the procedures and techniques that lead to legislative victories—and it became even more imperative to master the arcane language of military strategy. Until new circumstances allowed a larger progressive alliance to reemerge, it fell to those of us inside the system to fashion arguments on the basis of logic and an appeal to the self-interest of our colleagues. We had to build legislative coalitions through ever more careful assessment and ever more patient education.

As the war ended in Vietnam, the United States proposed to deploy a nuclear weapon system that would escalate the nuclear arms race. Thirty years earlier, the U.S. nuclear attack against Japan had launched the world on a path that at times would threaten its very existence. Much has been written about that action, but I believe it was avoidable. Any invasion of Japan was surely at a time of our choosing, and other opportunities existed to demonstrate that continued resistance was not in the Japanese national interest. Moreover, any view that such an action was desirable as a means of either downgrading Soviet influence in Asia at the postwar reconstruction table or attempting to "awe" the Soviets into acquiescing to larger U.S. interests was naïve. All the complexities of the Cold War that was to follow notwithstanding, the use of nuclear weapons to destroy whole cities represented a failure of morality and imagination. As the war crimes tribunals established, by 1945 the legal conventions of war had matured to the point where they required every possible effort to avoid civilian casualties in the application of force. The nuclear bombings exceeded those boundaries, especially given that Japan was on the verge of surrender.

Following the end of World War II, the United States and the Soviet Union became locked in a global competition that precluded efforts to halt the expanded deployment of nuclear weapons. Today, as we approach the end of a century marked by global conflict, we should shudder at the consequences of our refusal to be more aggressive in containing the nuclear genie—and wonder about the opportunities for peace that are being missed in this new era of deadly strife throughout the world.

One such lost opportunity was the U.S. decision to pursue MIRV technology—employing multiple warheads on missiles, each of which could be individually targeted. With the strengths the Soviets enjoyed in rocket science, it was obvious that any successful effort on their part to master MIRV technology would allow them to confront—probably sooner than later—the United States with massive numbers of very heavy missiles, each capable of carrying tens of warheads. In my view, it was as much in our strategic interest in the late 1960s to prevent the deployment of such systems by negotiating a total ban on MIRV missiles as it would be three decades later to negotiate for the elimination, destruction, and replacement of such systems.

Had we acted to ban these weapons before the systems were deployed, we could have avoided billions of dollars of needless expenditures. Nuclear bombs were not being exploded in the jungles of Vietnam or other surrogate conflicts, but the financial impact of building and maintaining them was being felt in the centers of America's cities. The search for smaller "circular error probabilities" and increased "throw-weight efficiency" caused a drain on the Treasury that thwarted crucial social investment. The result: continuing domestic devastation in the burned-out centers of Newark, Los Angeles, Detroit, and other cities.

Although the United States had enjoyed the early lead on MIRV technology, within a decade it was argued the nation had to respond to the Soviet "advantage" in MIRV forces, caused (not surprisingly) by their advantage in heavy missile technology. It was postulated that the USSR could achieve a successful first strike against the U.S. arsenal of fixed-silo, land-based MIRV nuclear weapons, destroying one leg of the "nuclear triad"—submarine-launched missiles, land-based missiles, and piloted bombers and cruise missiles. It was argued that this would leave the United States defenseless, unable to respond—resulting in a so-called "window of vulnerability." The proposed solution: make the land-based missiles mobile, so the Soviets could not target them. Its proponents also argued for making the U.S. missiles larger, so that they could carry more warheads. However, the plan to deploy such MX missiles would put more Soviet targets at risk; the vicious logic of an arms race always increases strategic instability.

Deterrence argued for restraint and for working our way out of the morass, moving back from the edge of the cliff. But some rejected deterrence and sought a near-term "strategic" advantage; they saw the increases in warheads and the accuracy of the new MX missile as critical to the development of a coherent strategy for fighting a nuclear war. Although they cloaked their argument in the garb of deterrence—that is, each leg of the nuclear triad must be capable of surviving a nuclear attack or deterrence would fail—any modicum of analysis showed that the United States had a credible deterrent, even if every land-based missile in the arsenal were to be destroyed. We had to fight the ascending spiral of the militarist view and prevent the deployment of such a world-threatening system. The dangers were enormous.

During debate on the military authorization bill in 1977, I introduced an amendment to delete funding for the MX. In support of the amendment I made the following arguments: the Cold War strategy was bankrupt; we needed to build upon the anti–ballistic missile (ABM) treaty by implementing strategic arms control and reduction treaties, and by negotiating further reductions in offensive systems; the MX missile was unnecessary in strategic terms, and it was destabilizing. I further argued that the nation could no longer afford unrestrained military spending when its cities were in despair.

One must always assume that an opponent will make a logical argument based upon their assumptions, so challenging an argument at the level of its assumptions is usually the most effective point of attack. The assumptions underpinning the argument for the MX would ultimately prove to be its fatal flaw. After undertaking an analysis of our nuclear deterrent force —including all elements of the triad—I concluded that Soviet military planners could not with any confidence plan a first strike against U.S. land-based forces. They had to comprehend that even if they wiped out the entire land-based arsenal, a massive, indeed cataclysmic, counterattack would be launched against the Soviet Union by the surviving U.S. bomber and submarine patrol forces. In other words, almost by definition, the synergy of our triad of nuclear defenses would deter the kind of attack that the proponents of the MX envisioned, no matter how threatening the "MIRVed" Soviet force might appear to be to our land-based forces.

In 1977, without a movement behind me, and still an "outcast" member of the House Armed Services Committee, I made the effort, but it failed miserably. Only eleven of my colleagues supported me on the floor—not enough even for a recorded vote.

Success required public opposition, and if public opposition to the MX was to grow, among the natural allies in the struggle would be those who were the potential victims of its basing modes. Individuals moved for their own reasons and their own self-interest, even conservatives might be led to understand that Soviet nuclear weapons were equal-opportunity destroyers, surely as capable of wiping out Salt Lake City as they were of leveling New York's or San Francisco's shipyards. Although my amendment to cut MX funding began to secure sufficient support to warrant a recorded vote, we were a long way from victory.

By 1979, dozens of schemes had been rejected or were under consideration for deploying the missile. Prominent among those was one in which the missiles would be shuttled around a "racetrack" and hidden in a series of shelters, forcing the Soviets to guess at where they might be. As I and others saw it, without arms control agreements to limit offensive forces, the most likely consequence of such a plan would be the further proliferation of warheads, in order to target even the empty bunkers.

One of the proposed sites for deployment of the racetrack scheme was in the high basin of Utah, where the prospect provoked strong grassroots opposition. Chad Dobson, an environmental activist working in the state against the missile's deployment, came to Washington to develop a national campaign against the MX. We met frequently to assess the strength of our effort, and I agreed to seek an audience with the leadership of the Church of Jesus Christ of Latter-day Saints—the Mormons—a powerful force in Utah politics.

In Salt Lake City, I first addressed the Utah state senate, at the invitation of state senator Frances Farley. Farley, a progressive woman in a male-dominated, conservative state was very engaged in the anti-MX effort. Meeting with the Utah-based peace activists was inspiring; there was a tremendous amount of excitement, enthusiasm, and expectation in the air. People tried to help me understand the huge local political significance of my meeting the next day with Mormon elder Spencer Kimball. In anticipation of the meeting I had said to my staff, "I want to meet this person because I believe that the weight of our ideas and our argument is compelling. I believe there is a potential for this person to see their validity and to embrace them. If he does, we may have a chance to turn this around." I felt that if I could present the argument well he would not only oppose the deployment of the MX in Utah but reject the entire the system itself.

I entered the large and elegant office feeling anxious to meet Kimball, but not nervous. He explained some of the history of the room, including the fact that every U.S. president for some years back had, during the course of his campaign, met with the church hierarchy in this very room. I thought of the import of the moment: a "Berkeley radical" sitting with a conservative leader in Utah, trying to seek common ground on an issue of global peace, in the sanctum of a very conservative religious organization. I wondered as well whether I was the first black man to ever enter this room.

First, I explained to Kimball the "synergy" argument and why, in my view, the proposed missile system was unnecessary to the defense of the nation. I also explained my view as to why its deployment would destabilize international security and therefore endanger our national security. I explained that by adding so substantially to our nation's war-fighting capability, such a move would unsettle Soviet military planners. Taken to its logical conclusion, the deployment of a new U.S. heavy missile would create "situational crisis destabilization." In an international crisis, Soviet military planners might feel compelled to launch a first-strike effort, to avoid having their missiles destroyed by a preemptive U.S. strike. MIRV technology was taking us closer to the precipice.

I sought to appeal to his self-interest by bringing the argument closer to home: the proposed deployment in Utah would make the state a natural target for such an attack. "Let's talk about deployment, and what will happen if it's deployed in Utah," I said. "The Soviets will know that it is in Utah—but maybe not exactly where—and any attack they make on the country will surely target the state. Its construction alone will devastate large parts of your environment. The logic of those who argue for this system—the faulty logic of fighting and surviving a nuclear war—does not justify the deployment. I hope you see that moving forward with such a system is dangerous per se to the United States, indeed to all humanity. We're talking about fashioning a dangerous and expensive solution to a problem that doesn't exist."

After hearing me out, he shared with me the fact that in his missionary work he had traveled to Hiroshima, and he had seen the devastation caused by the atomic attack on that city. "I know the awful devastation that nuclear weapons can inflict. I'm impressed by the arguments you've made; you've brought me a lot of important information today, a lot of food for thought." With that, he pledged to think about what I had said.

Without knowing what he or the church would do, I felt confident that the educative effort we had made was the right political strategy. If Mormon leaders entered into the public debate against the MX, their stand could provide important support for colleagues who felt reluctant to approve the scheme but worried about appearing weak on defense.

In May of 1981, the Mormon church officially came out in opposition to the deployment of the weapons system. That year, as I did each year after 1977, I was offering an amendment to eliminate the MX funding and knew that the church's statement that day would make an important contribution to creating the political climate necessary to end the weapons development program, something that had never happened before in response to public pressure and which the national security establishment was determined not to allow. With public alarm spreading about the newly elected Reagan administration's dramatic defense spending increases and seeming willingness to consider actually fighting a nuclear war, broader public opposition to the MX began to grow.

In 1983, six years after I had first advocated ending the program based on the "survivability" inherent in the synergy of the nuclear deterrent triad, President Reagan appointed General Brent Scowcroft to chair a bipartisan "blue-ribbon" commission of defense establishment experts to assess the MX issue. After careful consideration of the various basing modes for the MX missile, all of that high-powered intellect, money, and effort produced an acknowledgment of the doctrine of synergy that I had earlier advocated. Indeed, the principle of synergy would become an accepted one within the mainstream of policy analysis governing any decision about modernization of the land-based force. Representative Norm Dicks declared to all who would listen, "Ron Dellums is the father of synergy," trying to provide me with some credit for what on the surface seemed to be an administration viewpoint, one I had articulated years earlier.

I understood that Scowcroft and the others had embraced synergy for more cynical reasons. They distorted this analytic principle in an effort to justify building a new land-based system, searching for a politically acceptable basing mode. And it was important to them that they not allow the growing nuclear freeze movement to appear to derail a major weapons system modernization effort. So they jettisoned as nonessential the most easily ridiculed aspects of the MX, its defensive mobility, in an effort to preserve its offensive capability. They tried to turn the tables on our argument: vulnerability would no longer matter as much as offensive firepower. When the MX's capabilities were aggregated with those of other proposed systems—the Pershing II missile, the European-based cruise missiles, the Strategic Defense Initiative, the more powerful and more accurate Trident D-5 warhead for submarine-launched missiles, and efforts to enhance our antisubmarine warfare capability against the Soviet fleet—it became clear that a very dangerous and strategically destabilizing war-fighting architecture was being constructed. The world seemed on the verge of becoming very insecure.

One day, after I finished arguing in the House for the elimination of MX funding based on this new aspect of our analysis, Representative Marvin Leath, a conservative Democrat from Texas who served on the Armed Services Committee with me, sat down beside me. He and I had never talked, although we knew each other in a casual and friendly way. "Look," he said, "I just wanted you to know that I just made a big mistake."

I looked at him, perplexed.

"I made the mistake of listening to you. Usually when you take the floor, I just shut off. I think, 'Oh, there goes that Dellums again on the MX or the nuclear danger.' I usually head back to my office, get a cup of coffee. Today, for some reason, I thought, 'Let me check this out.' So I stood back behind the rail, smoking a cigarette, and listened to your speech.

"That was my mistake. I want you to know that that was the finest exposition on the MX missile I've ever heard. You're saying something not only about the missile but about the dangers of nuclear weapons that everybody needs to hear—even *my* constituents."

I thanked him and he asked, "Do you have a minute to get a cup of coffee?"

I was pleased. Finally someone from the conservative wing of the party had chosen to take the time to hear me. If he could accept me as making a credible argument, then others, for whom the ideological gap might not be as large, could be persuaded as well. His second point also impressed me, accepting the need for different communities to be educated on these issues. My effort to become expertly informed had just received its biggest validation.

When Leath reached out to me that day, he began a process that eventually led to a close friendship between us—although we would continue to disagree on more issues than not. He once lamented that we had not struck up a friendship earlier, joking that he had seen me as the KGB and I had probably seen him as the KKK. We came to respect each other's commitment to principle and enjoyed many honest arguments. In particular I enjoyed the challenge of engaging an analytical conservative on the issues, rather than just trying to make a deal, divide the issue, or seek the middle ground.

Leath even invited me to his central Texas district, to the town of Killeen, where he introduced me to his "bunch of good ole boy" buddies (his words, not mine). He started by stating the obvious: "Everybody must be wondering why I would bring a black radical home to meet my redneck constituency." Murmurs confirmed this. "First of all, he is my friend," he said, and with that he bridged the gap between the two of us and between them and me.

He repeated the story about how he had chosen not to walk away that day—the "mistake" he had made—and continued on to state that what I had said that day made a lot of sense. He was cloaking me with his hometown credibility and, in doing so, risking some part of that credibility, which is critical to a politician. What I saw that day was a man changing, burdened by his new knowledge but acknowledging it publicly. I admired him, for not all people assume responsibility for the knowledge they possess.

As I faced Leath's constituents I realized that I would never get his vote to cut a weapons program unless he could see himself explaining the position to them. For the moment, though, it was enough that he gave me a shot at trying to change their views by expressing mine—blessed by his introduction.

I will never forget that day. Leath's courage to face change would return to me in the 1990s, at a time when I had to confront a changed strategic climate that cried out for new thinking—and for the peacekeepers who might prevent genocide.

In 1983, the Nuclear Weapons Freeze Campaign was nearing the height of its worldwide strength and secured congressional support for their freeze resolution. The advocacy of the Left was combined with support from conservatives and conservative organizations such as the Mormon church, and with growing public concern about the administration's pursuit of a nuclear war fighting capability.

The Democratic Caucus was becoming increasingly insistent that its leadership oppose the MX, and members like Nick Mavroules of Massachusetts and Charles Bennett of Florida indicated their willingness to offer their own amendments to the authorization and appropriations bills. Similar developments occurred in the Senate, and the debate over the MX became a major political battlefield for several years.

Now my role was different. I had to keep up the pressure on the debate from the left and continue to advocate for the elimination of the program while others were seeking to cap funding, dictate basing modes, or keep the number of missiles below a strategically destabilizing level. Such positions were useful enough—and surely the prevention of a first-strike capability was by itself significant—but I was still awaiting the "peace dividend" we had looked for at the end of the Vietnam War. That promise had faded in the last year of the Carter presidency, and seemed to evaporate altogether during the rapid escalation of military spending under President Reagan. Terminating the MX program "at zero" held out the greatest hope of returning scarce resources to the cities, which were locked in an ever-advancing state of decline (with an explosion of cocaine use under way, Charlie Rangel's worst nightmare about the devastation wrought by drugs was becoming a reality).

Now that more moderate members of Congress had picked up the MX issue, I turned to other programs—the Pershing II, the SDI, and the military budget as national policy—in an effort to push the debate further to the left, further towards peace and disarmament. During the health care debate of the 1970s, many groups had stayed mobilized in support of the progressive alternative; as the military policy debate continued, I was disappointed when many progressive colleagues sought an early alliance with the House leadership in pursuit of middle-ground deals—deals which, in the end, would waste billions of dollars desperately needed elsewhere.

I was so disappointed at one point that I asked for a meeting with the peace and disarmament community's D.C.-based lobbyists. Confronting them with the fact that their lobbying flyers failed to even mention my amendment to terminate MX funding altogether, I asked, "How is it being for peace to support forty or fifty missiles instead of the original hundred?" Having watched Reagan raid domestic program budgets to fund his outrageous military buildup, I was angered that the peace community was apparently unwilling to fight to stop the scaled-back proposal for a "lesser deployment mode," which would still run into billions. Being for peace, I argued, was not just about preventing the deployment of a system that, because of its scale, was strategically destabilizing; we had to identify all wasteful military expenditure and divert as many of those funds as we could into our vital social agenda. Lobbying for a proposition the upshot of which would be spending billions for a system of no apparent military utility was a failure of political will, in my view.

We all understood that at the end of the day the deal would be made in the center, but defining that center was the key to victory. I argued strongly that support for complete termination of the MX program was the best way to move the leadership forward, because it would compel them to take account of legislators and constituents to their left. Our effectiveness inside the rooms where the legislative decisions were being made was reduced whenever my colleagues could turn to me and say, "But your peace movement constituency is with us on this issue."

Despite certain disappointments, I knew in the quiet of my heart and mind that I had made a difference by staying "out there" on this issue during the lonely years. With the help of others, and with a powerful nuclear freeze movement at our backs, we had fought the administration and

91

the MX proponents to a weary standstill. Although billions had been wasted, we succeeded in preventing the deployment of a missile system that would have significantly destabilized the strategic environment. We had achieved the very event that Scowcroft and others had sought so much to avoid, although they would never admit it publicly—we had used sound research and analysis to mobilize public opinion and to bring it to bear on issues of military policy and national security. We had not accomplished all our goals, but our ability to affect the system was increasing.

chapter four

Challenging the Nation

When I arrived in Washington, D.C., for orientation at the end of 1970 (already suspecting that no amount of orientation could prepare me for the changes I was about to face), I began to search for comrades. One set would arrive on my doorstep, in the form of Washington-based groups representing the activists of the progressive movement. My arrival had been trumpeted by the Agnew attack, and they quickly sought out their new ally. The other set would be those of my congressional colleagues-to-be who were like-minded or empathetic. Meanwhile, many members and former members of the House offered me recommendations and advice about constituent service, managing our budget, how often to return to the district, newsletters, caucuses to join, and how to arrange the myriad priorities of running what amounted to a small company on behalf of my district.

I knew some of the people I wanted to hire. The urbane and intellectual Don Hopkins became my district director and was widely regarded as one of the most politically astute black thinkers in the Bay Area. Barbara Williams, a young black attorney and social worker I had met professionally, came aboard as my administrative assistant in the Washington office. Mike Duberstein would provide progressive brilliance as my legislative director. Al Lowenstein, a progressive from New York who had left the House to run for the Senate, recommended a young Hoosier who had worked in his office, Marilyn A. Elrod; Mae, as we all came to call her, started in my office as a caseworker and would eventually serve as staff director of the House Armed Services Committee. My staff reflected my politics: progressive, multiracial, young, and determined to change the world.

Most relationships between legislative colleagues, as important as they are, remain informal and largely centered on friendship or mutual respect. In 1971, the thirteen black members of the House decided to make our particular relationship more formal. Bound together by race—and the experience of race in America—we believed that we needed to work with each other to more forcefully advance our common agenda, and we announced the birth of the Congressional Black Caucus, known as the CBC.

At that time, several members of the new group had already achieved substantial seniority and committee influence, including Robert Nix from Pennsylvania, Gus Hawkins from California, and Charles Diggs from Michigan. Others—like John Conyers from Michigan, Bill Clay from Missouri, Lou Stokes from Ohio, and Shirley Chisholm from New York—had not yet achieved that status but had served long enough to learn some of the ropes. Then there was the new crop, elected in 1970, including George Collins and Ralph Metcalf from Illinois, Charlie Rangel from New York, Parren Mitchel from Maryland, Walter Fauntroy from the District of Columbia, and me.

Black membership in the House had expanded significantly with the 1970 election. Nonetheless, and sadly, the thirteen of us, 2 percent of the House, had the burden of representing a far larger constituency—the 12 percent of the United States population that was black and which had historically been underserved by government and was still underrepresented in Congress. With Senator Edward Brooks, a Republican from Massachusetts, sitting as the only black member of that chamber, we had our work cut out for us.

By forming the CBC, we hoped to be able to establish a regular process of sharing information to better educate ourselves on the issues and more effectively use our individual strengths on behalf of our constituents and collective goals. Largely made up of urban-based members, the CBC was fairly uniform in its focus on securing funding for housing, transportation, health care, education, and economic development—on solving the problems of the cities and addressing the crisis of urban decay. But we were aware of other issues, and did our best to be advocates for rural blacks and those in the South. Civil rights and social justice goals constituted the "non-budgetary" portion of our domestic priorities focus. And we were determined to raise the profile of Africa and the Caribbean in the debate on United States foreign policy.

By the time of the CBC's establishment and functional operation in 1971, the Democratic leadership had already made committee assignments for the Ninety-second Congress, and we were left to use our assignments as best we could to cover the issues of concern to our constituents.

Prior to my arrival in Washington, I had given some thought to the matter and had decided to seek a seat on the House Education and Labor Committee, which had jurisdiction over many of the War on Poverty programs that remained in operation. Given my professional expertise and the experiences I brought from serving as a local elected official, it was on this committee that I believed I could make my greatest contribution. People within the social work community and the manpower training and organizing professions with whom I discussed this, including former colleagues like Roz Kane and Ernie Howard, were bursting with excitement to imagine that we might be able to take our expertise directly into the legislative process. I also thought that working with Gus Hawkins would be a treat for me personally; his reputation in California had reached me before we met, and, after all, I had come to Congress to implement progressive domestic legislative initiatives.

But the Democratic leadership advised me that there was no Education and Labor seat available, placing me instead on the House Foreign Affairs Committee, to fill the "California vacancy" created by John Tunney's election to the Senate. Speaker-designate Carl Albert also placed me on the District of Columbia Committee, based upon my city council experience. (A few ironies later emerged. After my disappointment at not having secured the Education and Labor Committee, I was often invited to testify before subcommittees in both the House and Senate which had jurisdiction over domestic policy initiatives; although I was recognized as enough of an expert in the field to testify, I was unable to employ that expertise in the drafting and committee "mark-up" of legislation, which is where the real work is done. And because of my commitment to community self-determination, I subsequently introduced the first legislation to propose statehood for the District of Columbia.)

Within two years I became chair of the District of Columbia Committee's subcommittee on education. I came to use that forum to investigate successful and failed urban education programs and to help develop potential solutions to D.C.'s education problems and, by implication, those of other cities. When I assumed the chairmanship of the full committee, in

1979, I accepted a mandate to address the wider concerns of the District of Columbia and, by extension, the full range of urban problems that affected all the nation's cities, such as health care, transportation, housing, pensions, and public safety. This allowed me to raise questions not asked in other forums and to inject a progressive analysis into the social policy debate.

By attempting to develop programs that could make D.C. a model city—and by promoting self-rule for its residents—my goal was to use the committee's developing expertise to make the transition from being the District's colonial overseer to becoming a full-fledged committee on urban affairs. There was as yet no forum in the House that sought to integrate fully the assessment of the problems that plagued our cities and the development of solutions to them; at the time these issues cut across many committee jurisdictions. It seemed to me that, like the Small Business Committee, which focused on the range of issues facing businesses, an urban affairs committee could develop the integrated programs necessary to maximize the impact of federal investment.

Assuming the responsibilities of the leadership of the House Committee on the District of Columbia changed my relationship with my legislative colleagues and my own view of the conduct of my office. First, it meant that I was a member of the leadership and was invited to attend meetings to discuss party policy. This provided me the opportunity to make my points more effectively, away from the hubbub of the floor. Second, I could bring witnesses to the committee hearing room who had not previously been given a voice in any official forum. If there was a terrible problem of infant mortality in the city, we did not need to hold an ad hoc hearing on the issue—as the CBC continued to do on racism in the military, governmental lawlessness, and other issues—we could schedule an official House hearing, require witnesses to attend, and, most important, bring new information to the debate.

Over the years, as my approach became quieter and more studied, some lamented what they perceived as a change in direction. What they saw, though, was growth, an adjustment of style and approach rather than a change in principle or substance. What they failed to understand was that this adjustment was for the better. As a freshman and junior member of the House, I'd had to be loud and challenging in order to make our point of view heard; as a more senior member, I had to change my strategy to reflect new opportunities. I could now command attention without screaming; colleagues were beginning to listen.

The D.C. Committee chairmanship was the beginning of this stage of my political education. It required me to discharge my responsibilities to both the House and to my constituency. These responsibilities were different, but they both demanded fidelity. It would prove to be a great training ground for the future.

As the Ninety-second Congress came to an end and the leadership turned its attention to organizing for the ninety-third, which would be my second term, the maneuvering for committee assignments began again, and it seemed possible that I would be able to obtain a seat on the Education and Labor Committee after all. I was still one of the only people in the Congress who had worked at all levels—line, supervisory, administrative, and consultative—in the antipoverty programs established in hope of achieving the Great Society. I had even gone to Washington, D.C., to draft administrative regulations. I knew what worked and why; I also knew what didn't work. My participation could better inform the committee's effort; accepting an assignment on the Education and Labor Committee was a natural.

But new thoughts interceded. Over the course of 1971 and 1972, I had come to believe that the House Foreign Affairs Committee was not where the key debate would occur on the important national security issues that affected budget priorities. Unlike the Senate Foreign Relations Committee, the House committee was not poised to confront the administration on the fundamental foreign policy issues of the day; instead, it was more involved in the oversight of foreign assistance programs. While these were important, I saw that the big money in the sphere of national security and international affairs was in the defense bills that were the concern of the House Armed Services Committee (HASC).

In my first two years in the House I had taken the floor many times to argue that we needed to free dollars from the military budget to fund social priorities. On more than one occasion a fellow member had come to me to say, "Ron, you speak eloquently about priorities; but you're talking about a world that doesn't exist. You're naïve. You don't seem to fully grasp the danger of the communist menace in the world. The East-West split poses a danger to our way of life. I may agree with you that we need to address these problems, but you're arguing naïvely that we can cut the defense budget. We need to maintain our ability to contain the Soviet threat."

I resented the fact that my colleagues perceived me as naïve, or worse, rhetorical, or even worse, uninformed. The only way to overcome this perception was to go into the heart of the matter and become a knowledgeable and credible analyst of the issues, strategies, and programs in question. I needed to learn how to argue from the vantage point of military requirements, in order to demonstrate that money existed in those accounts that could be redirected to meet our urgent domestic priorities without damaging our national security. I needed to challenge the assumptions and the policies that underpinned the military budget. I needed to learn their language, their argument, their assumptions, and their way of thinking.

In part because I thought of myself as a peace advocate, I had not learned enough about "forward deployment," "missile throw weights," "strategic defense," and the myriad other concepts (and buzzwords) that dominated the debate when it came to military policy and budgets. By not being "expert," I and other peace movement activists had lessened the chances that our ideas would be taken seriously. As far as many were concerned, our relative ignorance had become just one more reason for not listening, not hearing, or not supporting the ideas we advanced. That excuse, in my opinion, had to be eliminated.

Although Education and Labor was ostensibly a better fit, I began to think it made more sense for me to try for a seat on the Armed Services Committee—the bastion of the national security apparatus. The arguments in favor of the latter course became overwhelming. I would have greater credibility for arguing the case against the war, for challenging it from an even more informed position. I would have a greater ability to argue for peace in its broader context, and to argue with more effectiveness and greater credibility for reduced military budgets. In addition, racism and sexism were rampant problems in the military, and being on the committee would allow me to become a better advocate for the improved treatment of women, blacks, and other minorities.

Lou Stokes had often observed that the strength of the Congressional Black Caucus resided in its diversity, and the members of the CBC decided to implement that observation by seeking placement on all of the committees. We would be able to widen our influence and share information, and in theory we would be missing no opportunity to advocate on behalf of our agenda. The CBC already had outstanding members on Education and Labor, I reasoned, and I was available to them to the degree they would find my expertise useful. Perhaps I could make my contribution to reordering national priorities and to covering the CBC's agenda in another context.

I went to our next meeting and discussed my interest in a seat on the House Armed Services Committee. None of the other caucus members expressed an interest or felt inclined to seek an assignment to that committee, so the group as a whole agreed to send a letter to the Democratic leadership in behalf of my appointment even though we understood that this going to be a difficult, uphill battle. In fact, nobody in the CBC really believed I had a chance of securing the appointment to the Armed Services Committee, because of my high-profile activities in opposition to the Vietnam War and in favor of reducing military spending.

I understood that if the party leadership bought into the principle of placing a black person on the committee, newly elected Barbara Jordan from Texas would be their logical choice. Texas was (and is) a big state, with lots of military bases and defense industry facilities. Jordan had a solid reputation and would be perceived as a good candidate for the committee. I called her and offered her congratulations on her election. Then I explained to her at some length why I wanted to serve on the Armed Services Committee. I told her how my interest in issues of justice and equality, and war and peace had led me to conduct the ad hoc "war crimes" hearings, to secure CBC initiation of hearings on racism in the military, and to offer numerous amendments to the national defense authorization bill when it came up for discussion and vote on the floor. I advised her of my keen interest in civil rights for men and women in the services. I impressed upon her how hard I was working to learn how to argue expertly for reduced military spending. Finally, I told her of how Dr. King had touched me with his call to seek non-military alternatives to solving the world's problems.

"I appreciate the phone call," she said. "I think you ought to serve on Armed Services. I will immediately sit down and write to the leadership to say that my desire is to serve as a member of the Judiciary Committee." (Her request for Judiciary was approved, and her activities on that committee later catapulted her into international prominence.)

The next step on the pathway to membership on a committee was to make a request through one's "zone representative" to the Ways and

99

Means Committee's senior members sitting as the "Committee on Committees" of the Democratic Caucus. (These days the Democratic Policy and Steering Committee makes these decisions.) By 1973, California was already big enough to be a zone by itself. I waited in my office to see what the outcome would be, and soon enough my staff advised me that Representative Jim Corman, my zone representative, was calling from the committee room.

"Ron," Corman said when I came on the line, "they've turned down your request for HASC. Do you want me to nominate you for Education and Labor? I need to know quickly because the committee's proceeding in alphabetical order by committee and Ed and Labor will be up soon."

Although disappointed, I was not surprised. "Why did they turn me down?"

Corman told me that the night before, HASC chairman F. Edward Hébert had called each member of the Committee on Committees to inform them that he did not want me on the HASC "under any circumstances." Corman had learned that Hébert's pitch had been that "Dellums is a radical from Berkeley" and placing me on "his" committee would be a "significant security breach." Hébert, a conservative Democrat from Louisiana, had argued that the HASC could never have a closed, classified session and be confident that the classified information would stay in that room. Corman advised me that the chairman's actions had weighed heavily on the members of the Committee on Committees; they were reluctant to place any member on a committee over objection of a chairman, although chairmen rarely exerted themselves in such a fashion.

He asked me again, "What about Education and Labor?"

"No, don't nominate me for Ed and Labor. I think this is wrong and I want to fight it. How do I do that?"

"You can do that, but I don't think you're going to win. I don't think the Committee on Committees will buck the chairman. If you don't let me get you on Ed and Labor, you could end up with no committee assignment at all."

"I'll take that chance," I said. "There's no legitimate reason for me to be excluded from Armed Services." I was angry that Hébert would act so undemocratically, and determined to make good on my pledge to take the voice of the peace movement inside the system; it was not enough to be in the House, I needed to secure a committee assignment that would give me real influence in the process of determining national priorities, and I'd committed to HASC.

I called Phil Burton, a savvy liberal colleague from San Francisco who was completely familiar with the operations of the House and an effective fighter inside the institution. I needed some good tactical advice. He was in and agreed to see me. I literally ran over to his office. I quickly explained the situation and how little time was available to achieve my goal. I told him, "I'm an outside guy, but I want to fight this decision as a matter of principle. You know this process well, tell me how to do it." He thought for a moment and then asked, "Who's chair of the Congressional Black Caucus?"

"Lou Stokes," I said.

The ever blunt and honest Burton said, "Lou Stokes is great guy, nice and polite. You need him, but you also need somebody who can be angrier than Lou will be, somebody who'll play the bad cop. You need to get Bill Clay as well. Have Lou call Carl Albert to demand an immediate meeting to discuss black membership on the Armed Services Committee."

Anticipating this moment, I had argued to the CBC that the day was over for allowing the leadership to pick who were "good blacks" or "bad blacks." We had to be able to choose our own leaders and to determine who among us would serve on which committees. We needed to inform the Democratic leadership that they should be responsive to our request, that this was a matter of principle.

I left Burton, fortified by his advice, and sought out Stokes and Clay. They were friends and "classmates," both having arrived in the Ninety-first Congress, two years ahead of me. That day they were having lunch together in the restaurant of the Congressional Hotel (now an annex of the House of Representatives). I burst in on them just as they were being served. "Sorry for the interruption, fellas, but my request for the Armed Services Committee has just been turned down." I explained that I needed Stokes to call Carl Albert and demand an immediate meeting to discuss committee appointments, then I needed both of them to come with me.

Stokes immediately agreed and went to the phone to call the Speaker, and Albert agreed to meet. Leaving their lunch behind, my two allies walked with me over to the Speaker's offices in the Capitol building. On the way, I explained to them Burton's good cop/bad cop theory. They agreed that Stokes should raise the issue of principle—that a black should be appointed to serve on the Armed Services Committee and I was the choice of the Congressional Black Caucus. Clay would be the angry militant: "We'll tell *you* who to appoint, not vice versa."

As we entered the Speaker's personal office he was very friendly. "We did well for you fellas. We got your people on all the committees they wanted, except for Ron. The chairman weighed in strongly and objected. The committee didn't want to overrule him."

"That's why we want to talk," said Stokes.

Albert asked us to wait "just a minute" and went to get the majority leader, Tip O'Neill, and Wilbur Mills, the Ways and Means chairman, who was also serving as chair of the Committee on Committees.

When they had all returned, Stokes, in his erudite and dignified fashion, laid out our argument. "Mr. Speaker, this is a matter of principle to us, that a black person serve on the Armed Services Committee. The CBC has made a collective decision to have Ron serve. Ron is the one person among us with experience, expertise, and interest in these matters." He reminded the three leaders of my ad hoc hearings on war crimes, of my leadership in the CBC hearings on racism in the military, and that I had taken up many issues regarding the military budget during floor debate in the House. He concluded his opening argument by noting that "black people throughout the country, both in the military and out of the military, recognize Ron Dellums for his leadership in this area. There is no reason to exclude him just because he's Ron Dellums. This is a matter of principle."

Throughout the discussion that followed, Clay provided the refrain. "There is no reason other than racism that Ron would not be allowed to serve on the committee. We want him to serve and he will serve!"

"Well, the chairman really doesn't want Ron on the committee," Speaker Albert said. The three of them evidenced consternation and discomfort. "What about Barbara Jordan?"

I had anticipated this move. "Mr. Speaker," I asked, "didn't you receive a letter from her seeking the Judiciary Committee? I've talked with her and she supports me for Armed Services. Moreover, she doesn't want to serve on Armed Services; she wants to serve on Judiciary. She's a distinguished lawyer and that's what she deserves."

The Speaker acknowledged Jordan's letter. "So," I said, "Barbara Jordan is not an alternative. What are the objections to my membership on the committee?"

The Speaker indicated that "the chairman believes that you would be a security risk," confirming the information that Corman had relayed to me earlier. The whole basis of the effort to keep me off the committee was the characterization of me as a "commie" threat to the nation.

Trying to keep my anger in check, I challenged Hébert's assumption. "I am a member of the Foreign Affairs Committee and have dealt with classified information before. What did Doc Morgan say about how I conducted myself on his committee?" (Thomas E. Morgan, D-Pennsylvania, was Foreign Affairs chairman.)

The Speaker had to acknowledge the truth. "He says he has experienced no breach of security and that you have conducted yourself professionally."

"How can I be considered professional on one committee but not another?" I asked. "I raised my hand and swore to uphold the Constitution and the laws, just like four hundred and thirty-four other members did. What makes anybody think I'm not prepared to deal honorably with my oath?"

Clay said, "If you don't put Ron on the committee, the CBC will call a press conference and denounce the party and the Congress as racist. There's no other possible explanation for excluding this brother from service on the committee."

Stokes finished up. "Mr. Speaker, Mr. Leader, Mr. Chairman, this is a matter of principle."

Looking back and forth between us, Speaker Albert said, "I'll go back in and see if we can't get the committee to reconsider."

At that moment I knew we had won. As we left the Speaker's offices, I turned to Stokes and Clay and thanked them for leaving their lunches. "I'm totally confident that we've done it—I will be appointed to the HASC. Once you got them to agree to reconsider, it was all over." I walked back to my office and forty-five minutes later Jim Corman called to say I had been appointed. I thus became the first black member of Congress in history to serve on the committee, and it would not have happened without the militant and principled stand of the CBC and its leadership. We had managed to succeed even in the face of our own doubt.

As the Congressional Black Caucus became more active and thus more visible during our second term, we were inundated with requests for hearings and intervention from black community leaders from around the nation. In order to avoid our becoming so busy and scattered as to become irrelevant, Stokes, an effective and eager chairman, set up a task force on the role of the CBC and asked me to take charge of it.

Our task force concluded that for the Black Caucus to be effective we had to acknowledge that we were legislators—albeit on a national level—and were not in a position to be all things to all people, nor should we try to be. The NAACP, CORE, SNCC, the Black Social Workers Association, the National Bar Association, the National Medical Association, other civil rights groups, the welfare rights organizations, and others at the grass roots—all existed to further the interests of their members and our communities. If we were to try to do the job of all of these organizations—without the mandate, the staff, or the responsibility—we would fail our constituents at the most fundamental level. It was no ego trip to recognize that we were the national legislative voice of a large and disparate community—with an emphasis on "legislative."

We also concluded that the CBC had to help its members to develop competence and effectiveness as legislators, working in conjunction with other black organizations at the national, state, and local level. We were a *part* of a larger whole, not its paramount leaders. We needed to give groups outside the Congress a clearer and more realistic view of what we could and could not do and what our—and their—responsibilities were. In addition, we urged our caucus members to think about how to build coalitions within the Congress, among our non-black colleagues. Obviously, no law could be enacted with the support of only a handful of congressional representatives—no matter how impressive the case could be made on behalf of the idea or program. We had to think about how we could be effective in bringing the street heat, the ideas, and the concerns of the community into the legislative arena and succeed.

As the Black Caucus began to work with groups throughout the country, we also set out to strengthen our coalition building within the Congress—with the Women's Caucus, the Peace and Disarmament Caucus, the Latino and Asian caucuses, and others. We evolved our "legislative weekends," in which black community leaders from throughout the nation would come to the Capitol to learn and teach on the issues of the day. We met regularly with each other to share information and approached our colleagues to find common cause on issues that cut across racial and ethnic boundaries. Although we were bound together by our racial identity, the Congressional Black Caucus was an urbane and intellectually rambunctious group. We all understood that many of the problems that afflicted the black community also adversely affected other minorities, and that economic and political powerlessness was a fact of life for many whites as well, especially for women.

Although the CBC was organized because its members were black, it became apparent that we were in pursuit of legislative issues that spoke to concerns beyond the black community, and the CBC was clearly the most progressive grouping of members within Congress. Because of our personal histories as individuals we understood the impact of racism; as members of a minority we also understood more broadly the discrimination that minorities face; as representatives of communities suffering from significant social problems, we could relate to those in the white community who also suffered from social and economic oppression. As Dr. King had noted, and as my caucus colleagues understood, the black experience in America offers us all an extraordinary insight into the necessary legislative agenda for promoting justice and the well-being of all our citizens. Representative Bill Clay has documented very thoroughly this extraordinary legacy in his 1991 book *Just Permanent Interests*.

Earlier on, for example, the Black Caucus had held two sets of ad hoc hearings that captured the potential of developing broader coalitions. I had brought the issue of racism in the military to the attention of the group. As a result, we convened a hearing in Washington on the subject, then caucus members fanned out across the country to take testimony at many different military installations on the same day.

Our strategy for raising this volatile and troubling issue gave it nationwide prominence, and I believe the effort contributed to a somewhat improved environment. The situation was not as extreme or blatant as it had been for me in Marine Corps boot camp, when I was obviously rejected for Officer Candidate School because of my race, but the problem of racism still plagued the military into the early 1970s—and beyond. I believe that as a result of the CBC hearings, however, many blacks and other minority personnel subsequently enjoyed greater advancement opportunities as officers and noncoms, which helped to create the environment in which Colin Powell—obviously qualified for the job—could become Chairman of the Joint Chiefs of Staff. It had never been the case that blacks and other minorities were not qualified—just that they were not being given the opportunities. Unfortunately, and despite successes like that of General Powell, and the vigilance of the CBC, racism and a lack of equal opportunity in the military would require us to return to the issue in the mid-1990s.

The Congressional Black Caucus had also held a set of hearings on governmental lawlessness, looking at constituency complaints agency by agency. The lack of regulatory follow-through to legislative mandates, the sequestering of funding in frustration of congressional policy, and personnel policies that denied equal opportunity were all identified as significant issues. I believe that these hearings helped to set the stage for subsequent congressional actions that improved government accountability.

By 1981, the CBC had operated under three presidential administrations—Nixon's, Ford's, and Carter's. Opposition to the Republican efforts to undo the Great Society experiment had been fairly natural for the caucus; working with a president of our own party proved more complicated. The politics and loyalties of the Carter years made consensus within the CBC more difficult, which in turn diffused our approach to allies within the Congress. The 1980 election of Ronald Reagan, though, ended that situation. There is no such thing as universal agreement within the black community, for it includes the full range and diversity of political opinion—socialist and capitalist, liberal and conservative, religious and secular. Nonetheless, the black community's distaste for Reagan's ideology was as near to unanimous as that diversity allowed.

The CBC, which constituted black America's national representatives, was well aware that we had now returned with clarity to being the opposition. We labored mightily to derail administration policies so mean-spirited and spiteful against poor Americans that even Vice President Bush would later feel compelled to campaign for the presidency as somebody committed to a "kinder and gentler" political agenda.

By the time Bush ran to follow him in office, Reagan's policies had shredded the economic "safety net" for millions and created massive homelessness. In early 1987, as an act of solidarity with those in such circumstances, I joined with Representative Tony Coelho of California, Joe Kennedy of Massachusetts, and my son Brandy in sleeping outdoors on a heating grate in the dead of winter. During the night, I looked at my son and saw how cold he was, even with all of the layers of clothing he was wearing. As we looked at each other, we acknowledged that we were not really prepared for this experience and later we agreed that we doubted we could survive it on an everyday basis.

From the beginning, Reagan, his cabinet, and his advisors had set out to systematically unravel the progressive victories of the 1960s and 1970s and to complete the unfinished work started by Nixon and Ford.

Professor Troy Duster, an incredibly brilliant sociologist at the University of California at Berkeley, the director of its Institute for the Study of Social Change, and an African American, was among the first to understand the horrifying implications of Reagan's agenda. As a social scientist, Duster also understood how critical it was to be able to assess and measure the impact of policy. What had escaped the attention of many was that Reagan's budget also proposed a dramatic reduction in social science research funding. Duster approached me to hold hearings on the potential consequences of that part of the administration's proposed cutbacks. We agreed, and organized a full day's hearing at U. C. Berkeley, taking testimony from the chancellor of the university and a distinguished panel of academic luminaries of all political persuasions. After the hearing, Duster was able to arrange for the publication of a transcript and we distributed it to every member of the House. The information and analysis contained in this slim volume helped to preserve funding for social research. As a result, social scientists like Duster and his colleagues would be better able to measure and monitor the consequences of Reagan's social policy revolution.

As he introduced his first budget to the Congress, President Reagan issued a challenge to potential opponents: "If you don't like or cannot support this budget, pose an alternative." Reagan perhaps understood that it is easier to oppose something than to make the effort to develop and successfully promote a comprehensive alternative. Especially for those used to being outside the system, it is significantly easier to concur in opposition than to unite with others to do the hard work of developing a program, building a constituency, and defending it against criticism. The CBC was not afraid. To its lasting credit, it alone took up the challenge to defend the notion that government existed to provide for the common good—for those still left behind and for those who would be harmed dramatically by the devastating social program cuts under consideration.

Under Walter Fauntroy's leadership, the CBC agreed to develop, draft, and propose an entire budget alternative. As I often said when speaking in public, "If I were to travel to a nation and could read only one document to prepare myself, I would read the budget. The budget defines the values, the principles, and the priorities of a nation. What a nation decides to spend its money on speaks volumes about what it believes is vital, valuable, and important." One might say that the political process is designed to answer the fundamental question of who gets what, where, when, why, and under what circumstances.

I was incredibly proud of the Black Caucus's decision to challenge the Reagan budget. With only our handful of staff and some Macintosh computers, we rose to challenge the legions and the computing power of David Stockman's Office of Management and Budget, as well as the Budget Committee of our own House. This was no easy task, for we had to play by the House budget rules, which demanded an accounting for out-year expenditures, projections of annual expenditures for authorization and appropriations, and all of the other minutiae and esoterica required to put a formal budget proposal together.

From that moment forward, the Black Caucus would play a role in shaping the political boundaries to the budget debate. If for no other reason than that the CBC budget offered one group of members an annual opportunity to say they voted against "the big-spending budget," and allowed them to vote for the middle-ground Democratic alternative, it helped the process of redefining the center in the debate over national policies both foreign and domestic. In addition, some members saw it as vote of principle and an opportunity to vote for their aspirations.

Speaking on behalf of all those suffering economic pain around the nation, the CBC offered a vision for America based on a balanced budget, a full employment economy, and a reordering of national priorities. It was a set of proposals in the best interest not just of African Americans but of millions of others affected by lack of attention to the social and economic problems they confronted on a daily basis. We set out to construct a plan for federal spending that could solve the human misery that we saw, defend the nation, and commit the government to a foreign policy that would make a more stable world for our children—and in my view we succeeded.

Regrettably, too many in the press and among Beltway insiders thought of it only as a "black" budget, and this tremendous and beautiful effort languished in the anonymity that is reserved for those whom the pundits choose not to consider among the "real players." Even some of our most natural allies needed to be persuaded to embrace up-front the CBC's budgetary leadership and, in turn, to help us organize early enough to hope to have an impact on our congressional colleagues and so at least move the center of the debate farther to the left.

Many of our colleagues chose not to read our alternative budget, or confront it, or debate it—including members whose political views should have made them sympathetic. I remember on one occasion standing on the House floor to make the point. Here is the CBC with a magnificent piece of work, prepared to debate and defend it, with nobody here to engage us on this most fundamental aspect of national priorities.

The press gallery was also empty; we labored in total obscurity. This was tragic, I believe, because the only way to make informed judgments is through confronting information, and if the citizenry is to be well informed about the options under consideration in their Congress, the press needs to provide that information. But in fact the public never was exposed to the assumptions that underpinned our analysis, the programs we proposed to fix national problems, the advantages and disadvantages of our approach to national security. I once stated in the House, "The CBC budget is one of the best-kept secrets in American politics." Unfortunately, it was not only unknown among the masses but in some recesses of Congress as well.

In choosing to take on the budget rather than remain exclusively focused on securing amendments to legislation, the CBC was also trying to win the battle where it would count most. Our experience had led us to understand that once budget allocations had been made to the various authorizing and appropriating committees, the money would stay there. In terms of reordering national priorities, it would not be enough to defeat an MX missile or a B-2 bomber; if we succeeded, the money saved would migrate to some other weapons development or military program. By choosing to fight on the battleground of the budget, we argued that Congress needed to reduce funds allocated to certain whole administrative departments—and increase funding for others—and then let the respective committees sort out the spending priorities within those departments in light of the new allocations.

The comprehensiveness of our effort also allowed us to reach out to form closer relationships with our Jewish colleagues. Initially, many of them saw our proposals for the foreign policy account as placing aid to Israel at risk because of our efforts to boost aid to Africa and the Caribbean. We sat down with them and resolved this issue in the context of the total budget for foreign assistance, which the Black Caucus was committed to expanding. This caused a number of previously hesitant representatives to take a new look at the CBC budget and, equally important, helped build solid new working relationships. Expanding the foreign aid budget rather than allowing ourselves to be pitted against other interest groups fighting for their share was a logical consequence of our recognition that people had to be brought into coalition on the basis of their own self-interest.

The habit of thinking in terms of budget politics was crucial in other contexts as well. The Black Caucus continued to aggressively promote a budget for encouraging full employment and economic growth, one that would expand the economic pie so that all could share. Through such expansionism, we would be better able to call upon the nation to maintain its commitment to use all the potential tools necessary to finish the unfinished business of ameliorating the economic, political, and social impact of racism and sexism.

As the reaction against affirmative action began to sweep the United States, I recalled conversations I'd had with colleagues twenty years earlier, when efforts to act in the affirmative to eradicate the ravages of racial discrimination were first being implemented. There was a consensus at the time that such action was necessary, although even then the guidelines and programs that resulted had their detractors, who claimed that affirmative action resulted in a quota system that was inherently unfair. Despite this argument (in my view unfounded), the undeniable reality of the continuing scourge of racism was enough to mobilize a consensus in favor of action—in part because jobs were plentiful and the economy was growing.

At that time, many of us would make the point that a commitment to a full-employment economy was an essential element of this aspect of the battle against racism and unfair discrimination of all kinds, for the purpose of affirmative action was not to deny anyone a job, it was to open the door and create equality of opportunity. So long as the pool of well-paying jobs was expanding, we could mobilize self-interest in favor of sustaining the effort and build coalitions to provide political support. But once the economic picture began to change, the doors began to slam shut as reaction set in.

Tragically, this drama continues to play itself out in the current moment. As of this writing, the Levi-Strauss company has announced layoffs of over five thousand workers in the United States and Canada due to plant closures. Like their brothers and sisters in the aerospace industry of southern California, in the textile industry of the South, in the garment industry of New York City, and in the newer high-tech industries, the white Levi-Strauss workers who have lost their jobs are not out of work because of affirmative action. They have lost their jobs because companies have downsized and moved offshore. White students not admitted to the University of California at Berkeley were not denied because of black or Latino enrollment—in the spring of 1999 it was announced that over twelve hundred students of color with straight-A grade-point averages and high admission-test scores had also been denied enrollment—there are simply not enough places for all students who are qualified to enroll.

The CBC, by proposing a budget based on a full-employment economy and expanded educational opportunities, was doing its share to create the climate for opportunity and equality. I was later particularly disappointed by some so-called progressives who dropped their commitment to the affirmative action portion of the equation while offering rhetorical support for full-employment strategies—especially if they had ignored the CBC budget effort. Upon close and careful scrutiny, their analysis seemed shallow and their advocacy rang hollow.

Like the long-distance runners who impress spectators simply by virtue of their determination to continue, the CBC's alternative budget efforts—year in and year out—began to draw the respect, if not the support, of key members of the House. To his credit, Representative Leon Panetta of California, during his tenure as chairman of the House Budget Committee, realized the significance of the CBC's alternative vision and would always encourage us to come forward; in addition, he argued that the Rules Committee should grant the CBC effort substantial time for debate. His actions confirmed to many that the outcome in terms of national priorities would slip significantly to the right if we were to abandon this work. More than once he stated his view that ours was the most significant budget effort before the body. As we knew, and he articulated, we had shown our willingness to "bite the bullet" on every major issue: complex tax matters, military spending, economic investment, social programs, allocation of budget surpluses, and deficit reduction.

The Congressional Black Caucus will always deserve credit for risking attack in order to educate and lead, and for making the budget debate more honest than it might otherwise have been. Each of the members of the CBC contributed by helping to write that portion of the budget that came out of his or her committee experience, expertise, and interest. My role was to put together the military portion of the budget—the so-called "050" or national defense function.

Initially, we chose not to get caught up in the numbers game but to support spending whatever was necessary for legitimate defense purposes. But that was the question. What was necessary? We set out to identify the wasteful, the unnecessary, and the dangerous. By eliminating those from the budget as a whole and adding support for day care, environmental restoration, and other under-funded programs, we would arrive at our total number.

We resisted the "let Mikey do it" machinations of the Gram-Rudman automatic budget cut approach for spending overall. I similarly rejected the popular formulaic approaches—let's add 5 percent, let's cut 10 percent—as too simplistic and not based on actual program requirements. Instead, we tried to root our decisions in a more complex mix of policy and analysis. In our budget proposals, funds were taken out or put in or adjusted based upon a given program's need and its priority. I argued, for instance, that the debate on military requirements should be driven by an honest threat assessment, not by political or commercial motivation. Recalling President Eisenhower's warning about what he called the military-industrial complex a quarter of a century earlier, we were trying to pull the rhetorical cover off the set of assumptions created by a symbiotic relationship between the defense industry and its military customers.

We attempted to be as rigorous with social spending as we were with military spending. And we noted that one cause of the budget deficit was high unemployment. Depending on the economist one consulted, we pointed out, each 1 percent drop in unemployment could result in a $30 billion to $50 billion reduction in the deficit. We did not argue that the nation should create employment in a vacuum, but that to the extent the federal government could solve social problems with coherent and humane national policies the by-product would be to generate employment.

We saw evidence that Reagan's massive transfer of funds from the social side of the budget to the military side was leaving too many people behind. Hope was being killed, and our children—the nation's future—were developing a sense of fatalism about their place in the economy and society that would lead them to make desperate and disaffected choices.

During the early and mid-1980s, the news media were ablaze with stories about farm families in crisis. Over the years I had not paid much attention to agricultural issues, focusing instead upon urban and military policy questions. But I clearly recognized the tone of distress and disaster behind the headlines, and I determined to become educated on the issue. When the farm bill came to the House in 1985, I made a point of staying on the floor to listen to the debate. As I heard speaker after speaker lament the condition on the nation's family farms, I understood that my constituents, who depended on small farmers for high-quality, relatively low-cost food, had a stake in this issue, and that, furthermore, the desperate victims of the crisis in rural America needed help.

I walked up to Representative E. "Kika " de la Garza, chairman of the Agriculture Committee and the manager of the floor debate on behalf of the bill. "Kika, give me some time."

He looked at me with despair. "Oh, Ron, you're going to kill us if I give you time." He knew I had never supported agriculture bills in the past because I hadn't seen it as an important priority. I said, "Trust me, Kika. Trust me. Just give me some time."

He relented, and I took the floor to admit my ignorance of the issues but also to say that I recognized the description of desperation and human misery in the statements that were being offered in support of the bill. I promised my colleagues that I was prepared to engage them on this issue, and invited them to "take me to school." As a result of this speech, the Black Caucus designated me as the member responsible for dealing with farm issues, until such a time when expanding diversity would bring members into our ranks who represented rural communities. In addition, Representative Steve Gunderson, a Republican, immediately wrote me a two-page letter inviting me to travel with him to his rural Wisconsin district. I readily accepted and within weeks found myself landing by helicopter in the middle of farm country with television cameras and microphones thrust in my face. When asked why I had traveled to a region so remote—in every way—from my own district, I answered, "I choose not to govern in ignorance, so I have come to learn and to help if I can."

For three days I moved around Gunderson's expansive district, meeting with farmers, bankers, civic leaders, editorial boards, and families. In that whole time I never saw another black person. I remember standing outside of a barn one morning, taking some fresh air during an event at which scores of families had gathered for an annual breakfast. Two ladies walked by. As they moved past me, I heard one say to the other, "See, there he is. I told you there was somebody from Washington who came here to help us." It didn't matter to her that I was black; what did matter to her was that I cared enough to be there. She was prepared to accept me as an ally in her struggle.

The day before we were to return to Washington, I sat up late into the evening talking with folks in the living room of a young farming family. As Gunderson started to wrap things up, I asked if I could make a request. I looked around the room, into the eyes of each person.

"Your representative is a good person and he represents you well. He works hard, and he sees the problems and understands the issues. Further, he's invited me here to elicit my support and he shall have it. Because I've been designated, at least for now, as the Congressional Black Caucus's representative on farm issues, I'll go back and attempt to relay these experiences to them and further educate my colleagues. So my one vote translates into twenty other potential votes.

"Now, in return for that effort, I would ask that you, the constituents of Steve Gunderson, free him up to stand with me when I bring proposals to the House to better the lives of my constituents, who are mired in the urban crisis."

They looked to me and then looked to Gunderson, and many smiled and some among them said, "Of course." On a number of issues, despite our ideological differences, Gunderson came to support our efforts as I had come to support a number of his efforts. Like my trip to Killeen, Texas, with Marvin Leath, this was a chance to begin to build a new coalition.

Making its arguments in the budget arena and being willing to stand the public scrutiny that comes with such advocacy remains the Congressional Black Caucus's finest achievement, in my view. It required courage and determination, for support did not come running to our doors. In 1989, during my chairmanship of the CBC, the *Boston Globe* described the 1990 fiscal year's CBC budget alternative as "the only honest budget to be voted on in Congress this year," adding, "It's fiscally honest, true to a coherent set of values, and it ought to make people think." Our budget alternative—which would have cut over $39 billion from military spending—was debated in May of that year, but received only eighty-nine votes, despite its magnificence and the general dissatisfaction that Democrats felt with the Budget Committee's alternative.

This budgetary approach forced our allies in the Congress and beyond to confront their own willingness—or unwillingness—to advocate for a saner approach to military policy and a better approach to national priorities at the most basic level. It challenged the CBC to be willing to lead in behalf of the entire nation. And it required the peace and social justice movement to recognize the leadership of African Americans in Congress; for a long period, we were the repository of progressive resistance to the madness of the arms race and the brutality of the Reagan administration's social policies.

Like many of my colleagues, I traveled around the nation to contribute to the massive antinuclear mobilization that was occurring in response to the Reagan military buildup and the administration's seeming rejection of arms control as a strategy to improve international security. At every stop I also tried to explain to both black and white listeners that many more issues were tied up in the peace and disarmament movement than just getting rid of the bomb. The value of the CBC budget was that it helped to frame the debate in terms of priorities, so that blacks and other racial minorities, along with low-income whites, could see more directly how the money issues tied together. I saw it as a major part of my role to assist in bringing people of color to understand that the whole debate around arms control was not just a white middle-class issue.

I believed—and still do—that irrespective of race or economic circumstances, people need to know about and understand their stake in the issues involved in the military debate. Even if national priorities were to be radically altered, the essential truth would remain: a nuclear weapon is an equal-opportunity destroyer. I often asked everyone to envision "right next to me, a huge, sleek, nuclear bomb in all of its 'magnificence.' Shining brightly, painted flag—the whole nine yards." Later in my talk I ask, "Do you still see the bomb? I know you're thinking about it. Can you imagine what would happen if it were to detonate? We would all die here, and far beyond these walls tens of thousands would die with us."

"In the shadow this bomb, we have all come to understand our mutual vulnerability. In the shadow of this bomb, we have come to understand our essential equality. We must sweep this monument to terror and madness off the stage—out of existence—and dedicate ourselves to building a new future of equality and justice in the full light of peace."

Back in Washington, the movement was cresting. A nuclear freeze resolution was passed, but the Reagan military buildup continued. Citizens in progressive communities around the nation convinced their local city councils and boards of supervisors to declare their jurisdictions nuclear-free zones, yet Congress was continuing to fund a military budget that would almost bankrupt the nation—helping to drive the national debt above five *trillion* dollars, with hundreds of billions per year of debt service that was yet another factor crowding out desperately needed social investment. Whatever the arms race might ultimately do to the Soviet economy, it was also a bad deal for the United States.

One night the House was debating military issues late into the night and I was speaking on behalf of our alternative military budget when Representative Newt Gingrich came to the floor. A Republican backbencher at the time, and reputed to be both conservative and confrontational, he surprised me by offering a compliment. "Although I disagree with your point of view," he said, "I want to compliment you on your commitment to elevate the level of debate. I believe that perhaps more than any other member, you deserve credit for trying to make this institution function to its highest and best."

It was extremely late when I arrived home that night, but what had just happened on the floor was so powerful and personally exciting that I woke my wife to tell her about it. I had suffered challenges since my first day; many of my colleagues had questioned my patriotism, my citizenship, my credibility. They had rarely gotten around to dealing with the my arguments themselves; they would often avoid that by personalizing the debate, dismissing my efforts as the "Dellums amendment," as if that were a political curse.

Gingrich's words made me see that this had begun to change, that by taking the risk to offer an alternative, progressive vision of government and backing it up with in-depth knowledge of the issues—and by working to build coalitions—I had earned the respect of more and more of my colleagues. It seemed that maybe in the future they would be more willing to debate on appropriate grounds—not on whether I was controversial or not, but on the substantive ideas.

It felt like I had crossed some kind of political Rubicon, like I had thrown off the yoke of being the Afro-topped, bell-bottomed radical from Berkeley. Although I knew I would always stand to the left of most, if not all, of my colleagues, I felt like I had finally arrived in the Congress.

"How long has it been?" my wife asked me.

"Fourteen years."

"That's a long time to have to prove yourself every day, day in and day out."

"Yeah, but it's done. Now I can move on." I knew it didn't meant that all of a sudden the "Dellums amendments" would be passing. But it did mean that more members would do as Marvin Leath had done. My constituency had asked me to do one thing: bring their ideas, aspirations, and point of view into the body politic. Their voices now stood a chance of being heard. I could even hope that my colleagues (some of them kicking and screaming) would someday arrive at the analytical street corner on which my constituents and I had been standing all the while.

As I had learned in the Marine Corps, when you take point, you will draw the harshest fire. Those days were not over for me, but the days ahead would be better.

At the end of the 1980s, the world changed with breathtaking speed. The Berlin Wall came down, the Warsaw Pact dissolved, the Soviet Union broke apart, and the Cold War came to an end. Managing the peace required new thinking. Enormous opportunities existed—even the Bush administration held out the prospect of a new world order. From my vantage point, the world had arrived at a new crossroads: we might hope for peace and opt for diplomacy, sustainable economic development, and an entire range of strategies to build a safer and more equitable world. All of this had occurred without a single nuclear weapon being fired by either of the principal Cold War antagonists. Now the confrontation that had spawned so many surrogate wars was over and the world could turn itself in a new direction. Never was there a greater moment to pursue the principles that had been advocated by the Congressional Black Caucus in its alternative budgets of the 1980s.

In the early years, the members of the CBC were all urban-based, and considered liberal Democrats—except for Senator Brooke, the moderate Republican Senator from Massachusetts (and of course the press and others had a special, if mellowing, nomenclature for me). Over years, as the CBC membership grew, its philosophical boundaries broadened significantly. Once our membership became more diverse—urban and rural, liberal, moderate, and conservative—we remained unified as long as we were focused on the issues of race: affirmative action, minority business set-asides, treatment of minorities by government agencies, government appointments. We were like any other broad-based black organization; there was agreement on these issues, even if differences existed on strategy.

With diversity, we had to grapple with issues, like tobacco subsidies, for example, that we had previously unanimously opposed as a caucus but which would now divide us. At a time when our numerical strength gave us increased influence when we could be unified, we had to deal with more political difference among our own ranks.

One issue that divided the Black Caucus was my effort to terminate funding for the B-2 bomber—an airplane designed specifically for fighting a nuclear with the Soviet Union. Over the years that I had fought to kill the B-2 program, I had forged a coalition with Representative John Kasich, a young, fiscally conservative Republican from Ohio. We had developed a strong personal relationship in the gym, as we were both physical fitness buffs. The friendship had led to discussions about issues; we argued and compared ideas. Kasich, who served with me on the Armed Services Committee, had come to oppose the B-2 bomber by asking the same questions I had asked: Do we need the plane? Can we afford it? Do alternatives exist that would enable us to pursue our military strategy without it? We had agreed: No; no; and yes. As with the MX missile before, we were able to win a partial victory—limiting the production of the planes, first to fifteen, then to twenty.

After the Democrats lost the chair of the Armed Services Committee to the Republican revolution of 1994, a renewed and concerted effort was undertaken by proponents of the B-2 to resume its production. In my judgment, any rationale that had earlier existed for the plane—though I never thought a sound one did—had expired with the end of the Cold War and the collapse of the Soviet Union.

Kasich and I met and plotted a strategy to resist this effort. We had in hand an independent analysis that confirmed that there was no need for the B-2—a study that I had brokered with Senator Sam Nunn, the former chairman of the Senate Armed Services Committee. Kasich indicated his belief that fifty or sixty Republicans could be enlisted to oppose the effort to renew production on fiscal grounds. Those votes would be more than enough to offset the small number of defections on the part of pro–B-2 Democrats. With the determined effort of the D.C.-based disarmament lobbyists working to shore up Democratic support, augmented by some grassroots presence, we were confident that we would win the fight.

When the roll call was over, however, we had failed by a narrow margin. Kasich stormed across the chamber. "Ron, I brought you even more votes than I thought I could." Indeed, he had brought over eighty Republican votes to the issue. What had gone wrong?

Scanning the electronic tally board high on the wall above the press gallery, I was shocked to realize that the margin of our defeat was less than the number of Black Caucus members who had voted to support the bomber. I had to accept the fact that I had made a terrible miscalculation. I went through the roof and confronted those of my CBC colleagues who were still on the floor in the wake of the hotly contested vote. "How could you possibly support this weapon system?" I demanded of those I could find who had voted for the B-2. "It's a thirty-billion-dollar hit on our communities!"

I had mistakenly assumed that since the scale of the B-2 program would make it financially disastrous to social programs, opposition to the weapon system was a foregone conclusion for CBC members. They replied, variously, "You didn't talk with me about why I should oppose the system," "I didn't have all the information you had," "I talked with so-and-so"—this or that B-2 proponent—"and he explained why it was still critical to the defense program."

I had to come to grips with the fact that I had erred in my assumptions and expectations regarding the CBC. I had assumed that it was still the group I had always known—that it, and all of its members, had always been and would always be progressive. I had failed to take into account the dramatic change in the diversity of the caucus's membership. Some CBC members had been "voting their districts." Some had voted at the behest of other colleagues seeking their support—colleagues who were committee or subcommittee chairs, or were from districts where the B-2 brought jobs; like any other representatives, they had struck politically important legislative deals for their districts.

It was not that I had taken them for granted because I thought they "owed" me their votes. The sin I had committed was a naïve lack of recognition that the CBC had changed.

I got on the agenda of the next CBC meeting. Standing before the whole group, I said, "I wish to apologize to you. I had made an assumption that you would be with me on the B-2 issue." I explained that I was not so much attempting to change minds on the B-2 (I knew that those who had voted for it once would likely do so again and it would be hard to articulate the reasons for doing otherwise in the space of a few weeks), but I felt I owed it to them, out of respect for each of them individually and their role as my political family, to be prepared to do better in the future when it came to discussing and debating the issues and sharing information.

Changing demographics and civil rights victories in the South had brought new thinking to the CBC, and gradually new understandings evolved. We understood that by having come together for the purpose of improving the condition of black people in America we had made a commitment to unity, but such unity would not survive if we threw down the gauntlet of political difference. To insist on defining one political philosophy as the only acceptable one, or to adopt an ideological litmus test for membership would divide us. We all knew that the one place where we could instinctively stand together was on the ground of vehement opposition to racial oppression and vigorous support of equal opportunity. Everything else was open to debate within the CBC.

The amazing thing about the Congressional Black Caucus was that despite its increasing political diversity, its members continued to forge a relatively strong progressive political agenda—articulated through its regular presentation of an alternative federal budget. Like coalition building in any context, holding the Black Caucus together required fluidity and flexibility, the constant search for common ground, and no rigid tests of membership; otherwise the fate of other caucuses and coalitions that had arisen during the same period—narrowing, atrophy, and dissolution—would have befallen the CBC as well. Despite its diversity—or maybe because of it—throughout my entire congressional career the Black Caucus continued to work with other groups and causes to strive to place an agenda in front of the nation that spoke to our highest values and our best nature.

With classmates from St. Patrick's (third row, third from the right). *Courtesy of Willa Dellums.*

With Cesar Chavez during the first campaign for Congress.

With demonstrators in support of the Americans with Disabilities Act.

Receiving the American
Public Health Association
award from Vic Seidel, for
my work on the National
Health Service Act.

With Japanese American activists, receiving a certificate recognizing my efforts in obtaining reparations for Japanese Americans illegally detained during World War II.

With the Congressional Black Caucus discussing our CBC alternative budget.

Press conference announcing *Dellums v. Bush*, our lawsuit challenging the unauthorized war in the Persian Gulf.

Speaking to a Washington, D.C., anti–MX missile rally.

Getting arrested during a demonstration against U.S. policy in Haiti.

President Clinton, here meeting with Oakland community leaders, responded to my challenge to make Oakland a showcase of military base conversion.

With Speaker Tom Foley and Arnold Schwarzenegger during the President's Physical Fitness Challenge.

With Nelson Mandela and Rep. Kweisi Mfume.

With Bishop Desmond Tutu.

With Yitzhak Rabin, whose willingness to take great risks for peace was an inspiration, and Rep. Floyd Spence.

With Mikhail Gorbachev, another who worked hard to bring peace to the world.

chapter five

The Struggle against Apartheid

In the very first year of its existence, the Congressional Black Caucus took on an enormous set of issues, and its thirteen members were spread across the lot, trying to respond to all the groups who looked to us to help them "petition for redress of grievances" while covering the full range of legislative action moving through the Congress. We met regularly, with scheduled agendas, working to ensure that we were well organized to meet these challenges. Based on committee assignments, political interest, or ideological orientation, individual caucus members took up the responsibility (or were assigned the task) of taking the lead on a particular issue. In an effort to become better informed on the issues, we also received briefings or heard speakers on occasion.

During that year, my first in Congress, I attended a meeting of the CBC that set me on a path toward what I consider to be my single most important legislative victory: the imposition of sanctions against the racist apartheid regime in South Africa.

As usual, the agenda for the meeting was packed and several members had prepared reports to present. But a group of workers from a Polaroid plant had come down from New England with the express purpose of meeting with members of Congress to discuss their concerns regarding their company's commercial engagement with South Africa. They had not notified us in advance but demanded to meet with the Black Caucus that day. Their militancy was palpable and they were in no mood to be turned away.

Despite our significant interest in the issue, the CBC decided that the other urgent matters before us had to be dealt with immediately and there was no time to add the Polaroid workers to the agenda. The caucus chairman, Charles C. Diggs, Jr. (D-Michigan), asked me to meet with the Polaroid workers and report back on their concerns.

In accepting the assignment, I thought, "This is like being in Berkeley working for Otho Green—send Ron out to meet with the militants, he speaks their language." In addition, though, I was a member of the Africa subcommittee of the House (also chaired by Diggs), so it made institutional sense for me to talk with this particular group. As I started toward the door, John Conyers said that he would come along with me. The two of us gathered the Polaroid people up and found another room in which to meet.

South Africa was of course a topic with which I was very familiar. A nation founded on the principle of racial superiority, it had enshrined in its constitution the basis for a system that far outdid the worst types of "Jim Crow" segregation. Some parallels between the struggle for the freedom of blacks in South Africa and the freedom struggle in the United States were obvious; the compelling difference was that in South Africa a minority was oppressing the majority. There could be no pretense to democracy, no pretense of electoral legitimacy by claiming "majority rule." Whatever the failings of the United States system to deal with the legacy of slavery and to promote human liberation, they were outdone by the totalitarian brutality of South Africa's continuing enslavement of the majority of its people in their own ancestral lands.

Racial oppression in South Africa had existed for centuries. In 1948, a transformative election brought the Nationalist and Afrikaner Party coalition to power, despite the fact that they had received a minority of the vote. The white supremacist system they advocated was soon enshrined into law. Committed to a complete separation of the races, the Nationalist/Afrikaner government passed a variety of statutory provisions controlling travel, work, marriage, education, and other aspects of life—rules and regulations that were designed to ensure white privilege and racial "apartness," *apartheid* in the Afrikans language. Among those provisions was the deceptively named "Blacks Abolition of Passes and the Coordination of Documents Act," which in 1952 rewrote the "pass laws" restricting travel by non-whites and required all Africans (the catch-all racial category for non-European, non-Asian, and non-mixed-race persons) to carry "reference books." What had brought the Polaroid workers to Washington was their concern that their company's product—the product that they produced through their labor—was being used as a tool by the South African regime to implement the pass law.

Polaroid cameras were taking the I. D. pictures that were then placed in the pass books, thus they were part of the system put in place by a brutal regime to oppress millions of black South Africans. The Polaroid workers wanted our help to force their company to cease doing business in South Africa. The company was not, on its own, going to walk away from this business opportunity. But for the workers it was a matter of conscience and urgency; they no longer wanted to be complicitous with oppression in South Africa. Conyers and I agreed to receive their petition and to take up their cause within the Congress; we also promised to use our good offices to bring their case for sanctions against South Africa inside the system in any other way that we could. One of our first opportunities to do so was when the CBC met shortly thereafter with President Nixon. We recommended that he use the power of the presidency to discourage U.S. firms from further investment in South Africa. It was clear that Nixon was not going to act, however, so we knew we would have to proceed legislatively.

My legislative assistant, Michael Duberstein, had attended the meeting with Conyers and me. The research and legislation-drafting tasks fell to him. By February of 1972 we had introduced a disinvestment resolution for consideration by the House. Committed from the first meeting, Conyers was an original co-sponsor.

Under the rules of the House, the resolution was referred for consideration to the House Foreign Affairs Committee, and then in turn to its subcommittee on Africa. Although the situation in South Africa warranted dramatic and immediate action, we did not believe that our disinvestment resolution would be an overnight success. (In fact, it would be more than a decade before the Congress was prepared to come to grips with ending U.S. complicity in the perpetuation of the apartheid regime.) Nonetheless, we had raised the issue before the elected representatives of the American people, and our resolution provided an organizing device for those on the outside to use to begin to build pressure on the Congress for legislative action.

For me, the meeting with the Polaroid workers also drove home the point that while the Black Caucus as a group and I as an individual representative could provide such a rallying point for issues brought to us by constituents, above all I was—we were—now in a position to do something *legislatively* to advance their concerns. They were not coming to the

CBC to ask us to help them with community organizing; they were asking us to legislate on their behalf. In doing so, they helped us to define our mission in those early days.

As I reflected on the meeting at the time, I remembered an earlier conversation I had had with tennis great Arthur Ashe. I had met Ashe shortly after my arrival in Washington and had taken to him immediately. In our initial conversation he impressed me as a deeply concerned and principled man, with the kind of quiet strength that a real warrior possesses. Ashe, deeply concerned about what was going on in South Africa, had become an activist on the issue. I was impressed with both his knowledge and his zeal about the need to do something; he had developed a passion regarding South Africa. He had made me think about what I could do; now the Polaroid workers had provided the framework for action.

By the 1980s, the situation in South Africa had deteriorated so severely that our legislative approach shifted. Instead of submitting the matter for consideration as a resolution—perhaps important as a consciousness-raising tool, but nonetheless essentially a rhetorical device—we began to craft a bill that would impose statutory requirements for disinvestment, economic sanctions, and other prohibitions against doing business as usual with the regime.

Other efforts were ongoing at the same time, most notably the years-long effort by the Reverend Leon Sullivan to compel U.S. companies doing business in South Africa to adopt a code of conduct with regard to their business operations. This approach raised a new set of questions. Many in the business and political world looked to the "Sullivan Principles" as a device that would place the United States on the "right side" of this historic moral struggle while allowing for the continuation of lucrative commercial arrangements with Africa's largest economy.

Introduced in early 1977, Reverend Sullivan's six principles were designed to promote improved conditions for black South African workers. Companies signing on to abide by the principles would agree to end workplace segregation, adopt fair employment practices, pay equal wages for similar work, provide job training and advancement opportunities, and set out to improve the sometimes squalid conditions in which workers lived, often separated from their families because of the pass laws. By 1979, it appeared clear to many people who thought about this issue carefully that the Sullivan principles were an inadequate, if not counterproductive, approach to the problem. In New York, in April 1979, the self-titled

International Freedom Mobilization Summit Conference of Black Religious Leaders on Apartheid resolved that the principles "though well-intentioned, are no longer sufficient and that the very presence of United States corporations in South Africa serves to legitimize the apartheid system of white supremacy." John Marquard, writing in *The Johannesburg Star* on March 31, 1979, had put it more starkly: "The pressures to get out of South Africa, coming from student and church quarters in particular, are staggeringly strong. From what I can see, there is only one stumbling block to the dominance of this point of view. That stumbling block is the Rev. Leon Sullivan."

In his message to the Congress on January 21, 1980, President Carter stated that "a peaceful transition to majority rule in Southern Africa continues to be a major goal of the United States." He went on to note that only recently, congressional support "to maintain sanctions on Rhodesia until the parties reached agreement on a cease-fire and [on] an impartial elections process [had been] instrumental in creating the conditions necessary for agreement." In my view, and in that of the growing anti-apartheid movement, the same would be true for South Africa. Carter had made a point of supporting human rights around the world, and his principal spokesperson on these issues was our former CBC colleague Andrew Young, from Georgia, by then the United States ambassador to the United Nations. Freedom was on the march in Africa, and it was past time for the United States to act decisively—even if such action affected U.S. companies doing business in the largest economy on the continent.

In 1981, Ronald Reagan's election as president dashed any hope that the executive branch might support an early sanctions effort. Developing its doctrine of "constructive engagement," the Reagan administration determined that the best interests of the United States would be served by maintaining a working relationship with the South African regime, and by opposing progressive liberation movements throughout southern Africa. The battle against this doctrine continued throughout Reagan's presidency, pitting the search for democracy, human rights, and freedom against the Cold War *realpolitik* that had informed so much of U.S. foreign policy since the end of the Second World War. Administration foreign policy managers characterized non-democratic governments as belonging to one or another of two camps, authoritarian and totalitarian. Authoritarian governments were necessary allies in the battle against totalitarianism; that is to say, we were prepared to align ourselves with fascist dictators—

authoritarians—in order to pursue our war against the perceived global communist menace—the totalitarians.

As the nuclear freeze movement crested and the MX missile controversy careened into the center of the national political debate, I determined to see that achieving sanctions against South Africa would remain a high legislative priority. I worked within a movement coalition to pull our nation, however recalcitrant, to the side of freedom and democracy. If there were to be peace in Africa, there would have to be justice. Change would come; the question the United States faced was whether it would work to reduce the potential for violence or, by leaving no other options available to a struggling people, ensure that bloodshed would be the only way out of the moral quagmire into which South Africa had sunk.

Public pressure was building throughout the United States for more significant action, and as my staff and I moved the issue of South Africa to the top of our agenda, we were able to bring a much more refined and developed set of legislative skills to the process. By then, Bob Brauer of my Washington staff had taken over the management of our legislative development of the issue and he assumed frontline responsibility for organizing the necessary political support and working with lobbying and grassroots organizations. As we became clearer about the nature of the entanglements that bound the United States in its alliance with the government in Pretoria, we attempted to catalogue the things that needed to be done in terms of significant sanctions against the regime: termination of airplane landing rights, a ban on the sale of South African gold and krugerrands, prohibiting intelligence cooperation, ending the provision of bank loans and credits, compelling disinvestment, and forbidding trade. We also understood that any sanctions legislation would need "escape valves" if it was to pass, but we drafted these narrowly in an effort to remain consistent with the principled view of ending all U.S. complicity with a government that officially stood for racial oppression. Our "time lines" were short; should the U.S. government make these decisions, we wanted the companies out quickly and we wanted the trade to cease forthwith.

Throughout the process, we in the Black Caucus sought to incorporate as provisions in our legislation those efforts that other colleagues were advancing in various committees of the Congress. In addition, some of the provisions that we developed for our bill were pulled and offered as freestanding amendments. The overriding purpose of this collegial interaction—to use every available means within the legislative process—was our collective decision that provoking economic disinvestment and curtailing U.S. trade with South Africa was the most effective way we could influence events in that country. CBC members on key committees—Foreign Affairs, Banking, Ways and Means, and Commerce—used their positions to seek to amend bills moving through their committees to that effect.

Such efforts included attempts to amend the Export Administration Act reauthorization in 1984. The proposed provision, included in the House version of the bill, would have prevented new commercial bank loans to the South African government and placed license controls on the export of high technology to government agencies in South Africa. The corresponding Senate bill contained a milder version of similar sanctions. The conference between the House and Senate produced a bill that contained only the prohibition on new bank loans—something for which Representative Steven Solarz had fought vigorously. Many of us in the CBC believed that the bill was too weak, and we wanted an opportunity to amend it once again and return it to conference with the Senate. With the legislative session coming to a close and members wanting to get back to their districts to campaign for reelection, the House adopted a rule for debate forbidding such an amendment; then, with many CBC members voting "present" in protest, it adopted the House-Senate conference report. The Senate never even voted on the report, and so even these minimal sanctions were not put into effect.

The Black Caucus was outraged that the Reagan administration was persisting in its do-nothing policy of "constructive engagement" and that the Republican-dominated Senate was either blocking or watering down House efforts to impose economic penalties on the apartheid regime. That fall, TransAfrica's Randall Robinson organized a series of demonstrations and civil disobedience actions at the South African embassy. These Washington-based activities reflected a growing militancy around the nation. Religious leaders and students were pressing disinvestment initiatives with local and state governments, and the International Longshore and Warehouse Union—the union to which my father still belonged as a retiree—refused to unload ships that had engaged in commerce with South Africa.

Dr. Mary Berry, Walter Fauntroy, and Randell Robinson were in the first wave of arrests.

A few days later I got a telephone call at home one morning. My son Erik answered the phone. "Dad!" he shouted. "Congressman Fauntroy is on the phone."

I knew immediately why Fauntroy was calling. "Hello, Walter," I said. "It's a good day to go to jail. Where do you want me to be and what time?"

He laughed. "How did you know?"

"I just knew that it would one day be my turn, so when you called it was pretty easy to figure out why."

He told me to meet him on Capitol Hill, so I put on my suit and headed across town to my office. He explained what the plan was, although I was pretty familiar with the technique they were employing. We got in the car and headed across the Mall and up Massachusetts Avenue to the South African embassy. Three of us were going to be acting together: Mark Stepp from the United Automobile Workers Union, D.C. council member Hilda Mason, and me.

When we arrived at the embassy, students, labor union members, clergy, and other activists were picketing. A police line had been set up that established the perimeter for the protest. At a certain point, Robinson and Fauntroy told the three of us that it was time to act. Linking arms, we walked past the police barriers and toward the embassy entrance. We rang the bell and sought admission. As we expected, the embassy personnel denied our request and asked that we leave the property. We refused, stood our ground, and started to sing the spiritual that had become the civil rights movement's international anthem: "We Shall Overcome."

Since we had now violated the law by refusing to leave embassy property, the officer in charge of the police detail issued us a warning that we should disperse. Of course we continued to sing. The officer dutifully gave us a second warning, which included the admonition that we would be arrested if we refused to leave after a third notice. We remained on the embassy grounds, arms linked, singing our anthem. Upon our third refusal to move, we were escorted away from the door, patted down, handcuffed, placed in police cruisers, and driven to jail.

Because of the timing of our arrest, we could not be arraigned that day, and so Stepp and I spent the night in the city jail. Like all the inmates, we were searched, and our personal effects were taken from us, including our belts and shoelaces. The noise and energy of the place and its population pulsated throughout the night. I got a firsthand look at the operations of the jail; many of the young men had been arrested on drug or minor robbery charges, and many of the young women had been picked up for prostitution, arrested on street corners scantily dressed in the middle of winter. It hit me again in a painful way that at least in some substantial part it was the dismal economic realities and the lack of opportunities that they faced that had driven many of these young people outside the law.

We did not get into court for arraignment until late afternoon the next day. By then my whiskers had grown to a noticeable stubble. As I stood before the judge, I decided that this growth would become my anti-apartheid beard; that I would keep a beard on my face as a sign of commitment until South Africa was free. Members of Congress often comment on each other's appearance, and my changed appearance did indeed open up constant opportunities to engage colleagues on the substance of my protest and this manifestation of it. (Later, when that freedom came, I considered shaving off the beard, and some people even said I ought to call a press conference and do it publicly, to draw attention to the work we had done. By then, however, the gray-bearded face had become my own.)

In 1985 we were prepared to press for a vote on our bill—thirteen years in the making, and by now a rigorous and demanding bill that would promptly terminate any U.S. economic support for the regime in South Africa. What would happen over the next four years is a political science story so compelling that every progressive should be heartened. Through patient adherence to principle, mastery of the process, and the mobilization of a constituency in favor of justice, a movement can contribute to events that change the world.

Throughout the early 1980s, my office was in regular communication with the liberation forces in southern Africa and with activists throughout the United States pressing for sanctions. Damu Smith of the Washington Office on Africa became one of our closest political supporters, in on the ground floor and working tirelessly on behalf of our effort to achieve a complete economic embargo of South Africa. International pressure was building, with the other major trading powers also beginning to feel political pressure to impose sanctions. Some people were still claiming that such an embargo would harm black South Africans more than help them, but the liberation fighters within that country were calling for sanctions, noting in reply that while sanctions might hurt, apartheid killed.

The bill, H. R. 997, had been written in a manner to manifest the demands then being made by Archbishop Desmond Tutu, the still imprisoned but steadfast Nelson Mandela, and other political leaders in and out of South Africa. I had met with Tutu and assured him of the Black Caucus's absolute commitment to ending the immorality of U.S. participation in support of the regime. At the same time, Representative Bill Gray, on behalf of the Democratic Caucus and the Foreign Affairs Committee, spearheaded an alternative approach—H. R. 1460—the focus of which was to prohibit new investment. The anti-apartheid movement was split on appropriate strategic next steps in the legislative arena. Some believed that they should strike to the center, support a more moderate bill and seek the "achievable" outcome; others wanted to press for maximum sanctions.

In addition to introducing a bill that reflected my own preference for the latter course, I had also co-sponsored the Gray bill, along with my CBC colleagues, in an effort to ensure that some action by the United States would be taken. I believed, however, that with our broad-based movement winning victories for disinvestment every day at the local and state level, we had the capacity to achieve more. I believed equally that disinvestment would be required to force South Africa's Nationalist Party regime to determine that it had no continuing self-interest in perpetuating apartheid. And finally, I believed it was necessary to keep the pressure on the U.S. legislative process from the left. I regretted that the movement would be split on these choices, and believed that it should have been prepared to support all of these efforts—as the CBC had—accepting compromise only at the appropriate time.

The Gray bill moved through committee and was eventually brought to the House floor for a vote. I offered my bill "in the nature of a substitute" to the committee bill. In 1985, only 77 supporters voted for this substitute, with 345 members voting against.

The Republican-controlled Senate passed a weaker bill, but both the House and Senate versions proposed to ban computer and nuclear technology transfers, as well as new bank loans.

Senator Richard Lugar, then chairman of the Senate Foreign Relations Committee, tried to forestall a conference on the bills and pressed hard for the House to accept the Senate version, even refusing at first to appoint conferees to discuss the differences between the two pieces of legislation. When the conferees were finally appointed the bargaining proved to be tough. Representative Parren Mitchell from Maryland, a CBC member and the only CBC member appointed to the conference committee, appealed personally to Senator Lugar for inclusion of the krugerrand ban in the conference report that would return to both chambers. In exchange, the House was compelled to withdraw from its position that there be an immediate ban on new investments. Before the scheduled August recess, the House approved the conference report on an overwhelming vote.

Throughout August and early September, Senators Jessie Helms (R-North Carolina) and Malcolm Wallop (R-Utah) threatened a filibuster, and on September 9, President Reagan signed an executive order implementing some of the sanctions contained in the legislation, but he maintained his threat to veto any legislation that would be passed. On September 11, in an effort to cut off the filibuster, CBC members walked over to the Senate chambers to lobby senators, without success. Once the effort to shut off the filibuster failed, chances of passing sanctions legislation in 1985 vanished.

Militancy and protest swelled in reaction to this legislative failure and to President Reagan's executive order. Many, quite appropriately, saw it as a joint effort to deflect the anti-apartheid movement from its prized goal—and in the short term it certainly had worked with the Senate.

Every day, after returning home from the Hill, I talked with my wife about events in South Africa. Because she was working from a home office, she had constant access to television news—daily scenes of the incredible repression occurring in South Africa as the regime attempted to suppress the increasingly militant struggle for liberation. "Ronnie, whatever you're doing it's not enough," she said more than once. "You've got to do more to end this." We frequently discussed South Africa and the anti-apartheid campaign well into the night.

At the time, my daughter Piper was a student at Berkeley, and she was participating in a shantytown demonstration on campus. She called me one night to say that events there had gotten out of control, and that the campus police had roughed up student protesters. In response to her call, I returned to the district for the express purpose of sitting down with the university's chancellor, Ira Heyman, in an effort to ensure that the students' peaceful protest would not be met with police overreaction again. I spoke with him as both a concerned congressman and a concerned father, representing both my constituents and other parents who could not arrange such a meeting. I made the point that we had struggled long in the 1960s and the early 1970s to ensure that students could make such peaceful protests, and that the community was not about to retreat from those victories at this time.

And I vowed to redouble my efforts in the next legislative session.

Congress meets for two-year terms, and 1986 was the second session of the Ninety-ninth Congress. Because bills carry over into the second session, the so-called Dellums and Gray bills were still alive, and the same fight that had unfolded in the House in 1985 was about to replay itself, but with a dramatically different outcome.

As in 1985, the Gray bill moved through the House committee process and provided the basis for the bill that was moved to the floor for a vote. The Rules Committee was going to provide for ten hours of debate on the bill, and we requested debate time for our bill as well. I remained convinced that ours was the better path for achieving our goal—which was not to impose sanctions per se but to end apartheid. Moreover, I understood from the health care, MX, and other debates I'd participated in that without continuous pressure from the left, the debate would slip even further to the right—and with Reagan in the White House and the Senate firmly resisting strong measures, we needed all the left-wing presence we could muster. The Rules Committee wrote a rule that made our bill in order as an amendment in the nature of a substitute to the committee bill, and granted it only one hour of time for debate—half of which would be given to those in opposition. Nonetheless, we had our chance to educate, to provide an organizing target for the Washington Office on Africa and others, and to help awaken the United States to its conscience.

At the end of the debate, the chair stated, "The vote now occurs on the amendment in the nature of a substitute offered by the gentleman from California, Mr. Dellums." At that moment, there were more Democrats on the floor than there were Republicans. Those colleagues who surrounded me on the Democratic side wanted to voice strong support for our effort—and the ayes rang out loudly. They clearly overwhelmed the more tepid nay votes that arose mostly from the Republican side of the aisle.

As I waited for a member from the Republican side to call for a recorded vote, I turned to Bob Brauer, a member of my staff who had worked diligently and capably on behalf of our effort. "At least we've won for a minute." I believed we would do better than we had the previous year, but in truth I thought it would be a significant move forward if we obtained 150 or so favorable votes, far short of a majority. If we got that number or higher I was confident we would have significant subsequent influence on the legislative process.

The chair kept announcing, "The ayes have it, the ayes have it," soliciting the surely inevitable recorded vote. I began to sense that something significant was underway. The Democrats on the floor did not want to ask for an official tally because most of them actually supported our alternative, and they too knew that a recorded vote would end in defeat. Those that did not support our position, on the other hand, assumed that the Republican member who had been controlling time, Representative Mark Siljander from Michigan, would rise and demand a count for the record. In that moment, Siljander made a decision that would accelerate the profound changes we were hoping for in South Africa. At that point he chose to stay quiet.

The chair of the proceedings informed the chamber that the ayes had prevailed. "The motion in the nature of a substitute is agreed to." Rushing into the chamber, Representative Barbara Boxer of California, a supporter and a Democrat, shouted to me, "You've won! You've won! What happened?" I told her, "I'm not exactly sure, but I know things will never be the same."

I walked down into the well of the House from the Democratic debate manager's desk, and Siljander came down to me from the Republican manager's desk. A political conservative and a religious, good-natured guy, he extended his hand to me. He smiled and said, "Ron, I made you a hero for a minute."

"What do you mean?" I asked.

"The reason we let this go on a voice vote on this side of the aisle is that we respect you. You never said you could guarantee sanctions could work, but only that you believed we had to try. You obviously believe that all of this might work, and you explained the reasons for it. We respect your honesty and sincerity."

But then he went on. "Frankly we're not that comfortable with the Democrats on Foreign Affairs." It seemed he was taking a little pride in tweaking the other party's members of that committee on this vote; the guy in the political minority had managed to upset the apple cart. "And I'm afraid you won't be a hero long," he offered.

"Why do you say that?" I asked.

"This bill will never see the light of day. It's too radical. You deserve recognition in the House, but it will never go anywhere."

But I sensed that in fact Siljander had loosed a tidal force by failing to call for a recorded vote. I had seen that no Democrat had the heart to oppose the disinvestment bill. It was also apparent that Republicans were reluctant to be seen as favoring apartheid. In fact, Representative Mickey Edwards, a conservative Republican from Oklahoma, had taken the floor during the 1985 debate to say, "Mr. Speaker, no nation which represses its citizens and denies basic human freedoms is a friend of mine or of the principles on which this country was founded." They were all caught in a conundrum.

"I appreciate your respect and kind words," I said, "but I think we on this side will have the last laugh."

"How's that?"

"I believe just the opposite will happen," I said. "You've placed a marker on the wall below which the House of Representatives will never be able to go. Second, members are going to figure out that there's no political price to be paid for having taken this position. Third, you've just placed some significant pressure on the Senate, because there's a movement out there and it will take heart from what happened today. The House passed the amendment. Now the Senate's going to have to take up this issue and pass something. They won't be able to bottle it up again. And they'll have to pass something fairly significant."

Siljander reflected a moment. "You may be right."

"I think I am, but we'll find out." With that we left each other.

The House went on to complete its work on the sanctions legislation. With passage of the Dellums amendment in the nature of a substitute, there would no longer be any debate on the "well-crafted" Foreign Affairs Committee bill. The House would now immediately vote on final passage—but the vote would be on the Dellums bill. Now the members of the House were caught in a dilemma. Once the voice vote occurred, would anybody then demand a recorded vote, which would identify members as being either in favor of or in opposition to the Dellums bill?

The drama began to unfold as the chair of the House intoned, "The question is now on final passage. Those members voting aye." Screaming loudly to add weight to the moment, I was joined by fellow Democrats who were marveling at this incredible turn of events.

"Those members voting nay." Once again, after the second part of the voice vote, the chair announced, "In the opinion of the chair the ayes have it." I held my breath to see whether or not Siljander, or anybody else, would demand a recorded vote. There was silence in the chamber. The Dellums sanctions bill had passed the House on a voice vote. Word went out around the nation and the world—the United States House of Representatives had passed a bill to impose a trade embargo and to force U.S. financial disinvestment from South Africa!

Many colleagues came up to me that day offering congratulations and praise for our work and for our success. Senator Joe Biden from Delaware undertook to walk over to the House side of the Capitol, a rare action for a senator, to offer his good wishes. He noted that "many people who spend their whole careers in public life never experience such a significant victory." As time went on I became more and more convinced that I was right and Siljander and the Republicans had miscalculated, and in fact it would turn out that by being persistent in our advocacy, and aided by Siljander's decision, we had helped to set in motion events that would help to alter the course of history.

In talking with colleagues and interviewers I expressed my belief that this victory was possible on this date—where it had failed a year before—because of the state of ferment in the nation. In communities throughout the country, voters were demanding that their representatives in Congress take a principled, moral stand to disassociate the United States from the brutal regime in South Africa. The presence of the anti-apartheid movement was so palpable that (Siljander's analysis notwithstanding) members of the House who opposed strong sanctions had been frozen out.

I remember getting home that evening emotionally overwhelmed, soaring from what we had achieved. I put on my running clothes and ran for miles to calm myself down. Finally, too exhausted to continue, I sat down on the curb at a street corner. I thought of all the death and misery that existed in South Africa and of the hope of freeing a people from that terror. I began to cry from joy and rage, exhilaration and determination. I thought, "Yes. Yes." We had all put so much energy into this—Brauer and Carlottia Scott on my staff, the unions, the students, the clergy, Damu Smith, my CBC colleagues—and there was so much more to do.

After the vote, Speaker Tip O'Neill sent Representative Bill Gray to meet the press on behalf of the Democrats. I was distressed with the Speaker's action because it seemed like an affront to the progressive wing of the party. Obviously, we had won few enough outright victories in Congress, but we *were* part of the party, an important part. I felt that the leadership had a responsibility when the party adopted positions from its progressive wing to allow us to express the party's view to the public.

I wrote a letter to the Black Caucus and to the Speaker, complaining of this affront. Lou Stokes was supportive and lent his credibility to my complaint. O'Neill met with me and explained that he had chosen Gray because Gray was on the Foreign Affairs Committee and therefore he was the leadership's point person on the issue. "I thought I was doing the right thing," he told me, but he apologized for the oversight. I responded, "I don't have any problem with your having picked Bill Gray. He's clearly a leader on this issue and he's a suitable spokesperson for the committee and the leadership. But, Mr. Speaker, I think you have an obligation to the left wing of the party as well, and we deserved an opportunity to stand up in front of the nation and be given credit for what we've achieved." In any event, the *New York Times* had gotten the point, and prominently featured passage of the bill on its front page.

As I had predicted, the Republican-controlled Senate did pass a bill, sponsored by Senate Foreign Relations chairman Richard Lugar and his colleague Senator Nancy Kassebaum. Lugar met with me to discuss what might happen if both bills were to go to conference.

"I don't want to be ham-fisted in this situation," he told me, "but I'm stating what I believe to be reality. If you force a conference with the Senate on your bill, we can't guarantee that we can get a conference report out of the Senate. The only way you can guarantee a piece of sanctions legislation passing the Congress is if you accept the Senate bill and don't go to conference." Several factors were present: conservative senators would again filibuster, perhaps even block the appointment of conferees, and any legislation more stringent than the Senate bill would not get enough votes in the Senate to override Reagan's threatened veto.

Shortly after my discussion with Lugar, a meeting was called to bring together Black Caucus and Foreign Affairs Committee Democrats, Democratic senators supporting anti-apartheid legislation, and members of the movement community. The meeting had an obvious purpose: to convince me and other hard-liners that we could not to go to conference on the bill. In the end, they all knew that how I approached Speaker O'Neill on this matter would have a substantial impact on the ultimate decision he would make on behalf of the House position.

After much discussion, I said, "I've listened carefully to everyone in the room. I first want you all to know that I have no pride of authorship here. My role has been to advocate the position of the grassroots movement on behalf of the people of South Africa, and to put that advocacy into legislative form. That is what I have tried to do. If it is the collective wisdom in this room that it is not advantageous to go forward now, I will not press the point." I understood that this was still a long-term battle, and although I believed that preserving our recent victory might be important in the anti-apartheid effort, in the long run, the people in this room were necessary allies for its ultimate success in the future.

My diplomatic and accommodating comments notwithstanding, I shared my disappointment with my staff as we walked back to the office. I believed that we had the leverage to work the Senate, but we still lacked the heartfelt backing of the leadership of our party and the unified backing of lobbyists on the Hill. Without these, we would be missing elements essential to success in the conference battle with the Senate. Making a concession for the moment seemed the right thing to do.

The dilemma involved a fundamental aspect of our governmental structure—the House and Senate must come to agreement on a bill before it can go to the president for signature or veto. In this case, forcing Reagan to act was critical; by stepping aside and allowing the process to go forward, we could increase the pressure brought to bear at the other end of Pennsylvania Avenue, in the White House.

In the end, Reagan's veto made a Senate bill that I and other activists felt was a weak one far more significant than it would otherwise have been. When the Republican Senate and the Democratic House both overrode the veto, a clear message was sent to South Africa—the people's representatives within the government of the United States had trumped the executive branch, and had taken control of the character of the sanctions that would be imposed. Ironically, because of the early publicity on the passage of the sanctions bill in the House, many people mistakenly thought that Reagan had acted to veto "the Dellums bill." Contemporaneously with the U.S. legislative effort, Japan, the Commonwealth nations, and Great Britain also imposed sanctions, eroding any claim that sanctions would harm the United States only to benefit other nations without helping to end oppression in southern Africa.

While we in the forefront had stepped aside to let the Senate bill become the basis of the law, we never intended to stop pressing for disinvestment and a fuller embargo. We had to keep pressure on the process every day until South Africa was free. We knew that since Reagan had used his veto power to try to kill the Senate bill, his administration would enforce it only half-heartedly at best. Over the next year, we would wait and plot, refine and update, preparing to move forward in response to the escalating repression, violence, and confrontation in South Africa.

Meanwhile, the November congressional election came and went, and not a single congressional representative faced a challenge—much less lost his or her seat—because the Dellums bill had passed the House. In fact, that event had benefited some. Members of the House no longer had to worry about disinvestment as a barrier to their reelection (and fear of defeat provides the greatest motivation for members in evaluating their vote on an issue). The mark we had put on the wall was now indelible, and when we brought the issue to the floor again, what had passed in 1986 would be the minimum we could achieve.

In December 1987, Representative Charles Rangel, a CBC member from New York who sat on the Ways and Means Committee—the House's tax-writing panel—secured an amendment to the Omnibus Budget and Reconciliation Act to prohibit "foreign tax credit" for U.S. business income tax filings. Although the "business of doing business" in South Africa was still not outlawed, another screw had been turned, another sanction had been added, a further disincentive to staying engaged in commerce had been put in place. Rangel's action was significant. In my opinion, it contributed to the momentum of the effort and the escalation of the pressure. Successes such as Rangel's gave us faith that we could ultimately prevail in the larger struggle; it fueled the optimism that is essential to the achievement of progressive action for change and equally necessary as an antidote to the cynicism that leads only to rhetoric and posturing.

As the 1988 legislative session began, I determined to introduce our disinvestment bill again. Now we would have the support of the Foreign Affairs Committee leadership, but given the breadth of the sanctions we were proposing, Foreign Affairs would not have exclusive jurisdiction over the bill; seven different full committees claimed jurisdiction as well. Offering the bill on the floor as an amendment did not require a referral from committee, and many advised us to take that course, predicting that the bill could not survive running the gauntlet before all of the committees that claimed it fell within their purview.

We chose to work through the committees. My staff and I were everywhere, working committee staff, members, and chairs. We sought to be educative, explaining the need and purpose of all of the bill's provisions. And the cynics were proven wrong. The bill not only survived the full committee process, but that process worked in its highest and best fashion to actually strengthen it.

One day, Ways and Means Committee chairman Sam Gibbons, a representative from Florida, asked to see me. Gibbons was one of the real gentlemen of the House, known to be willing to fight for his beliefs, but he was not of the liberal wing of the party. Getting through Ways and Means was an important and difficult test. It would be a barometer for dealing with the concerns of other committee chairs—including those of Chairman John Dingell of the Commerce Committee, who was concerned about the impact of the bill on Michigan's automobile industry, the key to his state's economy.

As we sat down, Gibbons said, "I've been looking at the international provisions in the bill. As I understand it, you want United States sanctions to trigger pressure in the international community as well. I think I've figured out a better way to do that than is currently in the bill." At that moment I knew that our chances at passage had significantly increased. If Gibbons was committed to "taking ownership" of the issues under his committee's jurisdiction and moving the bill forward, we could not be stopped.

This year we would not have to offer the bill "in the nature of a substitute," as we had done in 1986; neither would we appear to be pressing a "quixotic" point of view, as had been the case that year. Through hard work, significant movement pressure, and legislative diligence we had seized control of the center; our bill would again become the House's bill, this time with fuller support. Although still ours in spirit, it would be managed on the floor by Representative Howard Wolpe, a progressive from Michigan whom I had come to know, befriend, and respect for his compassion, his diligence, and his commitment to freedom, human rights, and economic development in Africa. As chair of the House subcommittee on Africa, he would control time during the debate.

I reflected on a 1986 meeting of clergy, students, and labor activists we had held in the Cannon Caucus Room, during which we had debated about approaches to legislating sanctions against South Africa. At that meeting, Wolpe, perhaps arguing against his personal position, had argued in favor of the Foreign Affairs Committee approach, "to do what is possible"; making the case for our divestment bill, I had argued in response that "what is possible is what we in this room decide is possible." In 1988, the consensus among House Democrats had changed: disinvestment and economic embargo in support of the liberation of South Africa was now in the realm of the possible. They were prepared to reach to the mark set on the wall in 1986, and through their receptivity, diligence, and hard work they had pushed the mark even higher.

Our three-pronged strategy had worked: first, consult with grassroots activists and provide them with the grounds from which to press in congressional districts for the most principled position possible—in this case, complete disinvestment and embargo; second, work with willing national organizations to generate a lobbying presence on behalf of bold government action—maximum sanctions, in the case of the struggle against apartheid—always creating pressure to move the middle to the left; third, engage congressional colleagues and educate them about the issues and the pathways for change (in this instance, it turned out that the referral of a bill to seven committees could be transformed into the perfect educational opportunity).

In conversations, meetings, and committee mark-ups on the bill, the apartheid apparatus had come under withering scrutiny. Members had been educated on the issues, and in becoming better informed they had become outraged. As Representative Mickey Edwards, our conservative Republican colleague from Oklahoma, had said on the House floor, our stated national values demanded that we reject any association with apartheid.

A few weeks before the floor debate was to commence, the Democratic Party held its presidential nominating convention in Atlanta, Georgia. One afternoon, I met a young man from South Africa. He was a delightful person, although thin almost to the point of frailty.

"Thank you for all of your efforts," he said. "I want to thank you on behalf of the millions of my countrymen who will never have a chance to meet you." It made me feel great. I'd been caught up in strategies and abstractions, but here was somebody who was telling me that our actions had made a positive impact in the real world.

Two days later, as I was sitting down with staff to eat some lunch in one of the lobby restaurants of our Atlanta hotel, I heard a commotion and turned to see the same young man, agitated and upset, struggling to get to my table. Looking into his face and seeing that he was quite troubled, I asked, "What's the matter?"

He said, "I want to help you pass this bill."

I said again, "But what's wrong?"

He struggled to be able to speak, and said, "I just received a call from my mother in Johannesburg. There was a bombing. My two brothers have been killed."

He struggled to fight back the tears, and I reached out to him. He was young enough to be my son. He looked me in the eyes, a look that I will never forget, and said, "There must be a better way. I have lost my wife and my child and now my two brothers." He fell into my arms and started to sob. "Come hell or high water," I vowed, "this suffering must be stopped."

Returning to Washington fortified with a new fervor, we set out to marshal our speakers for the floor debate. I was seized with the power of the moment. The House of Representatives was on the verge of making a conscious act to place the liberation of a people ahead of commercial gain or strategic advantage. I tried my hardest to reach to my colleagues, to touch their minds and their hearts with the hope and then the pain I had seen in the face of that young black South African. When I finished my floor speech, the concluding argument for our bill, I went to the Democratic cloakroom to call my wife at home. I told her, "I tried to express the pain and the rage we both feel."

As I left the cloakroom, Representative Norm Sisisky pulled my coat. Sisisky, a genial member from Virginia, would be among the Southern conservatives to join in support of the bill. "That was the finest speech I have ever heard in the chamber," he said. At that moment I could honestly respond that what he had heard was the voice of a movement, using me as its means of expression.

Although we were confident, the outcome was not foreordained. But history was with us, and on August 11, 1988, the United States House of Representatives, on a vote of 244 to 132, went on record for the second time in favor of disinvestment and other strong sanctions against the apartheid regime in South Africa—and this time nobody could second-guess what anybody's vote, or that of the House as a whole, was meant to achieve.

Once again, conservatives within the Senate prevented action on this sanctions legislation. But a foreign journalist who later visited my office shared with us the benefits of his research on the international anti-apartheid effort and its impact on political developments in South Africa. It was his view that "the Dellums bill had hung over South Africa like the Sword of Damocles."

In March of 1990 I boarded an airplane with a number of congressional colleagues bound for Lusaka, Zambia, to meet with Nelson Mandela, who had recently been freed from prison, and his comrades in the African National Congress Party. I had never had an opportunity to travel to any part of Africa before arriving in Congress, and even since then, official business had never taken me south of the Sahara. After a lengthy flight, we arrived late at night and were driven, tired and exhausted, to a modest hotel in Lusaka. Early the next morning, I awoke, got out of bed and walked to the window to draw back the drapes.

I looked out into an enormous and stunning vastness. Sunlight glistened in the dew on the windows and around the grounds. My heart swelled and my eyes moistened. I thought, "My God, I am actually home. I am in Africa."

Suddenly I remembered a conversation I had had with my mother when I was a child, and the scene was blurred by my tears. She had said to me one day out of the blue, "Ronnie, you know what my greatest dream is?"

"No, Mom, what?"

"My greatest dream is to travel to a nation where as high as I can look, to the highest office in the land, the person looking back at me would look like me. Do you know what I'm saying?"

"Yes, Mom. I do." On the morning I awakened in Zambia, where a black person sat as president, I had lived to fulfill my mother's dream. As I gazed at the endless sky, I thought about how, of all the Dellumses and Pooles and Terrys, throughout all the generations of my family who were part of the great African diaspora, I was the first to ever return to Africa. My heart was so full at that moment that I found it hard to take a breath. I felt that I had returned home for all of them. I could not wait to share this sensation with my family, my children, and especially with my mother.

I sat down in a chair and reflected on how it had happened that I, personally, had come to be here to experience this joy. And I vowed to return to my district to thank my constituents for this privilege.

That morning, our bipartisan congressional delegation met with the ANC leadership. The delegation, appointed by the new Speaker of the House, Tom Foley, was led by Representative Bill Gray, the Democratic whip, and included Howard Wolpe and a number of other colleagues. We made a presentation regarding the history of our effort and explained the political situation in the United States.

At the time, President George Bush was considering lifting sanctions to "reward the regime" for its "progress"; we had responded that as laudable as the developments he cited might have been, they did not warrant such an action. During a meeting with the Congressional Black Caucus, Bush had asked what circumstances, then, would qualify. Our collective answer had been simple and straightforward: "Sanctions should be lifted only when the oppressed people of South Africa say that they should be lifted." All this was covered in our presentation to the ANC, including our hope that our trip would help solidify bipartisan congressional support around that position.

After the meeting, I was introduced to Mandela. I was riveted. Suddenly *there* he was—a person who had loomed larger than life for all of us. As I had crisscrossed the nation, shouting "Free Mandela!" at countless rallies, I had dreamed of but never fully visualized meeting him. I realized I was in the presence of an extraordinary being—maybe truly larger than life. Sizing me up with his gaze and taking my hands into his—the large hands of a prizefighter—he said, "I have heard much of you. You gave us hope. We know of your good works." We embraced and I stepped back.

Looking into Mandela's warm face for that brief moment, I sensed a serenity and strength that I had never seen before in a human being—nor have I seen it since. I felt I had met probably the strongest person I would ever meet during my life, a person of awesome balance and tranquillity. The moment reconfirmed for me my determination to be a man of peace.

Later, Joe Slovo walked up to me and introduced himself. "I'm glad that you came and made that presentation," he said as we shook hands, "because not everybody here is aware of the history of the struggle to end apartheid in the United States. But knowing that history is important."

We left Zambia for South Africa, visiting Johannesburg, Soweto, and later Capetown. The palpable pain of the inadequate housing, sanitation, and health care in the townships was appalling. Mandela's release and the "unbanning" of the ANC had created a sense of hope and possibility that a new South Africa could emerge from the ashes of this tyranny, but the reality on the ground clearly argued that a second stage of U.S. and worldwide commitment to end apartheid would be required. We would need to provide the financial assistance necessary to help meet the legitimate material expectations that democracy and liberation would bring to these impoverished communities.

As we stepped off the bus at a Soweto clinic, the overworked black doctor in charge came forward to greet us; he actually jumped when he heard my name. "Congressman Dellums, the man white South Africans love to hate. I am honored," he said.

Later, sitting across the table from Foreign Minister Pik Botha, I did indeed see hostility, even anger, in that white South African's eyes. When it was my turn to speak, I looked at him and said, "We have not undertaken our actions in order to bring South Africa to its knees, but to bring South Africa to its senses." During the meeting, the South Africans acknowledged that sanctions were having a major impact on their policies. I told President de Klerk that I was prepared to pause in the push for more stringent sanctions if he and his colleagues could demonstrate "in word and deed" their commitment to an early, total dismantling of the apartheid system. But I also stated unequivocally my view that the current sanctions must be kept in place until the major conditions of the 1986 sanctions law passed by Congress had been met and a process established to achieve that transition to a democratic, nonracist society. I concluded by saying, "That would be my counsel to my colleagues and to President Bush."

One evening as I entered a banquet hall, I saw a young black man lean over to a colleague and heard him ask, "Who is the snow man?" referring to my gray hair and beard. "That's Congressman Dellums from the United States," his dinner partner answered as I walked past. The young man jumped to his feet and rushed toward me—a bit disconcerting considering how quickly he was moving.

He grabbed me by the arms and introduced himself as Patrick Lekota, but went on to say that people called him "Terror" because of his prowess on the soccer field. He hugged me, then stepped back and told me of his imprisonment on Robben Island, where Mandela had been imprisoned for twenty-seven years. "I would like to shake your hand. I want to thank you. You kept us alive, you brought us hope," he said. It was an encounter nearly as moving as meeting Mandela himself.

In that brief speech, he confirmed what I have always seen as the role of the progressive; whether in victory or defeat, the challenge is not so much to prevail at the moment as it is to remain faithful to the ideas and to the struggle, and to refuse to yield to the powerful temptation of cynicism. People often ask themselves, "Will this succeed?" "Will this be effective?" My response has always been, Whether I have been successful or effective I leave to other people to assess. Others ask, "Why bother? You can't change anything." At the end of the day, I never felt that I could guarantee the effectiveness of an action, or control an outcome. What I did have control over, however, was my own faithfulness to the ideas and principles of our movement, and a willingness to do my work diligently in pursuit of the legislative goals that could achieve them. Simply put, showing up and being prepared for the fight is the first step, and sometimes that alone has powerful unanticipated consequences.

By moving from optimism, idealism, and hope rather than succumbing to cynicism, we had believed it possible to help bring change to South Africa. By our having kept faith, this young man had kept hope. He had not given up, and we had done our part to sustain him through the trials and tribulations of his imprisonment on Robben Island. He is now a member of Parliament in the post-apartheid government.

One night in Capetown, Representative Vic Fazio, a California Democratic colleague, and Representative Jim McCrery, a Republican from Louisiana, and I decided to take a walk down by the waterfront. We strolled together for a while, soaking up the beauty of the city's geographic setting and watching the rise of an enormous full moon that looked as if it were sitting right on the ocean waters.

After walking for a time, we talked about getting something to eat. But could a black man and two whites eat together in South Africa? "Do you think we can get into a restaurant?" one of the others asked me. "Maybe they'll try to put you in jail."

"I don't know," I said. "Let's go try it and find out." We picked a place that seemed to be filled with college students. The hostess walked up immediately and asked, "Three for dinner?" We said yes, and she asked us to follow her. We were pleasantly surprised. Things *were* changing.

We were halfway across the room when I heard somebody shout "Ron Dellums!" I was startled; it was as if I had walked into a coffee shop on Telegraph Avenue in Berkeley. A young white man stepped up to us and identified himself as an American citizen who had served as a congressional page. He had decided to learn more about what was happening in South Africa and was spending a year abroad, studying and living with a family in a black township. He was part of the change.

On the long plane ride back from Africa, members of the delegation talked with each other, sharing their reflections about the meetings, their experiences, and their observations. It proved to be a very important journey, one that bonded us together; the delegation came to the unanimous conclusion that sanctions should not be lifted. I believe that my articulation in our meeting with the South African government officials of a willingness to pause in my quest for more stringent sanctions had created the space for this unanimity. In essence, my conservative colleagues were saying to me, "Since you are willing to step back from pressing further, then we have to be willing to step forward and maintain the current sanctions law." When we returned to Washington, that unanimous message was delivered to President Bush: not enough had transpired to warrant lifting sanctions; change was coming, but pressure needed to be maintained on the South African regime in order to support and hasten that change.

Mandela traveled to the United States, reiterating the point at both the White House and the Capitol. Then he toured the nation to thank the U.S. anti-apartheid movement and to raise funds for the ANC's political campaign, which was to follow. I was elated when he agreed to come to Oakland and attend a rally in our municipal stadium. With tens of thousands of community activists filling the ballfield and the stands, Mandela was greeted with thunderous cheers. Being able to bring Mandela home to my community and introduce him to my people brought to my mind the words of a popular rap tune: "Can't touch this."

As he looked out into the stadium at the multiracial gathering, Mandela leaned over to me and commented on the powerful lift to his spirit that the assembly had provided. Not only had the "rainbow coalition" gathered there that day kept faith with him and his comrades throughout their long struggle, it stood for the promise of a peaceful and just multiracial society in South Africa. I felt overwhelming pride at being a part of this marvelous community—one that twenty years earlier had sent a black man from an overwhelmingly white district to Washington, D.C., to advocate on its behalf. The poetry of the moment was unavoidable.

Eventually President Bush issued an order lifting the sanctions, but not until July of 1991. Many in the movement wanted to reimpose them legislatively, and meetings were called to discuss strategy. It was my view that such a course was not appropriate. A campaign for legislation for sanctions at this hour could only weaken our position, I believed, because we might well fail. And meanwhile the mere threat that sanctions might be reimposed put pressure on the South African government and gave strength to the anti-apartheid parties in the negotiation process going on within the country.

By November of 1992, a date for the South African elections had been set: April 27, 1994. A legislative effort in the United States to repeal the 1986 sanctions law followed, this time supported by the ANC and other forces in South Africa. Many in the movement were set to oppose that effort, and we met to discuss how we should proceed. During the meeting, I reminded people that we had told President Bush not to repeal sanctions until the South Africans said they should be repealed. I urged them to consider the other side of the coin. We had not secured sanctions as an end in themselves; we had secured sanctions to end apartheid. If liberation fighters in South Africa believed that their political goals—reconciliation and a pathway for a successful nonviolent transition—would be aided by United States economic investment, who were we to tell them otherwise? On November 23, Bush signed legislation repealing sanctions.

Afterwards, Representative Steve Solarz of New York, a ranking member of the Foreign Affairs Committee, came to me to say, "There is still unfinished business in South Africa. We need to develop an aid and investment program to support the transition process there." He drafted a letter for our joint signature to send to our colleagues to impress upon them the urgent need to help the new South Africa address the enormous social and practical problems—the lack of housing, educational facilities, health care, and transportation—that could impede political process. We shared the letter with the White House as well, challenging the executive branch to join with us in this effort. A constant struggle followed, over the next few years, with Senate conservatives, who resisted cooperation with the ANC and other progressive forces in South Africa. The Gore-Mbeke bilateral commission operating in South Africa today is directly descended from this early effort.

On October 6, 1994, I had the honor of helping to escort President Nelson Mandela onto the floor of the House of Representatives to speak before a joint session of Congress. I had attended his inauguration a few months earlier, and at that great event had stood once again—this time among throngs of cheering Africans of all races—in a nation with a black president. On both occasions I again recalled my mother's words and the sense of privilege that I had felt in standing on African soil for her and for generations of my family, for my constituents, for my movement, and for my nation. The enormity of the African sky was matched by the heart of this magnificent leader—now rightfully taking his place on the world stage to carry his message of progress and human dignity.

I had not gone to Congress in 1971 to take up the banner of ending apartheid, but I had been swept into the fight. More than two decades after introducing that first disinvestment resolution, I could see the worth of the long-distance run that had begun with that effort. At the height of the anti-apartheid struggle, in the mid-1980s, my wife had once said to me, "Ronnie, I think that your work on South Africa will be the thing for which you will be remembered the longest."

I am proud to think that might be true.

chapter six

Waging Peace

The successful 1973 effort by the Congressional Black Caucus to secure me a seat on the House Armed Services Committee was not greeted with warmth by committee chairman F. Edward Hébert. Having called every member of the Democratic Party Committee on Committees to prevent the appointment of a "black male bomb-thrower from Berkeley"—a security risk and a radical—he was personally affronted at the fact that Speaker Albert and the leadership had forced my appointment on him.

Representative Pat Schroeder, elected in 1972 as a peace candidate, also secured an appointment to Armed Services. Hébert called her "the white woman bomb-thrower from Denver." He was clearly distressed at the idea of both of us being on the committee. On the day the body met to organize, adopt its rules, and pick its subcommittee chairs, Schroeder and I arrived in the hearing room early. As we looked at the nameplates we noticed that there was only one chair available for the two of us at our adjoining places on the dais.

I was outraged and so was she. The committee chair controls everything in the management of the hearing room—was it possible that he had allowed or even directed the staff to insult members of the House with such a petty gesture? We were all equal in the Congress, our presence validated by the mandate granted by our constituents in an open election. As I contemplated what to do, I thought back to my childhood. "Never give the other guy the knowledge that he can goad you into anger. It gives him the upper hand," Gram and my mother had said. "Always keep your head, no matter what the provocation."

I turned to Schroeder. "Let's not give these guys the luxury of knowing they can get under our skin. My mother once said to me, 'If you can take their thunder away an insult becomes a meaningless strategy.' Let's sit here and share this chair as if it's the most normal thing in the world. If it's all right with you, it's all right with me." And we did, sitting through the entire organizational meeting of the committee cheek to cheek. (Years later, upon hearing this story at a public gathering, Representative Barney Frank of Massachusetts referred to the incident as "the only 'half-assed' thing Ron and Pat ever did in their political lives.") At the next meeting of Armed Services, we both had chairs, but our lack of welcome at the committee had been made abundantly clear.

In light of Hébert's belligerent attitude toward me, I attended committee meetings armed with the book of House rules. Normally members should not have to fight for their rights. Decency, mutual respect, and comity are the necessary ingredients of a successful legislative process. A chair who fails to recognize the requirement for these elements of fair play is, in my opinion, a poor chair, and Hébert was such a chair.

I was prepared to assert my prerogatives as a member. My constituency had a right to be represented in the legislative process at this level—where the hard and detailed work of national military policy is formulated. They did not have the right to win every debate, but they did have the right to try—the basic right to be heard—and I was their voice. But sometimes even the rules would not be enough. Late one afternoon during committee deliberations, Hébert announced that the committee would proceed to discussion and vote on an item that had not been previously brought to the attention of the members. Common sense—and the committee rules—generally required that matters for "mark-up" be made available to the members in advance. The issue in question was not earthshaking, but it was important enough to be deserving of some measured consideration and deliberation by members. I secured recognition from Chairman Hébert and asked that he postpone the matter until the next day's session, so that I and other members would be better prepared to evaluate the information and thus cast informed votes. He first ignored my request. I pressed him further, to which he angrily responded, "I want to say to the gentleman from California that we have been doing it this way for a long time and we are going to continue to do it this way. The gentleman from California got on this committee through the back door and any time he wants to leave the committee, he can use the front door."

With as much professionalism as I could muster, I responded—still pressing my point. In the end, he prevailed, but I had the satisfaction of refusing to back down in the face of his publicly stated animosity.

After the mark-up was adjourned, a Marine Corps officer who had attended the proceedings approached me. He introduced himself and said, "Representative Dellums, I've been coming to these meetings for many years, but I've never seen anything like that kind of behavior from a chairman. I'm glad to see you're still a marine, still a fighter. I respect you for standing firm and fighting back." He shook my hand and walked away.

Throughout Hébert's chairmanship I would have to struggle constantly to preserve my rights and prerogatives. The early days of my committee membership turned out to be one of the most difficult periods of my political life. Pat Schroeder and I were waging a lonely battle against the insanity of the nuclear arms race, unneeded weapons systems, wasteful procurement practices, and a bloated military budget that was helping to bleed our cities of vitally needed sustenance.

Initially appointed to the subcommittee dealing with pay, promotion, retirement, and other benefits and a special subcommittee on "human relations," I picked up the effort that the Black Caucus had started with its hearings on racism in the military. With the issuance of our report and that of the Pentagon's Task Force on the Administration of Military Justice, I introduced legislation to reform the military justice system. Over the course of the next few years, my subcommittee assignments changed as my seniority allowed me more choices earlier in the selection process. Soon I found myself dealing not only with issues of military personnel and equal opportunity, but with military construction and early decisions made in the research and development subcommittee regarding weapons systems options for implementing military and foreign policy. Over time, I worked hard to become educated in the full range of military policy issues.

No matter how diligently I applied myself to my assignments or to learning the issues, however, Chairman Hébert would never deal me a fair hand. When Representative Mel Price of Illinois took the reins of the committee, he called me up and invited me to his office. "Ron," he said when I arrived, "I know that your life has been very difficult on the committee. I want to assure you, as the committee's new chairman, that situation will change. I feel badly about the way you've been treated." He promised me that he would do all he could to help me. Whatever I wanted or needed, he would work with me to the extent he was able. And, most importantly to me, he said, "I want to assure you that I will deal with you with respect and will respect your rights and prerogatives as a member." That was all I had ever wanted, on behalf of my constituents—to be treated with respect and given a fair hearing. I thanked him for that.

In 1985, Les Aspin from Wisconsin—leaping past several of the committee's more senior members—successfully challenged Price in the Democratic Caucus for the chairmanship, ostensibly on the grounds that the elderly Price was too infirm to run the committee. I believed that Price continued, though with some difficulty, to discharge his responsibilities in the exact manner required of a chair. I also wanted to thank Price for having reached out to me, when simple fairness would have sufficed. I thought, "Let's give Price an opportunity to go out with his pride and dignity and respect, the same things that I was demanding as a junior member." So I opposed Aspin's challenge.

Aspin and I would always understand each other. We had sat side by side on the committee for more than a decade. He was incredibly bright, and he delighted in the intellectual exercise of exploring military and foreign policy. He was also a skillful and shrewd legislator, always seeking to "work the deals" among the members. By the time Aspin became chair of Armed Services, I had been head of the military construction subcommittee for two years and, using the experience of my District of Columbia Committee chairmanship, had "moved out smartly," earning praise from my colleagues for my fairness and commitment to consensus building. "Get Dellums on your team," several of Aspin's lieutenants advised him. "He knows how to run a subcommittee. Given his philosophical view, he's not going to give away the store. He's going to argue for or against programs on merit and substance. It's better to have him with you than against you."

In very short order, Aspin generated serious concern within the Democratic Caucus for his stewardship of the committee.

In 1985, when Aspin assumed the chair of the HASC, Reagan's military budget effort was approaching its zenith. The Reagan investment in "strategic systems"—which euphemistic term covered nuclear weapons, conventional systems for fighting a nuclear war, and the architecture of missile defenses—was enormous and growing. The various elements of these systems were designed to move beyond nuclear deterrence and toward a war-fighting strategy, that is, they were aimed at the insane objective of ensuring the capacity of the United States to "fight, win, and survive" a nuclear war with the Soviet Union. (In 1982, Robert Scheer, the man who had once run as a peace candidate for the congressional seat I now occupied and was now a columnist for the *Los Angeles Times*, captured the insanity of the Reagan nuclear war-fighting budget in his brilliant book *With Enough Shovels: Reagan, Bush & Nuclear War*.)

The principle elements of the nuclear war-fighting machine were the deployment of the ten-warhead MX missile in the United States, the highly accurate Pershing II missile in Europe, and the submarine-launched Trident II missile, equipped with the D-5 warhead. These thousands of warheads were to be combined with nuclear-tipped air-, land- and sea-launched cruise missiles. The final offensive weapons component was the arsenal of nuclear bombs carried by the venerable B-52 bomber and in the future to be carried by the seemingly incapable B-1 and the proposed B-2 stealth bomber. The horrifying theory was that, when added together, these thousands of offensive warheads would be able to attack Soviet land-based missile targets with enough devastating power to make a first strike by the United States feasible.

Reagan's strategic defense initiative—the ABM-treaty-breaching "Star Wars" plan—was also a key element of this nuclear buildup, as were advancing efforts in antisubmarine warfare capability (ASW). Admittedly incapable of defending the civilian population of the United States from a large-scale missile attack by the Soviet Union, the Star Wars plan proposed by Reagan would, in theory, be able to destroy a significant percentage of any surviving Soviet missiles that might be launched in response to a U.S. first strike. The ASW component would hunt down Soviet strategic missile subs—as was depicted in the popular movie *The Hunt for Red October*.

While I opposed the Reagan administration's nuclear war plan with every ounce of intellectual strength I could bring to the argument, I recognized that it was—despite its folly and danger—a comprehensive vision. Therefore, since each individual element was part of the whole, the more of these we could defeat, the farther back from the brink of potential disaster we could pull the world.

Aspin was on the wrong side of this fight. The Democratic Caucus—a rambunctious and liberal-leaning group whose leadership was now emerging from the "Watergate class" of 1974—pressed the leadership of the party harder on the MX, on Central America, and on other military and foreign policy issues. Aspin's use of the Armed Services chairmanship to thwart the caucus's effort to terminate the missile system, and his support for the Reagan-backed Nicaraguan "contras," distressed many in that group.

In the wake of the 1986 elections, Democratic members of the House began to discuss a challenge to Aspin. Representative Marvin Leath, the man who had taken me into his conservative Texas district to discuss nuclear arms control issues and the MX missile, decided to take the lead. Leath came to discuss with me whether or not I—certainly the most leftwing member of the Armed Services Committee and perhaps of the Congress—would support the candidacy of somebody as conservative as he had been on many issues. I had given the question some thought and had already decided to support him.

My reasons were several. First, while Aspin did not abuse members on the committee in the way that Hébert had done, neither did he run its deliberations with open solicitation of the views of all. He was a loner in many respects, and those with whom he did consult were often not members of the committee.

Second, although I did not believe that my policy disagreements with Aspin should serve as the basis for opposition to his chairmanship, I shared the concern of others that he allowed his own point of view to skew his stewardship of the committee. In my opinion, given the key role that legislative committees play in the process of policy formation, the test of a good chairperson is his or her commitment to the fairness of that process. All legislators need to stand their ground on the issues, advocate for their positions with force and vigor, and vote for their points of view and those of their constituencies, as is their duty as elected representatives of these constituencies. But once the product of a committee consensus has developed, a chairperson must advance the committee's position at each subsequent step in the process—on the floor of the House and in conference with the Senate—reserving, of course, the right to take off the leadership hat and speak as an individual when appropriate. I had confidence that Leath would discharge his responsibility as a committee chairman with the openness and fairness required.

Phil Burton had warned me that if we ever made leadership in the House contingent upon an ideological or popularity test, members of other political views would always outnumber those such as myself who held minority political views. Furthermore, members had to have confidence that those discharging leadership responsibility would subordinate their politics to their institutional responsibilities—because those members could never be expected to abandon the politics of representing their districts. I had confidence that Leath would handle the chair with the fairness required, and would not insist upon putting his conservative stamp on committee policy.

Finally, and very significantly, I saw in Leath a person who was trying to grow intellectually and to develop a broader perspective on the question of arms control.

Many members were surprised when I supported Leath's challenge. Some liberal colleagues and some within the CBC were wary of supporting somebody whose record was so conservative on so many military and domestic policy issues. I tried to explain to them the potential I saw here for broadening the consensus against the insanity of the Reagan arms buildup. Our position would be greatly strengthened if Leath were to embrace arms control and then raise these concerns on the Sunday-morning talk shows from the perspective of a conservative. Building such a coalition would allow us to transcend ideology—hawk versus dove—and rest the debate on U.S. military policy on the proper grounds: how to build a military force that promotes rather than degrades the security of the nation and the world.

I pointed out that many of the committee chairs for whom my liberal colleagues had voted were just as conservative as Leath. We were not electing him to be Speaker or majority leader, but chairman of a committee. Despite his conservatism, I believed that Leath's potential chairmanship of Armed Services was an opportunity—like Nixon going to China—to have a conservative become part of the effort to reverse a misguided and seemingly "locked in" set of policies. Many liberal members understood the significance of this opportunity and supported his candidacy; some did not.

Leath's challenge pulled two other candidates into the field. One was Representative Charles Bennett from Florida, the panel's second most senior member, who recognized that if another member leapfrogged over him into the chair, he would never attain it. The other was Representative Nicholas Mavroules, a liberal from Massachusetts who, like Leath, was even less senior than I was.

As a result of these challenges, on January 7, 1987, the Democratic Caucus unseated Aspin from the chair by six votes, 124 to 130. All four candidates—Aspin and his three challengers—then faced the caucus in a series of votes. In the first two, none of them received a majority and the candidate with the lowest tally was dropped; the final vote was between Aspin and Leath. During the two weeks between the votes, Aspin, who was a master strategist and very adept at building deals in the House, spent a good deal of time campaigning to save his chairmanship. He prevailed on a vote of 133 to 116, sufficient to win but close enough to force some change in the nature of his approach to the committee and his relationship with the Democratic Caucus. Significantly, Aspin and I went on to develop a closer working relationship; at first this seemed ironic to me, since I had supported the effort to unseat him as committee chairman, but later I realized that I had earned his respect by making my points without attacking him personally.

As part of his effort to become more inclusive and communicative generally, Aspin made it clear that he intended to keep in touch with me in particular. I said, "I'm willing to be your eyes and ears on the committee in terms of letting you know if members are feeling cut out of the process. I can only do that, though, if we're in serious communication and you're really willing to listen to what people have to say." I told him that one of the problems we who had challenged him had seen was his consultation with others to the exclusion of his own committee's members. "I walked in the door fighting against exclusion, and I refuse to go back to those days. I hope you'll move forward from this in a constructive and positive way— and if you want to do that, I'm willing to help." From then on, Aspin style was far more inclusive.

In addition, the events of that January solidified my relationship with conservative members of the House. My support for Leath had demonstrated that while I was totally committed to my views on substantive matters, I respected the constituent mandate granted to each of us and believed that fairness and professionalism, not ideology, were the prerequisites of leadership.

In 1971, when I arrived in Congress, the nation was embroiled in a full-scale war in Vietnam, a tragedy that had been set in motion not through legislative deliberation, as demanded by the Constitution, but through the kind of executive action that had been feared by the Constitution's framers.

During my first term in Congress, the Foreign Affairs Committee deliberated at length on this war powers issue. Unlike the moral imperatives that confronted the nation—feeding the hungry, ending a war, ensuring equality—the issue of who holds the power to wage war under our system of government was (and remains) a profound legal and policy question. It was not something I could answer intuitively—except that I understood the importance of slowing the march toward war, the very reason that the framers gave the war power to Congress.

When the Congress returned to the debate in 1973, I was ready. I had immersed myself in the complexities of constitutional doctrine and had determined that the framers' clear intent was to require prior congressional approval of any military action in the name of the nation. They understood that long-term and sometimes unintended consequences flowed from acts of military violence. As Professor John Hart Ely and others have observed, the Constitution's drafters could have limited the constitutional grant of war-making power to the Congress to "declarations of war," limiting congressional engagement to certain undefined but large-scale events. However, they included mention of the issuance of "letters of Marque and Reprisal," a clear reference to private or public military actions of lesser scale. This makes it clear that the framers intended to prevent a president—a single individual—from entangling the United States in even small or "short-term" conflicts that might create adverse foreign policy consequences.

As I studied the War Powers Resolution put before the House in 1973, I concluded that it constituted an unwarranted grant of authority to the executive branch. By allowing a president to commit troops for a specified time period, it invited presidential war-making; in effect, it constituted a permanent version of the Gulf of Tonkin Resolution.

The legislative situation was complicated. During the Foreign Affairs Committee mark-up of the resolution, Representative Lester Wolff from New York had succeeded in adding a provision that would start the clock running with reference to the Vietnam conflict. This strengthened the support of the antiwar members for the resolution, who held the hope that the measure could end the Vietnam War through a back-door mechanism. I argued repeatedly with liberal colleagues like Representative Bella Abzug, also from New York, that their support of the measure was misguided. We debated back and forth heatedly; it was one of those moments when I believed that by pursuing a short-term "victory" we would lose the larger objective.

Despite significant pressure from colleagues, I voted against the bill. The Wolff provision had been stripped from the resolution during debate on the floor, ending its explicit application to Vietnam; but since a sixty-day limit on the authority of the president to commit troops without congressional approval remained, many liberal and progressive colleagues nonetheless voted for its passage, still convinced that by doing so they were "boxing in" President Nixon. As expected, Nixon vetoed the compromise bill that emerged from the House-Senate conference as an unwarranted intrusion on the powers of the presidency—powers nowhere set out in the Constitution as belonging to the president.

As the House and Senate moved toward votes to override the veto, liberal members faced enormous pressure. The conference report had passed with fewer votes than the two-thirds needed for an override. Liberal members were assigned to "whip" those of us who had voted no.

Abzug was assigned to me. I respected her a great deal; she was a staunch progressive. But I had to tell her, "Bella, we just have to agree to disagree on this one. And I have to tell you this—I think supporting passage of this is wrong and dangerous. It is an expedient liberal effort. It won't end the Vietnam War and it won't prevent future presidents from committing us to military folly. It's not enough for me to hand Nixon a defeat. Someday he'll be gone and we will have created a monster for some new president—maybe a Democrat—to use in the future. I think you're going to come to regret this vote."

Conservative members wishing to preserve presidential flexibility also voted against the override, which passed by only four votes (some would claim by only one vote, as three Republicans shifted their votes from nay to aye in the last instant, when the override was assured). Whether or not it was legitimate to consider this a symbolic victory against the Vietnam War and against presidential war-making generally, I believe the resolution did dramatic harm to the constitutional balance of power.

Years later I traveled to New York to speak at a fund-raising event for a Democratic colleague. My long-standing and dear friend Bella Abzug showed up. We had not seen each other for a while; in the interim she had left the House of Representatives to run unsuccessfully for the Senate. Taking me aside at one point, she said, "Ron, you know, you were right about war powers. I was wrong. I wish I had voted with you then." We smiled at each other and hugged—nothing else needed to be said on the matter.

Asia was not the only region that invited presidential overreaching. The tide of United States intervention and interference in the domestic politics of Caribbean and Latin American nations had risen and fallen, but with the advent of the Reagan administration in the early 1980s, it reached new heights. The tiny island of Grenada would feel the bite of a full-scale U.S. military invasion. Grenada's prime minister, Maurice Bishop, captured the absurdity of the Cold War mentality in a comment he made during a trip I took to the island to investigate the ostensible cause of the subsequent invasion, the construction of an airfield: "Suppose we had some big guns or airplanes and blew a U.S. warship or tanker out of the water? Where then would I take my island and hide from the greatest superpower on the planet? It's like an elephant stomping a flea."

As with Salvador Allende's election to the Chilean presidency in 1971, the success of the Sandinista revolution in Nicaragua in 1979 provoked a concerted reaction from the U.S. administration, which encouraged and financed the counterrevolutionary contras. In response to this and the administration's actions in neighboring El Salvador, and with Vietnam still on members' minds, limits were placed on administration conduct.

In January 1983, alarmed by persistent reports that contra forces were receiving training at U.S. military bases, I wrote to Attorney General William French Smith under the Ethics in Government Act and asked him to initiate the process of appointment of a special prosecutor to investigate the Reagan administration's conduct. Working with lawyers from the Center for Constitutional Rights (CCR) and the National Lawyers Guild (NLG), we presented evidence that the administration was violating both the Neutrality Act, passed by Congress in 1793, and the Boland Amendment, adopted by Congress in 1982. The attorney general's refusal to act on my request led me to file a lawsuit in U.S. District Court in July of 1983. On November 3, Judge Stanley Weigel ordered the attorney general to begin the preliminary investigation that I had requested nearly a year earlier.

Eventually the Ninth Circuit Court of Appeals upheld the view of Judge Weigel that the Ethics Act "imposes mandatory duties" of investigation on the attorney general. Although the court reversed and dismissed the case "on standing"—saying that private citizens did not have a right of challenge—we had made the point. By then, Judge Lawrence Walsh had been appointed as special prosecutor to investigate these and other allegations of what would become known as the Iran-Contra Affair. On February 4, 1987, I forwarded our files on the case to Walsh's office. Three weeks later he wrote to thank me as he commenced a process that would lead to the indictment of numerous high-ranking members of the Reagan administration for their illegal conduct in support of the contras.

On August 1, 1990, elements of the Iraqi army crossed into Kuwait and occupied that nation. Mobilizing quickly, President George Bush dispatched U.S. military forces to halt any further Iraqi advance and to achieve the stated goal of reversing the occupation of Kuwait. Although no president had ever acknowledged the binding character of the War Powers Resolution, Bush, like his predecessors, notified the Congress of his decision to deploy without seeking congressional permission.

This was not a situation in which the United States had been attacked and the president, as commander in chief, was clearly acting within his constitutional role in having ordered troops or naval forces to respond. This was an enormous foreign policy decision, and it was deserving of debate and authorization by the Congress. But the horse was out of the barn, and so the next question was asked: Was the sixty-day war powers clock ticking? Upon its return from recess, the Congress began to hold hearings and to deliberate the issues and developments.

Appearing before a joint session of Congress on September 11, Bush announced that Iraqi aggression "will not stand." By then, more than a hundred thousand troops had been deployed and more were being metered into the region. Bush was marching forward toward a mobilization capable of launching a counteroffensive to dislodge the Iraqi forces from Kuwait.

I began to discuss with my colleagues my concern that Bush was getting ready to take the United States into full-scale war without congressional approval. I believed strongly that commencing offensive military actions in Iraq—as opposed to preventing further aggression—was wrong and unnecessary. I also believed that if the matter were debated broadly in the public arena—and that was the purpose of the framers' decision to place the power to authorize war in the hands of Congress—a decision for sanity would prevail and the drumbeat of war would be stilled. Many colleagues agreed with me, including Representative Tom Foglietta from Pennsylvania, who worked tirelessly as we organized members for both legislative and legal action throughout the crisis.

I began to publicly decry the president's path and to prod my colleagues into action against it. On October 9, thirty-two colleagues and I sent a letter to the Bush administration urging the president to use diplomacy, mediation, and other available options to achieve our policy objectives and those of the world community. I firmly believed that war was avoidable and that the economic sanctions imposed by the Security Council of the United Nations, representing a world unanimous in its condemnation of Iraq's actions, would eventually compel the liberation of Kuwait. Bush's apparent readiness and willingness to go quickly to a massive military option—even against the advice of some of his military advisors, who believed sanctions should be given a longer chance—remained alarming. Other presidents before him had asserted nearly absolute power to commit United States troops to battle, but the combined scale (half a million military personnel) and swiftness of this "operation" was unprecedented.

In addition to the United States mobilization, the administration had organized an international coalition of forces under the United Nations' mandate. The irony was overwhelming—Bush was prepared to seek United Nations authorization while resisting coming to Congress in compliance with the Constitution he had sworn to uphold and defend. On October 26, I secured the signatures of over eighty members of the House on a statement of concern sent to President Bush and the Speaker of the House, demanding that the Congress act before any offensive military action. With congressional adjournment for the fall election season at hand, this was a profoundly dangerous time, and our statement was intended to signal to these two national leaders that the U.S. Constitution should not be one of the early casualties of military action in the Gulf.

I returned home to my district the weekend before the elections, and everywhere I spoke, I urged my constituents to mobilize against Bush's plans. Unfortunately, most continued to believe that "common sense would prevail" and that "war would be averted." Nothing I knew about the events unfolding in the desert led me to believe such a rosy set of predictions. Bush was committed to war and only the people could stop him; by inserting the people's representatives into the process more forcefully, we could gain time, I hoped, and have a chance to mobilize public opinion in favor of other options.

Then a new strategy came to mind. On the day before the election I called my office and asked members of my staff to contact the Center for Constitutional Rights in New York City, to determine whether the CCR believed that seeking an injunction against the President Bush would be worthwhile. (They and the National Lawyers Guild had done terrific work on the Iran-Contra case nearly a decade earlier.)

In response to the conversation held between CCR and my counsel, we decided to press forward immediately with plans for a suit. I quickly contacted those who had signed the October 26 statement of concern and urged them to join with me in thwarting the president's attempt to subvert the Congress's authority over issues of war and peace. On November 20, along with fifty-two House colleagues and Senator Tom Harkin of Iowa, we filed suit in U.S. District Court in Washington, D.C. In addition to vindicating the Congress's authority, I was trying to buy time for the mobilization of a peace movement. Without some action, Bush was going to go to war, either on his own or, even if we could compel him to seek approval, with the blessing of Congress. By mobilizing a grassroots effort we might have a chance to prevent congressional approval. It was the only chance to stop the war.

The American Civil Liberties Union and a group of preeminent constitutional law scholars ably led by Professor Harold Koh of Yale Law School filed amicus briefs in support of our constitutional claim. As had happened on previous occasions, our lawsuit, *Dellums v. Bush*, veered off on civil procedure grounds. Judge Harold Greene nonetheless concluded in his December 17 opinion "that, in principle, an injunction may issue at the request of Members of Congress to prevent the conduct of a war which is about to be carried on without congressional authorization." Although he ruled the issue was not ripe for injunctive relief, he further concluded that the proposed offensive action in the Gulf was a "war" within the meaning of the term as used in the Constitution. "[T]he Court is not prepared to read out of the Constitution the clause granting to the Congress, and to it alone, the authority 'to declare war.'"

Within short order the president and the congressional leadership were discussing whether and how to conduct a debate on what came to be known as the Persian Gulf War, a discussion still underway when the new Congress was sworn into office in January. The administration never conceded that the arguments in Judge Greene's opinion affected their actions, but I believe that the lawsuit strengthened the hand of our congressional leadership in dealing with the executive—forcing them to move beyond mere consultation and setting the stage for the full-scale debate on war that the framers had envisioned.

On January 4, 1991, the Senate commenced debate on the situation in the Persian Gulf, and four days later President Bush sent a letter to Congress requesting approval for proposed military actions—the first time a president had done so since the Gulf of Tonkin Resolution was passed, in 1964. In the debate that ensued, members of Congress rose to the occasion in both chambers, arguing for prudence and restraint, citing constitutional questions and the long-term interests of the nation.

Significantly, this conflict represented the first test of foreign relations powers and policy in the post–Cold War world. In our view this was a chance to bury the analytical framework that posed all confrontations in military terms; it was time to test new modalities of engagement. Even President Bush acknowledged, in his September 11, 1990, speech to the Congress, that "we are now in sight of a United Nations that performs as envisioned by its founders." With such an opportunity and such a broad consensus throughout the world community to constrain Iraq until its aggression was reversed, many of us argued, there was no need to press immediately to war. Most analysts had agreed that it would take twelve to eighteen months, perhaps longer, for sanctions to compel Iraq to withdraw from Kuwait. Yet here we were, debating going to war less than a half year since Iraq had invaded and the world community had reacted with near unanimous condemnation. For decades, the Security Council had been paralyzed on serious issues by the political geometry of the Cold War; the end of that era allowed for broad consensus and unanimity among the five permanent members of the council, an incredible development. Choosing the military option now, we argued, would squander the first opportunity of the post–Cold War world to use the international machinery established at the end of World War II to respond to such aggression.

The debate, though serious and on point, was not enough to persuade a majority of either chamber to oppose the administration. On January 12, authorization for war narrowly passed in the Senate (52–47); a handful of changed votes would have altered the course of history. The margin in the House for the use of military force was larger (250–183). Very importantly, the House had earlier that day passed a resolution stating that it was the "sense of Congress" that the president required congressional authorization before commencing military actions. That vote passed by an overwhelming 302–131, but its legal significance was beside the point for now.

Four days later, when I heard on the television that cruise missiles had attacked Baghdad and that the coordinated military offensive—Operation Desert Storm—was underway, I was overcome with sadness as I thought of how close we had come to preventing this. Sitting at home that day, I thought, "If we'd only had a few more weeks to mobilize a peace movement, we might have found the necessary votes—in the Senate at least—to put Congress on the record against military action." With that, we could have returned to Judge Greene for an injunction to prevent what was unfolding before my eyes. The issue would have been ripe for judicial action because the House had declared its view that congressional approval was necessary before military action could be undertaken, supporting the underlying legal argument of our suit. But none of that had happened, and it seemed to me that scattered among the ashes of the tanks and planes that littered the battlefield of the Iraqi desert were the once glowing prospects of global organization to combat aggression without a ready resort to massive violence.

Upon becoming chairman of the House Armed Services Committee in 1993, I proposed to Representative Lee Hamilton of Indiana, then the new chair of the House Foreign Affairs Committee, that the Congress should revisit the issue of war powers—an issue that was under the jurisdiction of Foreign Affairs. Hamilton was receptive and our respective committee staff counsel began to discuss the issue. At the same time, we began to discuss with the National Security Council staff of newly elected president Bill Clinton that some better arrangement for the "shared responsibilities" of the two branches of government was appropriate. These conversations led to an informal agreement to attempt to regularize a process of interactions between the president and the relevant leaders in the Congress on military, intelligence, and foreign policy issues. I believed that through regular consultation we could begin to slow down the leaps to judgment that seemed to characterize executive action. In addition, through this informal arrangement we might be able to develop a framework for formal consultations that both branches of government could agree to use when they found themselves in conflict over these vital issues.

We also began to discuss with Republican leaders and with the Democratic leadership the possibility of a legislative effort either to repeal the War Powers Resolution while explicitly reclaiming for Congress the authority to commit the country to war, or to substitute a new legal framework that would implement more accurately the Constitution's war powers provision. We hoped to open up a pathway to public debate and clearer expression of public opinion on questions of war and peace.

These consultations went forward during the brief period of time when the two political branches of government were controlled by one party, but, like so many other important initiatives, they were stalled when the Gingrich-inspired "Republican revolution" captured the Congress. Relations between the branches quickly soured, and discussions of modifying the war powers structure came to an end.

In fact, rather than focusing on recapturing the Congress's war powers authority, the new majority made repeated efforts to constrain the president's role as commander in chief. Because of their antipathy to the United Nations and to U.S. military involvement in international peacekeeping efforts, the Republican leaders attempted to prohibit the president from placing U.S. military personnel under the command and control of non-NATO United Nations commanders. Although I thought the Congress should fight to preserve its war powers, I also understood that the framers of the Constitution had rejected the idea of command by committee. As Hamilton said, the president is "first general and first admiral" of the nation; the Congress had no business trying to dictate command and control relations. It was a sad irony that the Congress came to be focused firmly on precisely the wrong issue, command instead of deployment. In doing so it was acting in the misguided tradition of the War Powers Resolution, injecting itself into the war-making process too late to contribute to the crucial decision that the framers had assigned to the representatives of the people: should the United States go to war in the first place?

The repeated failure of the Congress to assert its full powers under the Constitution provided for me a constant source of anguish. Too many people all around the world—including United States military personnel sent into the maw of violence—had died because one person had signed a finding or ordered a deployment. The moral issues were enormous and the failure of Congress to assume its responsibility was tragic. Over and over we have witnessed the consequences of congressional unwillingness to insist that a president secure permission from the people's branch of government before undertaking killing, whether in Asia, Latin America, Africa, or the Middle East. This is one of the most important powers entrusted to the Congress, *expressly* to prevent the executive from using it single-handedly, and every time Congress has failed to insist upon its power—whether in Vietnam, in Nicaragua, or with the bombing of Libya—not only have people died, but our national interest has been ill served. The ongoing bombing of targets in Iraq, ostensibly based on the War Powers

Resolution, is but one current example; too much time has lapsed since the 1991 congressional authorization of the use of military force—not to mention the U.S. victory in the Gulf War and the surrender terms negotiated with Iraq—to renew either sporadic or sustained military bombing without explicit congressional authority.

Except for 1991, when the Congress discharged its responsibilities to authorize war in the Persian Gulf, it has failed throughout the years following World War II, and into the present, to live up to its obligation to prevent the nation from embarking on military adventures without the consent of the people. And most often, as John Hart Ely observed in his book *War and Responsibility,* Congress "ceded the ground without a fight."

I had sought membership on the House Armed Services Committee in order to become knowledgeable about the assumptions, plans, and programs of the Department of Defense and its supporters in the Congress and industry, with an eye toward being able, ultimately, to pose appropriate and informed alternatives. During my tenure on the committee, my education progressed as I served on a wide variety of its standing subcommittees, including those on military personnel, pay and compensation, military procurement, research and development, and military construction. I also served on a variety of task forces and special subcommittees called into being when important issues arose, including panels to assess the Strategic Defense Initiative, naval training at the Puerto Rican island of Vieques, Indian Ocean forces, defense burden-sharing, and the North Atlantic Assembly, as well as Chairman Aspin's defense policy panel.

Early on, a position on the military compensation subcommittee allowed me to follow up on quality-of-life issues confronting military personnel and their families. In addition, I was appointed to a special subcommittee on human relations, a panel designed to investigate the recurring problems of racial injustice and unrest in the services. Coming on the heels of the Black Caucus's ad hoc hearings on racism in the military, this was a perfect assignment—it gave me an opportunity to pursue this important issue. Based on the CBC hearings, the subcommittee inquiry, and the information contained in the report of the Pentagon's task force on the administration of military justice, I offered legislation to change the military justice system from the ground up.

In the wake of the resignation of President Richard Nixon, Congress continued to investigate the abuses that came to be known collectively as

Watergate, including the insidious threats to the liberty of all in the United States posed by federal intelligence and law enforcement agency misconduct. I believed strongly that it was important for somebody from the Left to serve on the select committee established by the House in 1975 to investigate the alleged misdeeds of the intelligence community, a committee chaired by Otis Pike from New York. The Pike Committee delved into the swampy waters of COINTELPRO—the FBI counterintelligence program that had targeted the Black Panther Party and other leftist groups—as well as into the areas in which the CIA had acted beyond its established mandate. The experience was a chilling one, providing new insights into the scope of the federal response to the cultural and political revolution of the civil rights and antiwar eras both domestically and internationally.

Some on my staff and among my CBC colleagues questioned my decision to serve on the Pike Committee in light of the death threats the office was constantly receiving. I responded, "My father once told me that if you're in a fight with somebody much bigger than you are, get in close and hug them. Nobody ever got knocked out by somebody pounding on their back." Anticipating that my effort to be appointed might well be met with the same type of resistance put up by Hébert a few years earlier, the Black Caucus declared to the leadership that one of its members *would* serve on the committee, and that the member would be Dellums; my CBC colleagues felt that because I represented a district that had been the target of such abuses perhaps more often than any other, it was especially important for me to be part of the inquiry.

During my first term on the Armed Services Committee, North American Rockwell Corporation came before us to tout the virtues of the proposed B-1 bomber, a supersonic aircraft designed to penetrate Soviet airspace for the purpose of delivering nuclear bombs. As an offensive weapon, it was part of the strategy that kept the nuclear arms race escalating. I was alarmed by the proposed acquisition program and learned all I could about the bomber.

At one point in the meeting a Rockwell representative turned pointedly to me—the only black member of the committee and a Californian—and said, "I know *you'll* be interested in this. The $20.5 billion we'll spend to build the bombers will hire 125,000 people—many of them in southern California, from cities like Compton and Watts."

I had my response to that argument ready. I could hire far more people than that with $20.5 billion, I told him. "In fact, I could hire a million workers at $20,000 a year or two million workers at $10,000." Those were reasonable wages in those days. I pointed out to him that Rockwell's projected 125,000 workforce would not all be on the job for the life of the program; but at $10,000 or $20,000 a year I could hire between 200,000 and 400,000 workers for five years, and have half a billion dollars left over to administer the program.

"So," I concluded, "don't ever try to sell this as a jobs program. Anybody could hire far more workers and employ them in more socially productive ways. The military budget is not a jobs bill. It's the money that must be spent to defend the country and you should defend your plane as a product that can help us to achieve those goals. If it can't or isn't necessary to our requirements, we should refuse to fund it."

I spent a good part of the rest of my career arguing with legislators who saw weapons systems as important to their district—rather than to the nation. This attitude was one element behind the defeat that Representative John Kasich and I suffered two decades later, in our effort to prevent further funding for the B-2 bomber. That jobs would flow from a decision to build a given weapons system was obvious and inevitable. A big part of our effort to stop the country from continuing to waste resources on unnecessary and sometimes destabilizing weapons was trying to break down the thinking of our colleagues that the military budget was a jobs bill.

Later I was appointed to a task force to look at the B-1 bomber, its development problems, and its utility. Our group met with President Carter in 1977, to present our findings, and I was pleased when he accepted our view that the program was "an unnecessary luxury and a waste of money." I was profoundly disappointed in 1980, however, and in 1981, as Carter was leaving the White House, when he proposed substantial increases in military spending. His proposal for fiscal year 1982 was to increase military funding by nearly $20 billion—to above $190 billion per year. This was in comparison to the fiscal year 1980 budget request of only $126 billion, already too high.

The arms race was speeding up again. When Reagan came into office in January he put the military budget "on afterburners"—tearing up Carter's already excessive increases and proposing instead to spend $225 billion on the military. This constituted a $50 billion increase in military spending in one year alone. And Reagan proposed to take all of this from the already

stretched domestic budget requirements. It was this set of events that provoked the first of our series of Congressional Black Caucus alternative
budgets to challenge the inhumane logic of what would become known as
"Reaganomics" or the "trickle-down" theory.

In January of 1982, in the wake of the first CBC budget effort, I wrote
to ask Armed Services Committee chairman Mel Price to expand the
Committee hearings "to examine a full range of policy issues and economic factors relating to the military budget." Typically the committee
would hear presentations from various Defense Department, State Department, intelligence community, and industry representatives during its
deliberations. In my view, we were avoiding the fundamental questions
that should drive defense policy, responding to proposals only on the basis
of the assumptions embedded in the budget requests. Price replied that
the committee did not have time to add new hearings to its schedule.

I discussed with my staff my concern that Reagan's military buildup was
occurring in a complete policy vacuum in the Congress and that the debate
was being driven by superficial considerations. Can we afford 5 percent or
10 percent increases, or decreases, depending on one's point of view, in this
program or that program? Worse, some seemed content to let budget cuts
be determined by automatic budget balancing provisions. Substance was
missing from the debate. I talked with a number of colleagues both within
and outside of the Black Caucus and decided to organize a set of ad hoc
hearings. Working with many peace organizations, we brought in some of
the nation's leading experts—and most brilliant minds—to spend six days
discussing the full implications of the military budget.

We asked the fundamental questions: Toward what ends should the
military budget be directed? What are the foreign policy, national security, and military goals it should serve? Where do current and proposed
systems fit in the context of these goals? What are the logical consequences
of the Reagan arms buildup? Will it contribute to stability throughout the
world—or undermine it? What will be left to defend if we ruin our economy and allow our cities and citizenry to suffer the economic pain caused
by these misplaced budget priorities? Finally, what are the moral implications of the administration's military budget, and what role can citizens
play in confronting those implications?

During the six days of hearings, many of my congressional colleagues
joined in, and they helped frame our discussion with the witnesses. We
plumbed the foreign policy and national security implications of the arms

buildup. We looked at what might flow from disarmament initiatives, as opposed to the probable consequences of arms escalation. We heard experts discuss the economic and employment implications of these budgetary choices. We investigated the impact of global arms sales.

The hearings provided some of the most enlightening testimony I would ever hear concerning this complex set of subjects. The witnesses we heard were so compelling that we published an edited version of their testimony in a well-received 1983 book, *Defense Sense: The Search for a Rational Military Policy.* In addition, I set out to draft an alternative military authorization bill, which later became the defense function portion of the CBC's alternative budget. Our plan for military spending was built on a new set of assumptions, a framework that we had conceptualized from the information presented in our ad hoc hearings and from all I had learned in the context of my Armed Services Committee work. After nearly a decade of mastering the issues and learning the facts, I was now well prepared to challenge the committee and the Congress to debate the entire range of issues—and to do so with confidence. I remembered all of the prodding by my parents, family, and community elders: "You know, Ron, you've got to learn to be smarter and better. Blacks will never get ahead being just as good—in this society you have to be better than the white guy." With the hard work of staff and the support of helpful colleagues, we were ready to challenge Reagan and those in Congress who supported his military budget programs.

We went to the floor of the House to offer a budget based upon the principles of nonintervention in the internal affairs of other nations, one which proposed to eliminate counterinsurgency and interventionary forces. This aspect of our plan spoke directly to our nation's misadventures in Vietnam and Chile, and to the crisis that was currently brewing in Central America. We set out unilateral initiatives that the United States could undertake to move back from the brink of nuclear holocaust—ending the MX, Pershing II, and nuclear cruise missile programs among others. One of our premises was that maintaining unnecessarily large forces would encourage intervention in smaller conflicts. We proposed lowering force structure levels to reflect the reality that we were in military alliances with other significant powers in both Europe and Asia. We proposed cutting back naval shipbuilding requirements to reflect the reality that a global confrontation with the Soviet Union would result in the very prompt destruction of most aircraft carriers with nuclear weapons capability—that the pitched naval engagements of World War II would not be replayed. We assessed bomber, fighter, and other aircraft requirements, eliminating those systems that were wasteful, needlessly redundant, or destabilizing to the world environment.

The military spending cuts we proposed—based upon policy and not budgetary requirements—amounted to a $50 billion reduction in the first year alone. We were confident that this was a prudent military budget, and with the Congressional Budget Office "scrubbing" our numbers, we knew it was financially accurate.

I requested that the Rules Committee make our bill in order as a substitute for the Armed Services Committee bill and provide for an hour's debate. Representative Richard Bolling, of Missouri, stated from the chair that although he had been an unrepentant "hawk" throughout the war in Indochina, he regretted that the Congress had never provided a significant opportunity for alternative views and legislation to be presented. He stated his view that the "Dellums alternative, in light of its breadth and seriousness" justified a "full and fair hearing on the House floor." Although an hour was hardly enough time to accomplish that, it was far better than grabbing five minutes here or a minute there during debate. It would allow those who supported our effort to speak to the nation about these important issues. On July 20, 1982, for the first time in the history of the Cold War, an alternative military budget was brought to the House floor for consideration. Equally significant was the fact that the effort had been initiated by a black man from West Oakland, the representative of a district that had stood well ahead of the nation in support of the ideas embedded in our proposal. In the course of the debate, Representative George Miller, from a neighboring congressional district in California, rose to say, "If the Dellums amendment does not succeed today, then let me beseech my colleague . . . [to ensure] that this amendment [will] continue to be a landmark amendment for the discussion of military spending. . . . It must be this amendment that the Congress must come to grips with, because it underlies the fundamental notions of what is security for this country and what is foolishness and what is the waste of money for this country that brings us no closer to a peaceful world."

In my final argument, I made a promise to my district, my colleagues, and myself: "We will be back next year and the year after that and the year after that until we right the wrongs in this madness."

In 1983, after ten years on the House Armed Services Committee, I had gained enough seniority to become a subcommittee chair, and so had Representative Les Aspin. Sitting down with my staff to assess my choices—military personnel or military construction—we began to think through the issues under each subcommittee's jurisdiction. Military personnel would allow for further inquiry into the issue of racism and equal opportunity in the military. I could work to ensure that the men and women who served in the military had better pay and better retirement, health care, and other benefits. I could return to the issue of equity within the military justice system. And because this committee dealt with "people issues," I would be able to use the chair to argue *for* programs rather than just being a critic.

On the other hand, every weapons system, troop deployment, force structure change, or basing decision has a military construction "tail"—a road, barracks, commissary, office, or truck repair facility. One cannot deploy missiles without silos, aircraft without runways, or ships without berths. If the Congress authorized purchasing B-2s, the Air Force would have to build hangers. Members tended to view the military construction subcommittee in traditional terms—National Guard armories, bowling allies, barracks, and other mundane facilities. An activist chair, with the opportunity to hold hearings, could help shed light on the policy implications underpinning force deployment, weapon systems acquisition, and other military activities, including the full range of quality-of-life issues for service members and their families.

One day as I deliberated on my choices, Representative G. V. "Sonny" Montgomery, an affable conservative Democrat from Mississippi, came to talk with me on the House floor. He and other members of the larger committee had been discussing my eligibility to become a subcommittee chair. He reached out to me in a friendly way. "I want to reassure you that there is no effort among committee members to prevent you from becoming a subcommittee chair, despite articles to the contrary in the *Post* and elsewhere." He confirmed that military construction ("mil con," for short) and personnel were the subcommittees with open chairs, and asked, "Which one are you thinking about, Ron?"

"Personnel," I said. "But obviously it depends on which one Les opts to take." Aspin would be entitled to choose first because of his seniority.

Montgomery smiled. "Great. That's where we were thinking you were going to go." Then he added, "Plus, you know, Ron, they're not going to let you have mil con—they're not going to put you in charge of the family jewels." What he meant was that many of my congressional colleagues would be appalled at the thought of having to come to me to request money for their local projects—I was the guy who was always out to cut the military budget. I knew there would also be consternation within the committee at the prospect of Aspin chairing the personnel subcommittee, because he had made some noises about "going after retirement" and making other controversial changes in compensation benefits. What Montgomery seemed to be suggesting to me was that if I were to strike for personnel, Aspin might have some difficulty in competing with me for that assignment. Committee leaders were trying to shape an outcome that would be to the overall benefit of their own agendas.

I went to talk with Aspin about his thoughts, and I told him that I did not want to be used to thwart any aspirations he might have for the chairmanship of the subcommittee on personnel. In the back of my mind, I was mulling over Montgomery's tidbit of information—the members of the House did not want to have to come to me as chair of the military construction subcommittee to secure funding for their projects. Why not? What would it be like if three hundred or so members had to take the time to see me, know me, and work with me regarding their districts' interests before that subcommittee? "How do you want to proceed?" I asked Aspin. "What do you think?"

On the day that the Armed Services Committee organized itself for the term, Aspin's selection of the personnel subcommittee surprised many and dismayed some: Dellums had inherited the "family jewels" by default, an outcome that only two people had been privy to when we all walked into the room.

At our first subcommittee meeting of the term, I explained to the members that they should not view the military construction subcommittee as a relatively small body with limited jurisdiction—the usual parochial view. "If you're willing to put in the time, we can become the most informed members on the full committee. Nearly everything the committee acts upon has a 'mil con' implication. Unlike other subcommittees, we are not pigeonholed; our work cuts across and interconnects with all the others." I announced my intention to pursue a wide range of issues.

"We may disagree on whether troops ought to be deployed somewhere or how many ought to be deployed," I said. "We may disagree on whether we ought to purchase and deploy certain weapon systems. I am more than prepared to debate these issues. But once we have to come together on a decision, we must be responsible for the human implications. People we deploy should not have to live in anything other than dignity and respect. The place where we all must come together is on the issue of ensuring a good quality of life for our military personnel. On the human side of the equation, we ought to be able to sit down in an intellectually honest and significant way to ensure that these folks have decent housing and reasonable accommodations." The ranking Republican on the subcommittee, Representative Bill Dickenson from Alabama, responded immediately to this appeal, becoming an ally rather than an enemy. When we agreed, we could work to craft an outcome; when we disagreed, we took our arguments to the subcommittee, the committee, and onto the floor of the House—each seeking to prevail on behalf of our respective points of view in open and fair debate.

The fact that the services were increasingly populated by married personnel with dependent children raised the urgent need for child care, playgrounds, and other facilities necessary to provide a reasonable environment in which families could live and prosper emotionally. We funded health care facilities. We brought new consideration to energy issues, promoting conservation through the use of cogeneration facilities and the use of renewable resources such as solar power. We came together naturally around these issues. Despite our differences on other policy matters—and everybody knew that the lines were clear—we made a palpable difference to the men and women who were serving their nation. As a progressive, I am proud that we helped move the larger committee forward in addressing the humanity of our personnel and their families—just as I felt the Congress as a whole should have been doing for families not part of the military community.

At the first hearing our subcommittee held, I announced to the panel of witnesses, "I am not an engineer or a person with construction experience. My job is to develop policy, and that's what I'm best equipped to do. Rather than discuss these projects in terms of board feet, cubic yards of concrete, tons of steel, lengths of runways, et cetera, let's discuss why these projects are needed. What is the requirement? Talk to me about the need that drives your request."

For years, witnesses had been used to discussing these requests in technical terms. Nobody had counseled them to be prepared to answer questions posed from this new angle. "I'm sorry, sir," one witness answered for the panel. "We haven't been asked those kinds of questions before. We want you to know we will be prepared to answer them the next time we come up here." From that point on, both the presentation and the dynamics of this subcommittee's hearings changed profoundly.

Serving as subcommittee chairman for six years allowed me to interact with a great many members of the House every year. This gave them the opportunity to get to know me as a person and to learn how I carried out my responsibilities as a leader. Most members beyond the Armed Services and District of Columbia committees had only seen me in the context of controversial speeches before the full House. Having to sit down with me or catch me on the floor or in the lunchroom to discuss their concerns and projects forced them to reconsider their one-dimensional view of me personally and of my politics. Although I had been a subcommittee chair since my third year in the House, and a full committee chair since 1979, my selection to chair the HASC's military construction subcommittee resulted in a more earnest "Hello, Mr. Chairman" from members and staff alike whether we met formally or just passing in the halls of the Capitol.

If you are around the House long enough, you learn its rules and customs and come to understand that no point of principle is served by remaining a permanent outsider. My constituency, like any other, had sent me to Washington to legislate. I owed them nothing less than my best. My election as "mil con" subcommittee chair gave me new influence. I had new opportunities to bring my congressional colleagues along with me. They saw me in a different light; maybe now they would hear me differently as well.

Critical to that potential was ensuring that my colleagues respected the way I conducted myself in a new role. I could not use the subcommittee to advance my personal politics—although I was entitled to advocate my position on issues, win or lose. My goal was to use the chair to advance the educative process and expose members to all points of view.

Thus it was that our subcommittee moved through its hearings and mark-up of the military bill under consideration that first year, deliberating and debating the issues, discharging our responsibility in behalf of the full committee, forging a consensus on the issues within our jurisdiction. I made my report to the full committee during its mark-up session.

When the bill reached the floor of the House, it was my responsibility as subcommittee chair to lead the debate on behalf of the Armed Services Committee's position. I controlled the time and presented the committee's arguments for the bill. Once that was done, I said, "I have now discharged my responsibility as the chair of the Subcommittee on Military Construction. This bill is a reflection of the consensus of our work. Now that I have carried out my institutional responsibility, I choose to ... [speak] as the representative of my congressional district. In carrying out my duties as a representative of my constituency in California, I am constrained to vote against the bill and will do so at the appropriate time." I then laid out my reasons for opposing the bill in question.

I had spent some time thinking through the problem of having conflicting responsibilities and how I would handle it on the floor, and I hoped that my colleagues would see my actions for what they were—an honest effort to carry out both my responsibility as the head of a legislative committee and my duty to vote for the position I and my constituents believed in, maintaining fidelity to each.

With the debate finished, the chairman called for the vote. (On legislation of such significance, members almost always want either to be on the record or to force other members to go on record in support or opposition to the legislation.) As with my effort in 1986 on apartheid sanctions, no member of the House demanded a record vote on the mil con bill. Later, several Republican and Democratic members would tell me that the decision had been made to forego such a vote as an expression of admiration and respect for how well I handled these twin responsibilities.

In 1989 I became chair of the Research and Development Subcommittee of HASC, positioned to gain insight at the earliest conceptual stages of new weapons systems and technology. I saw this as an opportunity to inject the bright light of policy scrutiny into what had once been dark rooms of collegial log-rolling. It also required Les Aspin, now the chairman of Armed Services, to work more closely with me on policy formulation. Once he accepted that, our relationship became one of intense engagement and mutual respect. He understood that I would always come prepared to best him in debate, and he worked hard to never lose an argument to me. Like two prizefighters training for a title match, we studied each other's moves and prepared to counter and parry.

"You make me a better advocate," I told him once. "When I go to bed I think, 'Aspin's going to be up at four in the morning, so I better be up at three getting ready.'"

"But I get up at two," he replied.

I got in the last word. "I was just trying to psych you out, man—I *never* sleep." Several people overheard this exchange and joined in the laughter; they too appreciated our annual ritual of debate.

One day Aspin turned to me during a committee meeting to consider force structure options for new the post–Cold War era. He and his staff had prepared a series of options—A, B, C, and D—in increasing order of scale. During the discussion, I had presented an even "leaner and meaner" force structure, still building on the basic ideas set out in my ad hoc hearings and alternative budgets. He leaned over to me and said, "I think you've come with option A-minus. Man, you know that you and I are the only guys on the committee who give a damn about this policy stuff." I looked at him and smiled. He was exaggerating; other members cared deeply about these issues, but all too often they gave in to the temptation to focus only on the bases and weapons systems that would have an impact in their districts or states.

Our relationship continued to grow. During conference, Aspin would turn to me and say, for instance, "Your responsibility is all of the strategic weapon systems." Such a "tasking approach" served two ends: it put all the systems in the hands of one person and it gave the chairman somebody with whom to discuss conference negotiations at the policy level rather than on the basis of the weapons per se. He also knew I would not be rolled on these issues.

Such tasking also served notice that I was Aspin's ranking Democrat, a person with agency to act on his behalf. I had his ear without having had to give up anything vis-à-vis policy—it was by the sheer force of persistence, diligence, study, and endurance that this door had opened. It was not that I would get my way, but the point of view that I had vowed to articulate within the legislative process was now smack in the center of national security policy formulation. And in 1993, twenty years after fighting to overcome Hébert's opposition to placing a "commie pinko Black Panther from Berkeley" on *his* committee, events took another turn.

With William Jefferson Clinton's election as president in November 1992, speculation began to gel around the prospect of Aspin's nomination for secretary of defense. Sonny Montgomery was more senior than I with regard to a vacancy at the head of Armed Services, but it was unlikely he would relinquish his chairmanship of the House Veterans Affairs Committee, and I was next in line. Media pundits and conservative commentators sounded the alarm. "The most antimilitary man in Congress is about to become chairman of the House Armed Services Committee. More on *Nightline* tonight," an advertisement for Ted Koppel's show teased. Offended, I called Koppel and asked him, "Why do you want to raise the hysteria level in the country by painting me in that alarmist way? Why do you call me antimilitary?"

There was a pregnant pause. "But you *are* the most antimilitary person ever elected to Congress, aren't you?"

"That depends on your definition of antimilitary. If what you mean by antimilitary is that I oppose the utilization of our military to deal with problems I see as nonmilitary in nature, then yes. If you mean that I don't believe we should deploy troops in places where I don't believe their presence is necessary, then yes. If you mean that I oppose certain weapons systems—weapons of mass destruction and increasingly sophisticated weapons that we don't need, or are fiscally wasteful—then the answer is yes.

"But if you're saying that I'm against people in the military because they wear a uniform, or I'm against the military per se, that's nonsensical. I wore a uniform; I am certainly not 'anti' myself. Your teaser is a non sequitur. If you're going to raise issues about what I am and what I stand for, then you need to express them with some specificity."

He said, "Your point is well taken and I apologize."

Aside from wanting to respond to Koppel directly, I was also reacting to my most recent experiences of what happens when the media—or political forces—are allowed to demonize an individual. Only two years earlier, Speaker Tom Foley had appointed me to the House Permanent Select Committee on Intelligence. It was an appointment reflecting my seniority on the HASC and rewarding my diligent work, and it was a nod to my wing of the Democratic Party. A tidal wave of furor rose up among conservatives, and my appointment became a cause célèbre for right-wing groups who routinely attacked me for their own fund-raising purposes. Predictably, the hate mail and death threats escalated, to the point where I confronted Representative Newt Gingrich on the floor and challenged him to "call off the dogs." I was angry. "My family should not have its safety jeopardized because of somebody's fund-raising schemes," I told him. I was no security threat and I deeply resented this issue rising up like some ghost from my political past.

Once it became clear that Aspin would take the Defense Department position, Montgomery called from his district in Mississippi to tell me that he would not seek the chairmanship of Armed Services. "You're my chairman," he said, and promised to support my candidacy.

My staff and I discussed how to proceed—cautiously and without presumption until Aspin's departure from Congress and action by the Democratic Caucus. On January 27, 1993, the Democratic Caucus voted 198 to 10 to elect me as HASC chair. Members of Congress and knowledgeable defense insiders were not surprised by the margin. After my brief acceptance speech, I was deeply moved when the overwhelming majority of my colleagues came down into the well of the House and embraced me with enthusiastic congratulations on a "well-deserved opportunity to serve," "gained the hard way." "This is something special," one of them said. The depth and breadth of the support my chairmanship received surprised only the ideological right and those in the media who had persisted in maintaining a one-dimensional view of me.

I named Marilyn Elrod as HASC staff director—the first woman to direct a defense or foreign policy committee staff in the Congress—and assembled the committee staff. "I do not believe that one person should have the unilateral authority to terminate people because the leadership of the committee has changed," I told them. "You're human beings with families, responsibilities, and commitments not unlike my own. Therefore, anyone here who wants to stay has a job. Your ability to continue in that job will be based upon performance, which will be assessed by your new staff director, Marilyn Elrod." Many stayed, giving additional confidence to my colleagues.

We believed that the most important task for our new team was to set out and adhere to a carefully developed four-year plan as stewards of the committee. From my point of view this meant the development of a set of hearings, task forces, and investigations that would provide the official compliment to the ad hoc hearings the CBC had held on the full implications of the military budget a decade earlier—but it was also imperative that I not forget my commitment to openness and fairness, or step out so far ahead of the committee that I would lose their confidence in my ability to speak for the House as well as for my district.

The fact that we were well into the post–Cold War era—a period of transition for which there were no experts and no established paradigms—made all of this imaginable. It was an opportunity to paint with bold strokes rather than tinker at the margins. Each step away from the fall of the Berlin Wall was a step further into this unnamed era and away from whatever confidence people may have had in their old analyses. The old conception of "hawks" versus "doves" no longer fit as peacekeeping rather than making war became the focus of debate within Congress.

Finally, the long-delayed peace dividend that progressive activists of all kinds had dreamed of during the 1960s and 1970s might be invested in our nation's domestic well-being. The window of opportunity was open; for how long was unknown, but it was certain to close as new threats were imagined, new fears propagated, opportunities for peace and stability lost, and as defense industry corporations established new arguments for maintaining their hold on the nation's treasury. Thus the four-year plan.

In the first year, my staff and I planned to concentrate on mastering the process of producing a committee bill and on beginning a new assessment of the important issues on the table: the use of force in the post–Cold War era and the situation in the former Yugoslavia. We rejected the Aspin approach of having a policy panel, determining instead that the full committee should address these issues. To me, it was counterintuitive to leave the assessment of policy to a small group of members. It behooved us to share information with all committee members, to engage them all in the debate, and to search for common ground together.

Many believed that Senator Sam Nunn, chair of the Senate Armed Services Committee, and I would be incapable of "closing the deal" on any legislation. From our vantage point, however, the entire success of a Dellums' chairmanship of the House committee depended on producing a bill in the first year—ahead of the Appropriations Committee. We set out to succeed by vesting the crafting of the bill—except for the policy sections—in the work of the subcommittees.

In the second year, we planned to ratchet up the number of hearings on policy issues, and bring in greater numbers of "outside" witnesses. Not all issues in front of the committee had ideological or parochial overtones; our hope was to educate and encourage confidence in our leadership and ability to articulate committee policy.

The third year was slated to be a period of major policy formulation. By then, we hoped to embark the committee on a full-fledged investigation of the whole range of defense issues—a "bottom-up review" of our own in response to that which Aspin had announced he would undertake in his new role as secretary of defense. We would increase my presence in the national media, not to pontificate but to explain the process of inquiry on which the committee was embarked.

In the fourth year, and on the heels of the preceding year's assessment, we would seek to convince the committee to make substantial changes to the defense authorization paradigm. Now would be the time for me, hopefully with the backing of a committee that had moved to a new vision of national security, to take to the airways to explain a point of view and a perspective that had been derived through constant assessment and investigation.

It was a sound plan, we all agreed, and we set out to put it into action.

With Aspin's Defense Department undertaking a bottom-up review of defense requirements, I called a meeting with key arms control and disarmament lobbyists. I urged them to become something more than naysayers focusing only on opposition to weapons systems or defense programs. I told them I was planning to embark upon a thorough analysis of defense requirements—it was my obligation as committee member and chairman—but I needed the Left, and the peace community in particular, to articulate their vision of what our military should look like in this new era.

Formulating a military plan requires making commitments which I knew would be difficult. Just as our alternative defense plans had lost support as members of Congress found we had cut a particular system they thought was important, we risked dividing the peace and disarmament community by including one thing or another in our new vision—and of course groups like the Quakers would be hard pressed to openly support a military bill of any kind. Nonetheless, I believed it was critical to try, because the absence of voices on the Left articulating what it meant to provide for the "legitimate defense" of the United States would needlessly skew the debate to the right. It was important to be against destabilizing weapons; it was important to be against waste, fraud, and abuse; it was important to be against a defense structure that lent itself to the inappropriate or excessive use of force—but the converse of all of that was that some things *were* appropriate. I needed help in defining what they might be.

Keeping control of policy within the committee—rather than letting the appropriators determine policy by their money decisions—was critical. During our first year, the chairman of the defense appropriations subcommittee, Representative John Murtha from Pennsylvania, tested our resolve by seeking to fund an aircraft carrier without HASC authorization—a violation of the House rules. I vigorously resisted this effort—despite support on our own committee for the carrier—and indicated that I would press a point of order if the appropriations bill carried funds for the carrier. We would not put the cart before the horse; too much money was at stake and I was determined that the debate on whether or not the carrier was needed would take place within Armed Services. Murtha told me that he would fight my point of order. "And I never lose a fight!" he warned.

I sat down with my committee members and told them, "I know we don't all agree on whether we should or should not fund a carrier in this year's budget. That notwithstanding, we should all agree that the decision to build or not build a carrier is a policy issue, and that means it's our decision, not that of the Appropriations Committee." They backed me on principle.

At the end of the day, Murtha himself moved to strike the aircraft carrier from the appropriations bill. We had passed the first important test of my leadership, and the committee had stood with me.

During the 1992 presidential campaign, Clinton had promised to change the military's policies regarding gay men and lesbians in the armed services. It was an important campaign pledge, one that came under immediate and sustained attack from within the military and the Congress. Aspin began to broker a compromise—"don't ask, don't tell"—the essence of which was that gays and lesbians could continue to serve, but only if they remained "in the closet" with regard to their sexual orientation. Where this would go was obvious to me: people who chose to come out of the closet would be persecuted, and those who didn't would serve their nation as second-class citizens, deprived of their constitutional rights to liberty and freedom of speech and association.

I urged the new president to hold his ground and act by executive order to lift the ban on gay men and lesbians in the military immediately. "Whether the American people agree or disagree," I said, "they will see that you kept your promise. Mr. President, you have many other issues to deal with. Let the Congress fight this battle. I know the dance. I know the music, and I'm prepared to take on the issue. If the Congress reverses your executive order, so bet it." We held hearings on the issue, inviting the leaders of other military and police forces that had abandoned anti-gay policies. Throughout that year, the progressive movement would be split on how far to attempt to push the issue, but in my view there was only one principled position, and that was against discrimination.

Aided by our extraordinary staff and the able support of several colleagues, the Armed Services Committee began a new, exhausting and liberating effort to explore the new geo-strategic terrain of the post–Cold War world—all the while working the authorization bill toward completion. We immediately locked horns with the Senate on the B-2 issue, but managed, in the first year, to preserve a cap on the number of bombers to be built. George Withers, once my legislative director and by now a professional member of the HASC staff, worked very effectively over a period of years to maintain a coalition against the B-2 bomber.

At the beginning of my tenure at the head of the HASC, I sat down with the Republican members of the committee and told them I was committed to ensuring their full participation in all deliberations—that I considered this to be an obligation of the chair. Even during conference with the Senate, I continued to meet with both Democrats and Republicans on the committee, seeking to keep all the members fully informed of conference developments. As we neared the end of the process—as happens so often—a dozen issues remained outstanding. The conferees determined to the kick these issues upstairs to the "Big 4"—the two armed services chairs, House and Senate, and the ranking Republicans—for final resolution. Meeting with the House conferees, ranking Republican Floyd Spence from South Carolina said, "I know where the chairman wants to go on the outstanding issues and I have absolute confidence that he will represent the House position. I don't see any reason for me to attend; I would suggest that the two chairmen work out the remaining issues." I was gratified that within this short time my colleagues had already gained that much confidence in my leadership, and I am convinced that this confidence was based upon my openness and willingness to communicate, and on their understanding that I would discharge my responsibilities professionally.

Senator Nunn and I met to determine the outcomes for this package of a dozen issues, just the two of us sitting in a room alone, without staff, late one night. After we'd finished the task, he stood and said, "Well, we've done it." He held out his hand. "I want you to know that I've been on the Hill twenty-some-odd years, but I've never met anyone quite like you. You stayed in communication. I could count on your word. You never sought unfair political advantage. You were very straightforward and always willing to debate the issues on their merits. I just want you to know that I appreciate that. I appreciate you and I respect you. It's a pleasure and privilege to work with you."

Once again I thought, "No one in Berkeley would believe this moment."

During the next year's budget cycle, the issue of the B-2 arose again, and it posed a threat to the completion of the conference with the Senate. Once again my House colleagues left the issue to Senator Nunn and me. "If Dellums and Nunn can work something out, we can all live with it," they said, and they collectively chuckled. But they were right, if we could find common ground, then everybody would have the "political cover" they needed. This would be a major challenge.

Throughout the days of discussion, the back-and-forth of meetings, Nunn and I kept trying to hammer out an agreement. He was determined to return the plane to production and I was equally determined to oppose that effort. Finally I proposed to him that we agree to a provision that would require an independent study of bomber requirements and that we each provide a set of questions to be answered. We came to agreement and fashioned a process that we both believed to be fair, comprehensive, and conclusive. We shook hands on the proposition that in the next budget cycle we would both agree to abide by the conclusions the study reached.

Some in the disarmament movement saw this as a capitulation and challenged me for having brokered the provision. I sat down with them and explained our confidence in the outcome. I opposed the B-2 because it was unnecessary, unaffordable, and there were military alternatives—not just because it was a program put forth by the military establishment. If we really believed in our analysis, and if an honest process could be developed to assess the issues, we should have the courage of our convictions. In my mind, I knew we had negotiated an honest process and I was absolutely confident of the outcome of the report. I was prepared to take the political risk of subjecting my analysis to scrutiny. After all, wasn't that why we had come this far and worked this hard? The study concluded that no new B-2s were required, and even after my time as HASC chair had been terminated by a new Republican majority in the House, Senator Nunn kept his word and did not support efforts to build more planes.

Earlier, when my tenure as HASC chair was just beginning, the United States military was engaged in an operation in Somalia that was, in my judgment, one of the first tests of military policy in the post–Cold War era. Deployed by the Bush administration and maintained by newly elected president Clinton to provide a secure environment for the delivery of food and other aid to the people of Somalia, the U.S. action was immediately denounced by many on the left as "U.S. imperialist interventionism." I saw it differently. I saw no particular strategic advantage to U.S. involvement, but the humanitarian issues were obvious: three hundred thousand Somalis had died of starvation only because civil war prevented the delivery of food. We were not intervening for or against a particular faction, only to ensure the safety of the relief workers.

Things took a turn for the worse over that summer, when the United Nations made the fateful decision to join in conflict with the Adeed faction because of an attack on a UN peacekeeping unit. I counseled against such a position. Perhaps the deployed units needed better force protection, I argued, but the taking of sides would soon begin to corrode the operational effectiveness of the peacekeepers. In the fall—with a full-scale hunt for Adeed himself in effect—units of the U.S. military were caught in a firefight, and some of our troops were killed. As the body of a U.S. soldier was dragged through the streets of Mogadishu by Somali fighters, I knew that incredible pressure would arise to withdraw U.S. forces from the country. Several members of Congress told me that their office telephones were "ringing off the hook" and that vociferous objection was being raised to any continued U.S. presence.

At a meeting with congressional leaders and the president's national security team to discuss the situation, I was deeply concerned by the palpable anger of my colleagues and the ineffectual presentation given by the president's national security people. I spoke my mind, voicing my concern that should an order of withdrawal be issued, based on this precedent the United States would, for a generation, refuse to participate again in peacekeeping or humanitarian missions.

Having thought about the meeting during the night, I awoke the next day still concerned with the lack of knowledge about the underlying issues displayed by the president's team. I was convinced that he could not be well informed if this was the advice he was receiving. I needed to talk with him directly and share my thoughts and views.

Not only was the future of Somalia at stake, if we blew peacekeeping in Somalia we would be unlikely to play that role again in the developing world. This was a watershed moment in the evolution of U.S. foreign policy and in assessments of the changing role of the U.S. military. When I arrived in my office that morning, I called the White House and requested to speak with Clinton. Later in the day, he returned my call (a member of his staff advised me that the president had wanted to be briefed before our conversation).

"Mr. President," I began, "I preface my remarks by indicating that in this post–Cold War era there are no experts. You are as expert as anyone else.

"Secondly, we are not at war with the Somali people. The hands that dispense food and humanitarian aid cannot be the hands that dispense death. We did not go to Somalia to conquer the Somali people, we went there to help them.

"I believe we have made mistakes in Somalia, because in order to play the role of peacekeeper we must adhere to two fundamental principles: take no sides and make no enemies. Both of those tenets have been violated in Somalia.

"Mr. President, the mark of a great nation is its willingness to admit a mistake. I counsel you to go before the American people and admit that we have made mistakes in Somalia, and make a mid-course change toward a new direction."

I concluded by making a number of specific recommendations, and provided him with information we had received during several hearings on Somalia and peacekeeping. "Finally, I would hope that you will not establish a date certain for withdrawal of American peacekeepers from Somalia. Succumbing to the political pressure from some quarters to make a premature withdrawal would be a major mistake, perhaps condemning Somalia to unnecessary chaos and anarchy."

The next morning Clinton assembled the military and foreign policy leaders of Congress along with his national security team at the White House. With the exception of establishing a date certain for withdrawal, he seemed to have accepted the arguments that I—and I would assume others—had made to him during the preceding days.

I continue to believe that the establishment of a date certain was a critical mistake. It allowed the factions to wait for the peacekeeping force to withdraw. At least partially in consequence, Somalia has "functioned" without a central government for the longest period of time of any nation in modern times.

Other challenges quickly arose and my worst fears were realized. In

Rwanda, hundreds of thousands died in a genocidal "civil war" without an effective response by the world community or the United States. Leaders of the fighting factions were tried criminally for crimes against humanity—yet we did not mobilize to stop the violence.

In Haiti, the United States threatened a military invasion to restore the duly elected democratic government. For months, pressure had been building for the United States to do something to return President Aristide to office. To draw public attention to the situation, I organized a group of several colleagues—including Representatives Major Owens of New York, Barbara Rose Collins of Michigan, Kweisi Mfume of Maryland, and Joe Kennedy of Massachusetts—to protest at the White House. We were ultimately arrested for refusing to disperse. TransAfrica's Randall Robinson came near death as he fasted to dramatize the plight of ordinary Haitians, whose democracy had been taken from them by military force.

Literally while the invasion was underway, the military regime agreed to the establishment of a peacekeeping presence to restore the elected government and lead to a new round of elections. Constant pressure to establish a date for withdrawal was present once again, and the HASC deliberated at length on the issue.

A fourth humanitarian crisis soon unfolded—in Bosnia—this one made extraordinarily complex by the multiple issues involved, but starkly appalling in the brutality of the warring parties and the near-genocidal campaign of "ethnic cleansing."

During this time, Professor June Jordan, a brilliant essayist and poet, contacted my office, pleading that I support military intervention in Bosnia. She pointed out that combatants were engaging in systematic rape of the female population. This was a war crime in her judgment, to which the world community needed to respond. Her phone call provoked a chain of events that would allow me to develop a more cogent analytical framework around the whole concept of peacekeeping.

I discussed the crisis in Bosnia with Lee Halterman, my long-term counsel, who was also by then the director of policy for the HASC. He proposed that we have a sustained conversation about peacekeeping with religious leaders and moral philosophers. We sought out and invited several leading theologians from the major religions—including a Quaker—and over a lengthy lunch we began to explore the issues that Jordan had raised.

During the lunch, the bell rang several times, calling members to the

187

floor for votes. Walking back and forth from my office to the House, I talked with colleagues about the incredible conversation I was having. Many wanted to return with me, as they too were in a quandary on the issues.

The positions taken by the theologians we talked to that day were slightly different, depending on the religious tradition they represented, but they cohered in one respect—individuals and nations had an obligation to mobilize in the face of inhumanity, especially when it rose to the level of genocide. The obvious questions were how and when? Although every situation demands its own examination, the luncheon had clarified my thinking. It had allowed me to understand that being for peace did not necessarily mean opposing to the use of military forces as peacekeepers. Other organizations and resources might also—or sometimes might best—be deployed to keep the peace. But when whole groups of people have been killing each other and each other's families, military or police action may be justified as necessary to stop the cycle of violence.

Eventually, the belligerents in Bosnia agreed at Dayton, Ohio, to a cease-fire and a political arrangement conditioned on the United States' willingness to keep the peace that the European community had been unable to maintain. Many in Congress—liberals and conservatives alike—argued, "It's a European problem. Let them handle it." For me, it was not enough to point out, as Defense Secretary William Perry ably did, that the United States had been drawn into two world wars when the peace failed in Europe. I argued that the moral dimension of a quarter-million dead—killed because of their ethnicity or religion—could not be ignored. The Bosnian conflict was a human rights catastrophe that demanded that we, as a nation, respond affirmatively when asked to help stop the killing by standing between the belligerents. Anything less would be a moral failure.

Professor Jordan and the theologians we consulted had escaped the Cold War paradigm, whereas some "doves" who argued against "intervention" seemed to be confusing peacekeeping with nationally self-serving acts to affect the course of political developments within sovereign states. If progressives stood for the United Nations, for internationalism, and for alternatives to war and violence, then we had to learn from the Nigerians and Canadians, the Pakistanis and the Norwegians, and others who had resisted the pull of Cold War ideology and recognized the role, value, and moral imperative of peacekeeping. As a progressive, I believed that we as a nation could not stand on the sidelines; we had to engage, and we had to be prepared to act as true peacekeepers—taking no side and making no enemies. In addition, I argued that our foreign policy had to "preventively engage" with economic, diplomatic, and other nonmilitary investments to prevent the conditions that gave rise to conflict.

Throughout 1993 and 1994 I felt that my staff and I were making significant strides within the HASC and in our own thinking. The task of reeducating ourselves and others seemed endless; eighteen-hour days were the norm, and many weekends were spent in research and preparation. We held numerous hearings on force structure issues, peacekeeping, and the use of force in the post–Cold War era in Somalia, Haiti, and Yugoslavia, and on a host of other, equally important subjects. The committee members joined in, responding to my injunction to make the full committee its own policy task force. Members knew they were being taken to school, and in the process they were "raising their game" to defend their own points of view, as Aspin and I had done during our intellectual duels.

As we began to approach the third year of my chairmanship of HASC, I met with Marilyn Elrod and Lee Halterman and we sketched out a series of staff task forces and a hearing agenda that would touch upon every major aspect of defense policy—bombers, naval forces, peacekeeping, industrial base, technology development, arms control, etc. By the fall, these staff groups had been assembled, briefed, and turned loose on their assignments. It was thrilling to see and feel the excitement they exuded as they set to their tasks. Every single member of the staff knew that he or she played an important part in this significant effort; all contributions were appreciated, and policy had moved beyond the "policy shop downstairs" in the chairman's office.

In November 1994, the Democratic Party suffered a crushing defeat. Newt Gingrich's "Contract with America" campaign plan had worked, and the Republicans would control the House and the Senate in 1995. On schedule and poised for our third year, our four year-plan—with all its promise and potential—was swamped by this political tidal wave.

A short time later, Representative John Kasich from Ohio approached me and said, "My colleagues and I were marveling that one day you were the chairman and the next day you moved over and became ranking minority representative, without missing a beat. What's the secret?" Although I had lost the chair of the HASC, I had by no means departed from the debate—in Congress or on the committee—on all the issues that mattered so much to me.

"There is no secret," I told him. "I've spent my whole life as a minority. And I've learned how to fight and win in the Congress as a political minority."

In my experience, it was the women and the racial minorities in the Democratic Caucus who most quickly adapted to our new status as the political minority. Flailing away or following a strategy based on denial was no way to deal with the shift in power; we still had to fight for our communities within the circumstances we now faced. I was disappointed but not fazed. This dramatic turn of events just meant that we would have to work harder—and I was prepared to demand the same fairness for the new Democratic minority as I had provided for the Republicans.

As the new majority set out to implement its Contract with America, my staff and I sat down to assess where we might be able to advance our ideas with help of the Democratic members of the committee behind me. I also had to think about where else I could carry on the effort more independently. Preserving U.S. participation in peacekeeping operations was one issue on which we could hope to keep the Democratic Caucus together—but it would require hard work. We also ended up defending the president's role as commander in chief, an ironic counterpoint to the effort we had initiated to regain congressional control of the power to authorize war.

We quickly found ourselves back in the B-2 debate, and I was disappointed with the split that occurred within the Black Caucus over funding this unnecessary weapons system. Reagan's Star Wars initiative was back as well; the majority planned to force the administration to spend more money on our national ballistic missile defense system—again in a manner that could breach the ABM treaty. As I assembled the Armed Services Committee's Democratic members to discuss strategy, I told them that I thought there was an issue here on which we might have some chance to score a victory. Star Wars was both controversial and expensive. Like the B-2, its acquisition could crowd out other systems of interest to members of Congress, and in addition I thought we might be able to bring some Republicans to our side over the general issue of arms control.

As H. R. 7—the defense plank of the Contract with America—came to the floor, we reached a consensus around our approach to the debate. Moderates and conservatives would lead in offering the handful of Democratic amendments, one of which would be designed to force the House to choose between Star Wars and other important defense priorities concerning military preparedness and quality-of-life issues for the troops. We went to the Democratic Caucus and secured their concurrence with our strategy, which was significantly different than that being implemented in opposition to other Contract provisions; whereas we were seeking to form a consensus among Democrats on issues that might draw Republican supporters, many of the dozens of amendments to the non-defense provisions of the Republican plan constituted a frontal assault on the majority and were therefore, we feared, doomed to failure.

The difficulty was in securing a clean vote on the issue. Floyd Spence, now chair of the House Armed Services Committee, would control the debate. In the usual course of events, he would be able to control its tempo and allow for majority amendments to any amendment. A constant process of offering amendments only to have them changed by the majority would never get us to where we wanted to go. Representative Ike Skelton from Missouri, who would succeed me as the ranking Democrat on the committee upon my retirement, turned to the staff and said, "This is what we pay you the big money for. Go figure out how we can win this!" After consulting with the parliamentarians, our counsel returned with a set of amendments to be offered in a particular order. The last one was to be offered by me as a perfecting amendment to one offered by Sonny Montgomery. The trick would be to secure recognition by the chair of the Committee of the Whole House immediately after Montgomery's amendment and before a senior Republican could be recognized.

It worked. As I took the floor to offer the amendment that would close off the "amendment tree," the Republican floor managers realized too late that we had outmaneuvered them, and in the vote on relative national security priorities that followed, we prevailed.

It was the first defeat of a Contract with America provision for the new majority. I felt a certain pride that it had been engineered by a black man— a fact noted by many. During all our years in the political minority, I and my staff and allies had never wavered in our belief that one must always fight to win on matters of principle, no matter how outnumbered or outgunned.

———

As I left the Congress, I was deeply saddened by our nation's failure to end Cold War–type military planning and the outsized military budgets and misguided policy assumptions associated with this mindset. I was especially disappointed by the Clinton administration's "nuclear posture review," which failed to steer a bold course to reduce the threat posed by nuclear weapons. Certainly instability and danger remain in various parts of the world, including Russia and the other nations of the former Soviet Union. Military modernization in China, Southeast Asia, Latin America, and elsewhere—including within the United States—should always give us pause. But in my view, none of this warranted the scale or direction of the investment we were making.

Humanitarian crises and instability throughout the globe will of course continue to require the involvement of the U.S. military at least in the near term—preferably through United Nations–sponsored undertakings in which the United States acts as a colleague who can bring special skills to the table. But we should not allow ourselves to be trapped into the belief that these challenges, only partially military in nature, require anything like our current force structure or modernization plans. And, as many military officers would admit, preparing our forces to become effective peacekeepers is the key to future military operations. Those who persist in the view that "we only do the big one" fail to understand how important it is to respond quickly any time an opportunity exists to deter, deflect, or prevent conflict—precisely in order to *avoid* having to fight "the big one."

As of this writing, U.S. planes are bombing Serbian forces in Kosovo and throughout Yugoslavia. Those operations provide a critical learning ground for what to do and what not do in such a crisis. It is my hope that by the time this book is published, that war—for it is a war, no matter what we call it—will have long been over. We can end such wars and convert our mission to peacekeeping only through concerted diplomatic efforts on all possible fronts. In the conflict over Kosovo, for instance, Russia must play a critical part, as it did in Bosnia, and the United Nations or the Organization on Cooperation and Security in Europe must provide expanded political and legal authority for a coordinated intervention.

Building upon the principles established by the United Nations with regard to Iraq, that in some cases internal human rights abuses are properly the subject of international intervention, the United States must work within the international framework to establish greater cohesion and coherence for these important actions. I worry that although working to prevent such horrors as ethnic cleansing and genocide is a proper function of the international community of conscience, in the case of Kosovo we have pushed forward too rapidly and in the wrong direction. I fear that we have made some of the same mistakes we made in Somalia and which we managed to avoid in Bosnia.

In the meantime, our cities are crying for redevelopment and the residents of abandoned and neglected communities scramble to end the nightmare of drugs, crime, and economic disintegration. What economic success does exist in our nation generates heightened gaps between the rich and the working or poverty classes, creating further social and political cynicism and despair. This is our real national security crisis. Our nation's leadership seems incapable of taking the peace dividend—and yes, there is a general peace at hand despite Kosovo—and doing what succeeded so well in the 1950s. With a Marshall Plan for Europe, the restoration of the Japanese economy, and large-scale investments in U.S. infrastructure, science, and education, we built a durable peace among former adversaries. We know that such investments bear fruit, and our Constitution's framers set the pursuit of peace and justice as among the highest purposes of government.

As Dr. King taught, wars do not arise in the abstract. Economic avarice; cultural, religious, or ethnic chauvinism; failed diplomacy; and political disputes produce them. They are often born of a failure to confront injustice, or to communicate effectively about issues, or to act to resolve them. Sustained diplomacy can end crises, if the diplomacy is backed by a willingness of neutral parties to play peace monitor, peacekeeper, and—sometimes—peacemaker. Private and public investment in sustainable international economic development—with a focus on broad-based economic benefits rather than the enrichment of narrow elites—can give individuals, communities, nations, and regions a stake in stability. It worked in Europe and with Japan, and it can work elsewhere.

One of my colleagues, whom I shall allow to remain anonymous, confronted me one evening with great anger. His palpable rage was misguided and inappropriate, for I was not the source of his problem; nonetheless, it led him to threaten me with bodily harm. Shocked and amazed, I suggested that we take this disagreement to a more private place. We stood alone just off the floor of the House, face to face. Seething, he continued his verbal assault. Without wavering or flinching, I stood directly in front of him and said, "There's nothing holding you back but atmosphere. Whatever you think you have to do—do it. You don't have to look for me. I'm right here, standing in your face." For a long moment we stood in total silence, wrapped in an envelope of tension and hostility. At a certain point, I broke the silence, saying, "Don't you think this is a bit stupid, for two old men to be standing here, poised on the brink of disaster?" He calmed down, I calmed down, and we were able to walk away from each other and away from the confrontation.

The next morning, as I walked onto the floor of the House, this man met me with tears in his eyes and said, "I thought all night about my actions yesterday evening. I want to apologize. I was wrong to be angry with you." We talked a while about what was really bothering him and how to deal with it. Then we shook hands and embraced each other.

I said to him, "Last night two men trained by this country to be warriors were poised on the brink of war with each other. But we both decided the price of violence was too high, so we stepped back. We chose a nonviolent path, and that led us to solve the real issues. We chose the path of peace. That's all I've ever been about here. Now I think you can better understand who and what I am."

I believe that belligerents—be they individuals, social classes, cultural groups, or nations—have the capacity to step back from their anger. In this era of heinous weapons and an enormously increased capacity for destruction, the cost of war is too high. There are other ways to solve problems, even huge and difficult ones. Everything that I learned on my journey through public life has underscored this view: when you solve the underlying economic, social, and political issues that give rise to war, you achieve peace.

chapter seven

Keeping the Faith, Fighting for Change

I awakened one morning in the spring of 1997 to the realization that I was over sixty and had served in elective office for nearly half of my life. I needed to assess where I was and wanted to be in my personal life. At that point I also realized that this would be my last term in the U.S. House of Representatives; if I did not make plans to leave after my current term, the chances were I would never leave on my own. While for thirty years I had been willing to accept the call to service, it was now time for me to recapture my life. I had never had any intention of being "carried out" of the Congress. I had always imagined returning to private life.

Over the next few days I wrestled with the uncertainty of what to do professionally or otherwise beyond congressional service. Then I received a phone call out of the blue from my former colleague Harold Ford of Tennessee.

Ford's call led to a meeting with a group of young African American men led by Anthony Cebrun of Nashville, Tennessee. We met and talked several times, and I came to appreciate Cebrun's brilliance, his character, and his vision. That vision was an interesting juxtaposition of the romanticism and clarity of somebody whose view of the world was shaped by the 1960s, bound up with a pragmatism born of his training as a lawyer, his experience as a businessman, and his compassion as a health care advocate. His global perspective and his comprehensive understanding of the interrelations among the many factors that impinge upon the health of individuals and communities were inspiring. The endeavor Cebrun and his colleagues were about to embark upon sounded exciting; it offered a new challenge, new mountains to climb, and new and important subject matter to master. As I contemplated their project, I knew it would be incredibly invigorating to be part of the effort.

The relationship born out of our meetings and discussions resulted in my agreement to accept the position of president of a fledgling international health care company—Healthcare International Management Company—whose initial focus would be on improving the quality of life in southern Africa through the provision of coordinated, accessible, and comprehensive health care based upon the strategy of wellness.

I had decided to take the job, but I determined that I could not leave the Congress in the middle of the defense authorization process. I wanted to discharge that responsibility through to the end, and not as a "lame duck." Then I could say farewell to my district and my colleagues.

As it happened, we did not finish the defense bill until November, right at the end of the session. In the meantime, friends and supporters from the Bay Area had taken it upon themselves to raise the funds necessary to have a portrait of me painted for display in the Armed Services Committee hearing room—in keeping with the committee's custom to accord that honor to its chairpersons. A community panel from our East Bay congressional district had conducted a search and chosen André White, a young African American suffering from a painful physical disability, from over sixty competing artists. On September 24, the portrait was unveiled at a ceremony that was dramatic testimony to how far my odyssey had taken me.

Both Dick Gephardt, my Democratic Party leader, and the Speaker of the House, Republican leader Newt Gingrich, participated in the celebration. Secretary of Defense William Cohen also took the time from his busy schedule, as did his former colleague Senator Strom Thurmond, who, despite his advanced age, stood throughout the lengthy ceremony. Marilyn Elrod, whom I had hired as a young caseworker and who had performed so ably as HASC staff director, was mistress of ceremonies. The imposing committee hearing room was filled with friends, former staff members, uniformed military personnel, colleagues and former colleagues, and people from the national security and foreign policy elite.

Throughout the night many of us had a hard time fighting back the tears. All of the pain of those long years washed over me as I felt the embrace of colleagues from both sides of the aisle and from across the ideological chasms that had often divided many of us present in the room.

While their tribute was focused upon me, I felt that in a very real way they were above all honoring the principles of democracy and fair play that I had attempted to live by. Speakers lauded me for my fairness, for my intellect, for my commitment to principle, for my willingness to bring substance and vigor to the debate on the issues, for my willingness to listen, and for my willingness to be a friend. Minority Leader Gephardt noted that most members "don't leave much of a difference behind . . . but Ron Dellums, day in and day out, stayed on the beam and argued passionately for his cause . . . and then we won it." Of course I appreciated the accolades, and I hoped that some measure of what they thought deserved praise would remain behind and inspire them to help improve the process of governance after I had left the House.

It spoke volumes that Speaker Gingrich agreed to participate in behalf of his party, already ably represented by HASC chairman Floyd Spence. Gingrich noted during his very kind comments that "in taking on apartheid in South Africa and taking it on and taking it on, starting as a lonely voice and gradually . . . changing the policy of the United States Government," I had hastened the advent of freedom in that nation. Having earlier alluded to the experience of racism in the United States, Gingrich offered that this act had "helped repay the debt" I owed to liberation fighters in my own country. I thought of the irony. I had nearly come to blows with Gingrich only a few years earlier, before he was Speaker, over Republican fund-raising tactics that vilified Speaker Foley's appointment of me to the House Select Committee on Intelligence. In the interim, Gingrich had taken the time to know me, and he accorded me respect for my work and my effort on behalf of positions with which he disagreed. He would pay me a similar compliment a year later by inviting me to the podium at a ceremony presenting President Nelson Mandela with the Congressional Medal of Freedom. As it would turn out, the portrait unveiling was the first of a series of formal and informal celebrations of my career in the Congress.

At the time, I still held closely my decision to leave. The deliberations of the conference committee on the national defense bill were dragging on and important matters remained to be negotiated. When our work finally ended in November, on the eve of adjournment for the session, I sought out certain colleagues to advise them that I would not be returning next year. The protests at the abruptness of my departure were overwhelming, and I was moved that colleagues from throughout the House chided me for not giving them an opportunity to pay tribute to the work I had done for the nation.

Finally, on Friday, February 6, 1998, my thirty-plus years in public office came to an end. I had written my last bill, offered my last amendment, negotiated my last agreement, and had taken the well of the House floor for the last time. Deeply humbled by the honor to have served and by the heartfelt embrace of colleagues whose predecessors had isolated me by their shrill rejection of both me and the politics of my community, I left the Congress for a new adventure.

I knew that I had maintained faith. I had upheld my end of the sacred contract I had entered into with my constituents. I had sought to rise to the leadership challenges laid out by Dr. King: I had tried to form a new consensus; I had been comprehensive in my moral concerns; I had sought to live and work from a perspective of peace; I had sought to link the quest for peace with the quest for justice. And I knew that by leaving Congress I was not ending my part in the struggle to make the world a better place for my children and grandchildren.

On the following Monday I flew to Memphis to formalize my relationship with Anthony Cebrun and Healthcare International Management Company.

It was exciting to be in a new job, heading a forward-thinking company looking to establish itself in an important arena of work. I had brought Charles Stephenson, my former legislative director, with me, and I hired Ann Brown to round out the "office of the president," based in Washington, D.C. We began to make the rounds and establish contacts: the administration, embassies, the World Bank, and other key organizations in D.C., and soon thereafter I traveled once again to South Africa. We were on a steep learning curve, digesting mountains of information about managed care, patterns of disease, and basic health care delivery. Every day was a new challenge; it may not have been Brandeis, but I felt that I was definitely going to school.

During the course of our work and assessment, I came to understand the dimensions of the health care crisis that is all too real for most people in southern Africa, from limited access to complete lack of access to primary health care. I also ran headlong into what I perceive to be one of the great moral imperatives of our time—the need to stem the human suffering associated with the rampant spread of HIV and AIDS in sub-Saharan Africa. It is anticipated that over twenty million people will die of AIDS in this region over the next ten years. That is morally unacceptable. The world cannot sit by and do nothing about this cataclysmic crisis.

As of this writing there are 7.8 million children in the region orphaned as a result of deaths due to AIDS. It is predicted that their number will reach 36 million within ten years. The psychological, sociological, economic, political, and security implications of millions of children orphaned in sub-Saharan Africa stagger the imagination.

Life expectancy is falling rapidly throughout the continent of Africa. It is reported that the life expectancy in Sierra Leone has reached a modern low of thirty-five years. In Zimbabwe, life expectancy has fallen into the mid-forties. In southern Africa generally, life expectancy has fallen into the mid-forties and continues to drop. This is the reality on the continent of Africa. This too is morally unacceptable.

In 1995 in the United States, the peak year for deaths from AIDS, over 50,000 individuals died. In 1998, approximately 18,000 people died. Data show a similar drop in mortality in Europe as well. The significance of these data are that treatment modalities have been identified and administered that can extend life for people who have contracted HIV and enhance their quality of life, as well as aid in combating the transmission of HIV from mother to child during pregnancy and birth—*if* they are available. A failure to receive such treatment is a sentence of accelerated death, and a failure to provide information and practical assistance for avoiding the disease dooms countless others in the future.

Between 80 and 90 percent of reported AIDS cases worldwide are in the so-called developing world, a large measure of them in Africa. The principle obstacles to delivering to people there the treatment modalities that are readily available in the developed nations of Europe and North America are accessibility to health care and the cost of treatment regimes.

The first step in confronting the moral dilemma before us is for the developed world to commit to a partnership with African nations and leaders to develop the infrastructure and provide the mechanisms to deliver the treatment and prevention programs. Many will argue that developing a solution to this problem is enormous and complex—and they would be correct. My view, though, is that we must make a start by focusing first on committing ourselves to enlisting the worldwide community in the development of a strategy to solve the crisis in Africa.

As I have become increasingly engaged in attempting to mobilize leaders around the world on this issue, I have challenged them to commit their governments, their businesses, and their international agencies to the development of an "AIDS Marshall Plan" for Africa. Such a plan would have to be large, comprehensive, and interrelated; in addition to funding education and prevention campaigns that are currently without necessary resources, there must be a treatment strategy as well. In that connection, we must understand that AIDS cannot be treated in a vacuum and only an investment strategy that deals with access to health care, infrastructure requirements, and other related issues will succeed.

Such a strategy would have huge implications for other worldwide health care and development issues. But what is demanded of us now is that we recognize and respond aggressively to the stark moral dimension of the issue: deaths can be prevented, the number of orphans can be significantly reduced, and life expectancy for people who are HIV-positive can be extended. It is a cause that the world must come to embrace if we are to be true to King's vision of peace and justice.

When running for the Congress in 1970, I campaigned on the strength of my belief that the youth of our nation held the greatest capacity for idealism and change. I was inspired by their militancy. The people who swelled the ranks of all the movements for social justice—feminists, environmentalists, civil rights advocates of every kind, disarmament and antiwar activists—were singing a common tune. They wanted to build a just society, based on equality, democratic principles, and mutual respect. These were noble ideas then and they remain not only noble ideas but great imperatives as well. Further, I am convinced that policies based upon them might end much of the pain and dysfunction in our society.

The generation that came of age in the 1960s believed we could change the world—and in many ways we did. We ended a war, prevented the deployment of the MX and Pershing missiles. We forced the Reagan administration back to the arms negotiation table. We secured passage of important environmental laws. We ended legal discrimination against racial minorities and helped to break down some of the barriers that limit the choices of women, gays and lesbians, persons with disabilities, and others who have historically been oppressed or exploited.

Everything we have struggled for remains under attack—and in some measure it always will. Some will always reject equality as a first principle and will do no more than pay lip service to the idea that the common good means including everybody. They will persist in the belief that individualism is a paramount virtue, and that government should not seek to level the playing field or break down the walls against opportunity. Some will always believe that war is the inevitable solution to international affairs, and will refuse to commit to strategies that avoid militarism and conflict as early or first options. Some will always seek to consume rather than preserve the environment, indifferent to our responsibility to be careful stewards of the planet for subsequent generations. And so it will go.

The current generation of young people has grown up in a cynical era in some measure culturally dominated by the proponents of reaction. They are removed from the era of our victories, of the time during which we moved history forward. It is my hope that this book has provided both a measure of inspiration and the evidence that principle married to determination can lead to success.

On the occasion of my leaving the Congress, many told me, "Dellums, you made a difference in the world." I had been audacious enough in my very first campaign to argue that one person could make such a difference. After over thirty years I have learned that one doesn't make a difference by oneself. Even as I listened to others say that my efforts on the anti-apartheid sanctions bill had helped to change the world, I knew that I did not make that contribution by myself. *We* did it, when millions of people took the time to coalesce into a mighty force that could bend the political process to its will.

At the end of the day, it is not about personalities. People come and go. Ultimately it is ideas that prevail and it is the commitment to those ideas that transcends everything. I came to the Congress for but a minute in the history of the nation, and I do believe with absolute confidence that I remained faithful to my sacred bond with my constituency and faithful to the progressive ideas they manifested through their activism and their outrage. Linking hands with them and with countless other activists across the nation and around the world in the service of their legislative agenda has been the highest privilege imaginable.

I arrived in Berkeley in 1968, a freshman at the University of California. I had been a progressive social and political activist while growing up in Napa, California—a relatively conservative small town in northern California. Berkeley seemed to me the very center of the social revolution sweeping the globe, and I was thrilled to be in the midst of the storm, living in Oxford Hall, a student-run cooperative house on the western boundary of the campus.

Already traumatized by the assassinations of Dr. Martin Luther King, Jr., and Senator Robert Kennedy, in whose presidential campaign I had volunteered to work, and by the debacle that was the 1968 Democratic National Convention, I became even more politically alienated by developments between 1968 and 1970. Declaring myself to be a conscientious objector to my local Selective Service board when I turned eighteen, I raged at the ongoing progress and expansion of the war in Vietnam, and at the social injustice that was manifest at home, generating the on-campus rebellion that was being played out across the nation.

When Berkeley was placed under martial law during the People's Park confrontations, I found myself, as Oxford Hall's president, confronting a police invasion of our building on the claim that snipers were on our roof. They were harassing us because we had the audacity to establish a medical clinic in the lobby of our co-op, to treat the victims of tear gas and shotgun pellets being fired at demonstrators by the occupying army of soldiers, sheriff's officers, and police. Never before in my memory had an overwhelmingly white city been occupied by the military; that had been an experience reserved for black and Latino communities, whose rebellion against oppression had ignited conflagrations in several of the nation's major cities.

By April 1970 I was completely turned off to politics and to school. I dropped out of the university and decided to go to Paris to perfect my French and write the next great American expatriate novel. I hitchhiked to Napa first, to ask my father to help me secure a job in the pipe mill—from which I hoped to earn enough money to save for my planned exodus. I was picked up by a young schoolteacher traveling from his home in Berkeley to his job in Vallejo. He had some "Dellums for Congress" literature in his car, which I took up and started to read once our conversation had subsided.

The literature grabbed my attention: "Ron Dellums says: 'First take care of business at home.'" Columns were headed with movement phrases: "Stop Repression!" "Withdraw the Troops!" "End Racism!"

By 1970, Dellums was a fixture of local politics. The only person on the Berkeley City Council to whom the students and community activists could turn throughout our many confrontations with the system, he stood in the political vanguard. He had opposed Governor Reagan's order for the National Guard to occupy the city and had worked hard to have them removed. His literature went on, "It is my hope that the idealism of young people will give rise to leadership of statesmen who are idealists, replacing the expedient politicians of today." His campaign argued that "one man can make a difference."

I felt the tug of personal challenge and thought to myself, "Okay. This guy has no chance in the world to win this election. But if Dellums is willing to run, I have to go to volunteer in his campaign. After his 'inevitable defeat' in the June primary, I can get the job in the mill. I'll just delay my plans a couple of months." After the weekend was over, I returned to my group house in Oakland and announced my determination to go work for Dellums. One of my roommates said he would come too, so we rode our motorcycles down to Fifty-fifth and Shattuck in North Oakland, walked through the door, and started stuffing envelopes.

Of course Ron won the primary, because of his dedicated effort to build a multiracial and politically progressive coalition—and because the war drove thousands of volunteers like me into his headquarters. I never left. By the end of the campaign I was deputy campaign manager, in charge of voter registration, precinct organizing, and get-out-the-vote—although I was too young to vote myself. For me the campaign was both politically and personally a salvation. With my cynicism washed away and my activism reenergized by Dellums's analysis, oration, and principled politics, I once again thought that maybe we actually had a chance to change the nation. Eligible to reenroll in the university, I made plans to resume classes in the spring.

One day Jeannie Rucker, one of Dellums's friends and the closest thing to a "transition manager" that he had, told me to set up a job interview with Don Hopkins. Hopkins, who would teach me so much professionally during his twenty-two years as Dellums's district administrator, was soon to be in charge of the congressional district office. Seeking a job in the congressional office had never dawned on me. I was too young, not finished with my education, and quite radical in my politics. But there it was, confronting me: a potential job offer. Would I take it? I went back and forth in my mind: "Do I really want to be around to watch this guy make the inevitable compromises that will tarnish the purity of his ideas, extinguish the fire of his idealism?"

Finally I decided that if Hopkins offered me a job I would take it. If people on the left weren't willing to enter the government when opportunities actually arose, then we really had no chance of achieving our goals; we'd be reduced to mere rhetoric. I hoped that I would recognize the moment—if it were to happen—that Dellums would compromise our politics, and that I would have the courage to leave.

Dellums never disappointed me. Over time, the insight of his analysis would become sharper, his skills would improve, and his comprehension would become more encompassing. He only ever asked his staff—an incredible collection of diverse, intelligent, and committed people—to "do what is right." "Don't worry about the political fallout," he'd say. "I'll handle that." If he was ever impatient with us, it was when we hesitated to do what was right or lacked analytical rigor. He was more than a boss to us; he fashioned himself our colleague. "I'm the only one who can vote on the floor or in committee; otherwise we're all in this equally," he would say to us time and again. He wanted our best because he knew it would take that and more to change the world and end the pain that was consuming our communities.

He took his cause for peace to many corners of the world—South Africa, the Middle East, Europe, and Asia. At the height of the Cold War, he went to Cuba with a delegation of citizens to meet with Fidel Castro. He tried to assess how the schism between the United States and that tiny island nation could be repaired—and he returned from the journey with an important message from Castro to President Carter about Cuba's role on the continent of Africa. Dellums never abandoned the effort to terminate the cruel and unnecessary boycott against Cuba by the United States. On the floor of the House and in committee he would sometimes remark sardonically, "I've tried to figure out how our nation decides which are the good communist nations and which are the bad ones, which are deserving of 'most favored nation' trading status and which deserve an embargo. I've come to the conclusion that if it's a big communist nation that can fight back, it's good; but if it's a small—and probably Third World—communist nation that cannot fight back, it must be bad."

It has been an honor to share this leader's public life, to be his colleague over the twenty-eight years between that first election and his retirement from Congress in February of 1998, and to become his friend.

His story is remarkable, if only for the astounding fidelity he maintained to the principles that sent him into public life. Those who have seen him speak acknowledge that his oratorical skills place him—in the estimation of his congressional colleagues—among the Websters and the Clays of Congress, among the Kings and the Kennedys of our day. Enthralled with his political leadership, many will never know the incredible pain and personal sacrifice he made on our behalf—suffered because of his commitment to a community and its values. Modest and self-effacing, his righteousness was always directed in pursuit of some higher good. Incredibly humorous in private, he could always find the resilience to persist, gaining solace from his belief that we all were serving a higher purpose, a higher ideal.

We have tried to tell the story of the public life of a man dedicated to principle and committed to knowledge and to persevering in his effort to educate a community and a nation. He has been prophetic in his assessment of the dangers inherent in our nation's misplaced priorities, its pursuit of weaponry capable of destroying the world, and the unwillingness of our government to seize the opportunities presented throughout history to rewrite the future. Here is the vision and experience of a man who heard Dr. King's call as a personal demand to dedicate his life to peace and justice, and to promoting the understanding that peace and justice must exist together or neither will exist at all.

I can say honestly that this book tells only a small portion of the story, the part that focuses on the process of effecting change at the national level.

Here is a man who was asked by national constituencies to seek the Democratic Party nominations for president and vice president, and who was nominated to run for president by the National Black Political Assembly. Here is a man who thought seriously about running for the Senate from California—and who could have won—but decided that the bicameral nature of the national legislature allowed him a better chance to accomplish his goals 'from the House, due to the seniority that he had accumulated there, in what some consider the less prestigious body.

Dellums's many large and small legislative achievements—such as creating opportunities for minority businesses in the nation's airport construction program or securing funding for a stunning new federal building to anchor Oakland's economic revitalization—demonstrate the development of the legislative skills necessary to the process of governance. His work as chairman of the District of Columbia Committee could produce its own volume, as he utilized the committee to explore the full range of problems associated with the urban condition. The spiritual uplift from his participation in the Longest Walk, a march organized by the Native American community to press for vindication of their shattered treaty rights, remained with him throughout his career.

At the local level, Ron Dellums set a new standard of excellence for the administration of a district constituent office. He gathered together a staff that would become expert in the ombudsman and community organizing functions of an ideal government representative's office and renowned for the length of its tenure; the quality of the work they performed elevated that of other offices at the local and state levels of government. Dellums implemented his vision of coalition politics by establishing a district advisory committee and giving it the responsibility to develop positions on ballot measures and candidates—an almost unimaginable ceding of political power back to the community. His visionary leadership in guiding his community through a round of base closures and putting in place the political mechanisms to make rapid economic redevelopment a reality have been hailed by Clinton administration Defense Secretary William Cohen as "crown jewels" of the nation's conversion effort.

Ron Dellums is a man who kept the faith, fighting for change throughout his career, with ideals firmly rooted in the progressive tradition that so many attacked through mischaracterization and misunderstanding.

I have seen the public man, strong and unyielding in the face of the political and personal attacks mounted against him in an effort to undercut his credibility and to marginalize the ideas he went to Washington to advocate. I have seen the private man cry at the sight of avoidable death and destruction, frustrated at our failure to prevent the horrors of war and violence.

And I have been privileged to know the Ron Dellums who always insisted, "I'm just a dude. I get up every morning and get dressed like everybody else. What has lasting value and public importance are the ideas we are trying to advance."

I hope that this book will provide some insight into that man, his passion, and his ideas. I pray that it will inspire some other nineteen-year-old somewhere, at some time, to take up the challenge of taking progressive values inside the system in an effort to pull the levers of power on behalf of peace and social justice. I know, in ways publicly apparent and in ways that can never be discussed outside of a secure room, that the world is a better and more humane place for my children—Joshua, Alexander, and Kimiko—than it would have been without the steadfast engagement of Ron Dellums.

One person did make a difference, and he gave others the chance to make our own contributions along the way.

Acknowledgments

Any book project requires the insight and partnership of many individuals. This is especially so when the object is to chronicle a public career and to catalogue and assess the meaning of its events and their lessons. With respect to this work, thanks must go not only to those who helped with the book, but also to those who helped to guide my way, who bore the sacrifices demanded by public service, and who toiled to give greater meaning, purpose, and effect to my own activism. That list is indeed quite lengthy, and it includes the thousands of anonymous individuals who marched in civil rights and antiwar demonstrations, those who built "shantytowns" during the anti-apartheid effort, and all those who through quiet determination have worked to make this world a better place.

Among those closest to me during my public career, I must acknowledge that my family made the greatest sacrifices. They bore burdens and wear the scars of my engagement with the political process. Having been uprooted from their community in Berkeley in 1971, they then had to endure my all-too-frequent absences. Few outside the process can ever know or fully appreciate the adverse impact that public life has on an elected official's household, but it is profound. The moral support alone that my family offered me can never be repaid; beyond the strength of purpose that such support gave me, throughout my public career each member of my family provided me with valuable and timely insights that informed and sometimes inspired the actions I took on public issues.

My early education in important public and political issues, and in the importance of serving the community, owes a great deal to my father, Verney, and my mother, Willa; my sister, Theresa; and my grandmother,

208

formally known as Estelle Terry, but "Gram" to me. Dignified members of the working class, they provided me with the discipline and inspiration to be a complete person—and to reject any notion that my race or class should bar me from any goal to which I might aspire. My uncle, C. L. Dellums, showed me what it meant—and why it was required—to sacrifice for the community and the nation. Without his example, my personal history would have been written differently.

Over the period of my public career, I came to enjoy the support and association of a second family: my congressional staff. I was among a very few elected officials who've been honored to have staff willing to commit to the long haul. Because of a shared passion for our ideas and ideals, they employed their significant intellectual and organizing talents on my behalf. They were not motivated by a desire to advance their personal careers; rather they sought to implement through government action a vision of a society based upon the principles of peace, justice, and equality. I gratefully acknowledge that the achievements for which I have been publicly lauded would not have been conceived so well or been so ably executed without this group. Many of them served with me for over a dozen years, several for over two decades, and a few for my entire congressional career. A book could be written about the contribution of each of them, so I must hope that by this acknowledgment they understand that I know all of this would not have been possible without them.

Among the longest serving members of my staff to whom I and the nation owe special debts of gratitude are Johnny Apperson, Nell Beal Barnett, Robert B. Brauer, Roberta Cheff Brooks, the Honorable Keith Carson, Michael Duberstein, Marilyn A. Elrod, Donald Ray Hopkins, the Honorable Barbara Lee (who succeeded me in the Congress), Ying Lee, Daniel Lindheim, Richard H. "Max" Miller, Carlottia A. W. Scott, Nancy Snow, Charles C. Stephenson, Jr., Sandre R. Swanson, Barbara Williams, and George O. Withers. George also provided valuable research assistance during the writing of this book. I want especially to recall and acknowledge the work of the late Joyce Williams; Joyce literally gave her life for the cause of humanity when, taking my place in 1989 on a delegation to investigate starvation in Somalia, she was killed in a plane crash, along with my dear friend from Texas, Representative Mickey Leland. Over the years, dozens of others also served and made important contributions while on my personal staff or on the staff of either the District of Columbia, Armed Services, or National Security committees.

H. Lee Halterman, my coauthor, joined my first campaign at the age of nineteen and served with me throughout my congressional career. Able to utilize his organizing skills directly within the congressional process, Lee ultimately served as both my general counsel and the policy director for the Democratic members of the defense authorizing committee of the House. He played an essential and successful role in translating my political progressivism to the committee and its staff, and to the public. Many of our successes were due to his unique blend of legislative acumen, intellect, and commitment to both the democratic process and progressive values. It is fitting that we have transformed our decades-long relationship into this collaboration. This book could not have been written without his insight and his strong hand in its development.

We thank Micah Kleit and the staff at Beacon Press in Boston, who enthusiastically embraced this project. Their encouraging support and editorial guidance provided important contributions to this effort. Chris Kochansky served our effort superbly with her editorial judgment as well. We also want to thank Willa Dellums, Ernie Howard, Otho Green, Margaret Russell, Cynthia Lewis, and Charles Stephenson for their timely reviews of all or portions of the manuscript. In addition, our agents Wanda Akin and Carol Randolph were similarly enthusiastic and have never flagged in their efforts to spread the message we were trying to communicate. I assume full responsibility for any of this book's failings or shortcomings.

Finally, Lee and I would like to single out for special thanks two people without whose love, support, and understanding this work could not have been completed—Margaret Russell and Cynthia Lewis.